more taste of home slow cooker classics

taste of home
BOOKS

REIMAN MEDIA GROUP, INC. • GREENDALE, WISCONSIN

A TASTE OF HOME/READER'S DIGEST BOOK
© 2010 Reiman Media Group, Inc.
5400 S. 60th St., Greendale WI 53129
All rights reserved.

Taste of Home and Reader's Digest are registered trademarks of The Reader's Digest Association, Inc.

Editor in Chief: Catherine Cassidy
Vice President, Executive Editor/Books: Heidi Reuter Lloyd
Creative Director: Howard Greenberg
North American Chief Marketing Officer: Lisa Karpinski
Food Director: Diane Werner RD
Senior Editor/Books: Mark Hagen
Project Editor: Julie Kastello
Art Director: Edwin Robles, Jr.
Content Production Supervisor: Julie Wagner
Design Layout Artist: Emma Acevedo
Project Proofreader: Victoria Soukup Jensen
Recipe Asset System Manager: Coleen Martin
Premedia Supervisor: Scott Berger
Recipe Testing & Editing: Taste of Home Test Kitchen
Food Photography: Taste of Home Photo Studio
Administrative Assistant: Barb Czysz

The Reader's Digest Association, Inc.
President and Chief Executive Officer: Mary G. Berner
President, North American Affinities: Suzanne M. Grimes
President/Publisher Trade Publishing: Harold Clarke
Associate Publisher: Rosanne McManus
Vice President, Sales and Marketing: Stacey Ashton

For other Taste of Home books and products, visit us at **tasteofhome.com**.

For more Reader's Digest products and information,
visit **rd.com** (in the United States)
or see **rd.ca** (in Canada).

International Standard Book Number (10): 0-89821-831-4
International Standard Book Number (13): 978-0-89821-831-2
Library of Congress Control Number: 2010932444

Cover Photography
Photographer: Rob Hagen
Food Stylist: Kathryn Conrad
Set Stylist: Deone Jahnke

Pictured on front cover:
Hot Fudge Cake (p. 275), Tex-Mex Beef Barbecues (p. 46),
Tropical BBQ Chicken (p. 233) and Special Southwestern Soup (p. 48).

Printed in China
3 5 7 9 10 8 6 4 2

table of contents

Slow Cooking 101

The original slow cooker, called a Crock-Pot®, was introduced in 1971 by Rival®. Today, the term "slow cooker" and the name Crock-Pot® are frequently used interchangeably, however, in actuality Crock-Pot® is the brand and slow cooker is the appliance.

Most slow cookers have two or more settings. Food cooks faster on the high setting, however, the low setting is ideal for all-day cooking or for less tender cuts of meat. Use the "warm" setting to keep food hot until it's ready to serve. The slow cooker recipes in this book refer to cooking on either "high" or "low" settings.

Some newer slow cookers seem to heat up faster than older ones. If you have an older model and a recipe directs to cook on low, you may want to set the slow cooker on the highest setting for the first hour of cooking to be sure the food is thoroughly cooked.

Advantages of Slow Cooking

CONVENIENCE. Slow cookers provide people with the convenience of safely preparing meals while being away from home. The appliances are readily available and budget-friendly.

HEALTH BENEFITS. As more people make better food choices to improve their overall health, slow cooking has gained popularity. Low-temperature cooking retains more vitamins in the foods and healthier cuts of lean meat will become tender in the slow cooker without using extra fats. Many slow cooker recipes call for condensed soups, but lower sodium and lower fat versions can be used. And, for many busy folks, knowing that a healthy meal is waiting at home helps home cooks avoid less-healthy, "fast-food" meals after work.

FINANCIAL SAVINGS. A slow cooker uses very little electricity because of its low wattage. For instance, it would cost roughly 21 cents to operate a slow cooker for a total of 10 hours. If you roast a pork roast for 2 hours in the oven instead of using the slow cooker for 10 hours, you would spend $2.51 to operate an electric oven or $1.49 to operate a gas oven. Plus, slow cookers do not heat the home as ovens do, providing summertime savings in home-cooling costs.

When Using Your Slow Cooker...

■ Slow cookers come in a range of sizes, from 1-1/2 to 7 quarts. It's important to use the right size for the amount of food you're making. To serve a dip for a buffet, the smallest slow cookers are ideal. For entertaining or a potluck, the larger sizes work best.

■ To cook properly and safely, manufacturers and the USDA recommend slow cookers be filled at least half full but no more than two-thirds full.

■ With many slow cooker recipes, the ingredients are added at once and are cooked all day. For make-ahead convenience, place the food items in the crock the night before, cover and refrigerate overnight (the removable stoneware insert makes this an easy task). In the morning, place the crock in the slow cooker and select the temperature.

■ Do not preheat your slow cooker. An insert that has been in the refrigerator overnight should always be put into a cold base unit. Stoneware is sensitive to dramatic temperature changes, and breakage could occur if the base is preheated.

■ After the recipe is finished cooking, if there are any leftovers, allow them to cool, then refrigerate. Slow cookers should not be used to reheat leftovers. Instead, use a microwave, stovetop burner or oven to reheat foods to 165°. This ensures that the food has been thoroughly heated and is safe to eat.

■ Following a power outage of less than two hours, you can finish cooking food from your slow cooker on the stovetop or microwave. If it's been more than two hours or you are unsure how long the power has been out, discard the food for your safety.

TIPS FOR TASTY OUTCOMES

• No peeking! Refrain from lifting the lid while food cooks in the slow cooker, unless you are instructed in a recipe to stir or add ingredients. The loss of steam can mean an extra 20 to 30 minutes of cooking time each time you lift the lid.

• Be sure the lid is well-placed over the ceramic insert, not tilted or askew. The steam during cooking creates a seal.

• When food is finished cooking, remove it from the slow cooker within 1 hour and refrigerate any leftovers.

• Slow cooking may take longer at higher altitudes.

• Don't forget your slow cooker when camping, if electricity is available. When space is limited and you want "set-it-and-forget-it" meals, it's a handy appliance.

• Reheating food in a slow cooker isn't recommended. Cooked food can be heated on the stovetop or in the microwave and then put into a slow cooker to keep hot for serving.

• Use a slow cooker on a buffet table to keep soup, stew, warm dips or mashed potatoes hot.

Useful Handles For Lifting Food

Layered dishes or meat loaves are easier to get out of the slow cooker using foil handles. Here's how to make and utilize them:

1. For a 3-quart slow cooker, cut three 20-inch x 3-inch strips of heavy-duty foil (or 25-inch x 3-inch strips for large slow cookers). Or cut 6-inch wide strips from regular foil and fold in half lengthwise. Crisscross the strips to resemble spokes of a wheel.

2. Place the foil strips on the bottom and up the sides of the ceramic insert. Let the strips hang over the edge. To prevent food from sticking to the foil, coat the foil strips with cooking spray.

3. Place food in the order suggested by the recipe in the center of the foil strips and lower until the food rests on the bottom of the slow cooker.

4. After the food cooks, grasp the foil strips and carefully lift the food from the ceramic insert. Remove the foil strips from the food before serving.

CONVERTING RECIPES FOR THE SLOW COOKER

Almost any recipe that bakes in the oven or simmers on the stovetop can be easily converted for the slow cooker. Here are some guidelines:

- Before converting your own recipes, check the manufacturer's guidelines for your particular slow cooker. Find a recipe that is similar to the one you want to convert and use it as a guide. Note the amount and size of meat and vegetables, heat setting, cooking time and liquid.

- Since there is no evaporation, adjusting the amount of liquid in your recipe may be necessary. If a recipe calls for 6 to 8 cups of water, try starting with 5 cups. Conversely, recipes should include some liquid. If a recipe does not include liquid, add 1/2 cup of water or broth.

- In general, 1 hour of simmering on the range or baking at 350°F in the oven is equal to 8-10 hours on low or 4-6 hours on high in a modern slow cooker.

- Flour and cornstarch are often used to thicken soups, stews and sauces that are cooked in a slow cooker.

A Melting Pot of Ingredients

BEANS. Minerals in water and variations in voltage affect different types of dried beans in different ways; therefore, dried beans can be tricky to work with in the slow cooker. As a result, dried beans should always be soaked before adding to a slow cooker. To soak beans, place them in a Dutch oven or stockpot and add water to cover by 2 inches. Bring to a boil, and boil for 2 minutes. Remove from the heat, cover and let stand for 1 hour. Drain and rinse the beans, discarding the liquid. Sugar, salt and acidic ingredients, such as vinegar, have a hardening effect on beans and prevent the beans from becoming tender. It's best not to cook beans with these flavorings, but to add them only after the beans are fully cooked. Lentils and split peas do not need to be soaked.

COUSCOUS. For the best results when preparing couscous, cook on a stovetop instead of in a slow cooker.

DAIRY. Milk-based products tend to break down during slow cooking. Add items like milk, sour cream, cream cheese or cream during the last hour of cooking unless the recipe instructs otherwise. Cheeses don't generally hold up over extended periods of cooking, so they should be added near the end of cooking. Condensed cream soups can be cooked in slow cookers for extended periods of time with minimal curdling concerns.

FISH & SEAFOOD. Since fish and seafood cook quickly in a slow cooker and can break down if cooked too long, they are often added toward the end of the cooking time.

MEATS. For enhanced flavor and appearance, meat may be browned before going into the slow cooker. Browning, although not vital, may improve the color and flavor of meat. When cooking a roast over 3 pounds, be sure to cut it in half before placing it in the slow cooker to ensure that it thoroughly cooks. Frozen meats should be completely thawed before being placed in a slow cooker. Trim excess fat from meat or poultry before placing in a slow cooker. A slow cooker retains heat, and large amounts of fat could raise the temperature of the cooking liquid, causing the meat to overcook and become tough.

OATS. Quick-cooking and old-fashioned oats are often interchangeable in recipes. However, old-fashioned oats hold up better in a slow cooker.

PASTA. If added to a slow cooker when dry, pasta tends to become very sticky. It's best to cook it according to the package directions and stir it into the slow cooker just before serving. Small types of pasta, like orzo and ditalini, may be cooked in the slow cooker. To keep them from becoming mushy, add during the last hour of cooking.

RICE. Converted rice is ideal for all-day cooking. If using instant rice, add it during the last 30 minutes of cooking.

VEGETABLES. Vegetables, especially potatoes and root vegetables (such as carrots), tend to cook slower than meat. Place these vegetables on the bottom and around the sides of the slow cooker and put meat on top of the vegetables. Add tender vegetables, like peas and zucchini, or those you'd prefer to be crisp-tender, during the last 50 to 60 minutes of cooking.

p. 23

soups & sandwiches

p. 15

p. 19

p. 39

turkey sloppy joes

PREP: 20 MIN. • COOK: 4 HOURS

Lisa Ann Panzino-DiNunzio
Vineland, New Jersey

Letting all the flavors simmer together in the slow cooker is the key to these mildly sweet sloppy joes. This recipe is sure to be a keeper, and since it calls for ground turkey, you can feel good about serving it to your family.

2 pounds lean ground turkey

1 medium onion, finely chopped

1 small green pepper, chopped

2 cans (8 ounces *each*) no-salt-added tomato sauce

1 cup water

2 envelopes sloppy joe mix

1 tablespoon brown sugar

10 hamburger buns, split

1 In a large nonstick skillet coated with cooking spray, cook the turkey, onion and pepper over medium heat until the meat is no longer pink; drain. Transfer mixture to a 3-qt. slow cooker.

2 Stir in the tomato sauce, water, sloppy joe mix and brown sugar. Cover and cook on low for 4-5 hours or until flavors are blended. Spoon 1/2 cup onto each bun.

Yield: 10 servings.

hearty taco chili

PREP: 30 MIN. • COOK: 6 HOURS

Julie Neuhalfen
Glenwood, Iowa

Ranch dressing mix and taco seasoning give this hearty mixture extra-special flavor. Folks will come back for seconds.

2 pounds ground beef

1 can (16 ounces) kidney beans, rinsed and drained

1 can (15 ounces) pinto beans, rinsed and drained

1 can (15 ounces) black beans, rinsed and drained

1 can (14 ounces) hominy, rinsed and drained

1 can (10 ounces) diced tomatoes and green chilies, undrained

1 can (8 ounces) tomato sauce

1 small onion, chopped

1 envelope ranch salad dressing mix

1 envelope taco seasoning

1/2 teaspoon pepper

2 cans (14-1/2 ounces *each*), diced tomatoes, undrained

1 can (4 ounces) chopped green chilies

Corn chips, sour cream and shredded cheddar cheese, optional

1 In a large skillet, cook beef over medium heat until no longer pink; drain. Transfer to a 5-qt. slow cooker. Add the beans, hominy, tomatoes, tomato sauce, onion, salad dressing mix, taco seasoning and pepper.

2 In a blender, combine diced tomatoes and green chilies; cover and process until smooth. Add to the slow cooker. Cover and cook on low for 6 hours.

3 Serve with corn chips, sour cream and cheese if desired.

Yield: 11 servings.

pulled pork sandwiches

PREP: 20 MIN. • COOK: 6 HOURS

Tiffany Martinez
Aliso Viejo, California

Preparing pork sirloin roast in the slow cooker makes it so moist and tender...it's perfect for sandwiches. The meat shreds so easily, and the cumin and garlic add just the right flavor. The sourdough bread, chipotle mayonnaise, cheese and tomato make these sandwiches complete.

> 1 boneless pork sirloin roast (2 pounds), trimmed
>
> 1 cup barbecue sauce
>
> 1/4 cup chopped onion
>
> 2 garlic cloves, minced
>
> 1/2 teaspoon ground cumin
>
> 1/4 teaspoon salt
>
> 1/8 teaspoon pepper
>
> 16 slices sourdough bread
>
> 1 chipotle pepper in adobo sauce, chopped
>
> 3/4 cup mayonnaise
>
> 8 slices cheddar cheese
>
> 2 plum tomatoes, thinly sliced

1 Place pork in a 3-qt. slow cooker. Combine the barbecue sauce, onion, garlic, cumin, salt and pepper; pour over pork. Cover and cook on low for 6-7 hours or until meat is tender. Remove meat. Shred with two forks and return to slow cooker; heat through.

2 Place bread on an ungreased baking sheet. Broil 4-6 in. from the heat for 2-3 minutes on each side or until golden brown.

3 Meanwhile, in a small bowl, combine chipotle pepper and mayonnaise; spread over toast. Spoon 1/2 cup meat mixture onto each of eight slices of toast. Top with cheese, tomatoes and remaining toast.

Yield: 8 servings.

small-batch veggie meatball soup

PREP: 10 MIN. • COOK: 4-1/4 HOURS

Charla Tinney
Tyrone, Oklahoma

It's a snap to put together this hearty soup before I leave for work. I just add the pasta when I get home, and I have some time to relax before supper is ready.

> 1-1/2 cups reduced-sodium beef broth
>
> 1 cup frozen mixed vegetables, thawed
>
> 3/4 cup canned stewed tomatoes
>
> 9 frozen fully cooked homestyle meatballs (1/2 ounce *each*), thawed
>
> 2 bay leaves
>
> 1/8 teaspoon pepper
>
> 1/2 cup uncooked spiral pasta

1 In a 1-1/2-qt. slow cooker, combine the first six ingredients. Cover and cook on low for 4-5 hours or until heated through. Stir in the pasta; cover and cook 15-30 minutes longer or until pasta is tender. Discard bay leaves.

Yield: 3 cups.

southwest chicken chili

PREP: 15 MIN. • **COOK: 6 HOURS**

Phyllis Beatty
Chandler, Arizona

Moist chicken thighs are a nice change of pace in this easy chili. I also include a smoked ham hock and fresh cilantro to add flavor and keep the dish interesting.

> 1-1/2 pounds boneless skinless chicken thighs, cut into 1-inch cubes
>
> 1 tablespoon olive oil
>
> 1 smoked ham hock
>
> 1 can (15-1/2 ounces) great northern beans, rinsed and drained
>
> 1 can (14-1/2 ounces) chicken broth
>
> 1 can (4 ounces) chopped green chilies
>
> 1/4 cup chopped onion
>
> 2 tablespoons minced fresh cilantro
>
> 1 teaspoon garlic powder
>
> 1 teaspoon ground cumin
>
> 1/2 teaspoon dried oregano
>
> 1/8 to 1/4 teaspoon crushed red pepper flakes
>
> Sour cream, optional

1 In a large skillet, brown chicken in oil. Transfer to a 3-qt. slow cooker. Add the ham hock, beans, broth, chilies, onion and seasonings. Cover and cook on low for 6 to 8 hours or until ham is tender.

2 Remove ham bone. When cool enough to handle, remove meat from bone; discard bone. Cut meat into bite-size pieces and return to slow cooker. Serve with sour cream if desired.

Yield: 5 servings.

italian beef sandwiches

PREP: 15 MIN. • **COOK: 7 HOURS**

Carol Allen
McLeansboro, Illinois

Before leaving for work in the morning, I often put these ingredients in the slow cooker. Supper is ready when I get home. This recipe is also good to take to a get-together.

> 1 boneless beef chuck roast (3 to 4 pounds), cut in half
>
> 3 tablespoons dried basil
>
> 3 tablespoons dried oregano
>
> 1 cup water
>
> 1 envelope onion soup mix
>
> 10 to 12 Italian rolls *or* sandwich buns

1 Place roast in a 5-qt. slow cooker. Combine the basil, oregano and water; pour over roast. Sprinkle with soup mix.

2 Cover and cook on low for 7-8 hours or until meat is tender. Remove meat; shred with a fork and keep warm. Strain broth and skim fat. Serve meat on rolls; use broth for dipping if desired.

Yield: 10-12 servings.

french onion soup

PREP: 15 MIN. • COOK: 8 HOURS

Kris Ritter
Pittsburgh, Pennsylvania

*It's hard to believe something this delightful came
from a slow cooker! Topped with a slice of French
bread and provolone cheese, individual servings are
sure to be enjoyed by everyone at your dinner table.*

1 large sweet onion, thinly sliced (about 4
cups)

1/4 cup butter, cubed

2 cans (14-1/2 ounces *each*) beef broth

2 tablespoons sherry *or* additional beef broth

1/2 teaspoon pepper

4 slices French bread (1/2 inch thick), toasted

4 slices provolone cheese

1 Place onion and butter in a 1-1/2-qt. slow
cooker coated with cooking spray. Cover
and cook on low for 6 hours or until onion is
tender. Stir in the broth, sherry and pepper.
Cover and cook 2-3 hours longer or until
heated through.

2 Ladle soup into ovenproof bowls. Top each
with a slice of toast and cheese. Broil 4-6
in. from the heat for 2-3 minutes or until
cheese is melted. Serve immediately.

Yield: 4 servings.

Sweet onions. Vidalia and other sweet
onions are mild-flavored onions that are
high in sugar and water content and low
in tear-inducing sulfur compounds.

southwestern beef tortillas

PREP: 25 MIN. • COOK: 8-1/4 HOURS

Marie Rizzio
Interlochen, Michigan

A boneless chuck roast makes for a savory filling in these satisfying tortillas. Cooked to perfection in a slow cooker, the beef is treated to an effortless jalapeno-flavored sauce.

  1 boneless beef chuck roast (2 pounds)

  1/2 cup water

  4 large tomatoes, peeled and chopped

  1 large green pepper, thinly sliced

  1 medium onion, chopped

  1 garlic clove, minced

  1 bay leaf

  2 tablespoons canola oil

  3/4 cup ketchup

  1/2 cup pickled jalapeno slices

  1 tablespoon juice from pickled jalapeno slices

  1 tablespoon cider vinegar

  1 teaspoon salt

  1/8 teaspoon garlic salt

  8 flour tortillas (8 inches), warmed

1 Place roast and water in a 3-qt. slow cooker. Cover and cook on low for 8-9 hours or until meat is tender.

2 Remove meat. When cool enough to handle, shred meat with two forks. Skim fat from cooking liquid; set aside 1/2 cup.

3 In a large skillet, cook the tomatoes, green pepper, onion, garlic and bay leaf in oil for 15-20 minutes or until liquid is reduced to 2 tablespoons.

4 Stir in the ketchup, jalapeno slices and juice, vinegar, salt, garlic salt and reserved cooking liquid. Bring to a boil. Stir in shredded beef; heat through. Discard bay leaf. Serve on tortillas.

Yield: 8 servings.

chunky chili

PREP: 15 MIN. • COOK: 5 HOURS

Jolene Britten
Gig Harbor, Washington

My family (especially my dad) loves chili. After experimenting with several recipes, I came up with my own version that uses ground turkey and is conveniently prepared in a slow cooker.

- 1 pound ground turkey *or* beef
- 1 medium onion, chopped
- 2 medium tomatoes, cut up
- 1 can (16 ounces) kidney beans, rinsed and drained
- 1 can (16 ounces) chili beans, undrained
- 1 can (15 ounces) tomato sauce
- 1 cup water
- 1 can (4 ounces) chopped green chilies
- 1 tablespoon chili powder
- 2 teaspoons salt
- 1 teaspoon ground cumin
- 3/4 teaspoon pepper
- Sour cream and sliced jalapenos, optional

1 In a large skillet, cook turkey and onion over medium heat until meat is no longer pink; drain.

2 Transfer to a 3-1/2-qt. slow cooker. Stir in the tomatoes, beans, tomato sauce, water, chilies, chili powder, salt, cumin and pepper. Cover and cook on low for 5-6 hours or until heated through. Garnish with sour cream and jalapenos if desired.

Yield: 8 servings (about 2 quarts).

forgotten minestrone

PREP: 15 MIN. • COOK: 7-1/2 HOURS

Marsha Ransom
South Haven, Michigan

This chunky soup gets its name because the broth simmers for hours, allowing me to work on my freelance writing. But after one spoonful, you and your family will agree this full-flavored soup is truly unforgettable!

1 pound beef stew meat, cut into 1/2-inch cubes

1 can (28 ounces) diced tomatoes, undrained

1 medium onion, chopped

2 tablespoons minced dried parsley

2-1/2 teaspoons salt, optional

1-1/2 teaspoons ground thyme

1 beef bouillon cube

1/2 teaspoon pepper

6 cups water

1 medium zucchini, halved and thinly sliced

2 cups chopped cabbage

1 can (15 ounces) garbanzo beans *or* chickpeas, rinsed and drained

1 cup uncooked elbow macaroni

1/4 cup grated Parmesan cheese, optional

1 In a 5-qt. slow cooker, combine the first nine ingredients. Cover and cook on low for 7-9 hours or until meat is tender.

2 Add the zucchini, cabbage, beans and macaroni; cover and cook on high for 30-45 minutes or until vegetables are tender. Sprinkle each serving with cheese if desired.

Yield: 8 servings.

barbecued beef sandwiches

PREP: 20 MIN. • COOK: 8-1/4 HOURS

Tatina Smith
San Angelo, Texas

A chuck roast makes delicious shredded beef sandwiches after simmering in a rich, homemade sauce all day. The meat is tender and juicy and takes minutes to prepare for a weeknight meal or potluck dinner.

3 pounds boneless beef chuck roast

1-1/2 cups ketchup

1/4 cup packed brown sugar

1/4 cup barbecue sauce

2 tablespoons Worcestershire sauce

2 tablespoons Dijon mustard

1 teaspoon Liquid Smoke, optional

1/2 teaspoon salt

1/4 teaspoon garlic powder

1/4 teaspoon pepper

12 sandwich buns, split

Sliced onions, dill pickles and pickled jalapenos, optional

1 Cut roast in half and place in a 3– or 4-qt. slow cooker. In a small bowl, combine the ketchup, brown sugar, barbecue sauce, Worcestershire sauce, mustard, Liquid Smoke if desired and seasonings. Pour over beef.

2 Cover and cook on low for 8-10 hours or until meat is tender. Remove meat; cool slightly. Skim fat from cooking liquid.

3 Shred beef with two forks; return to the slow cooker. Cover and cook for 15 minutes or until heated through. Using a slotted spoon, place 1/2 cup on each bun. Serve with onions, pickles and jalapenos if desired.

Yield: 12 servings.

bavarian meatballs

PREP: 15 MIN. • COOK: 3-1/2 HOURS

Peggy Rios
Mechanicsville, Virginia

I use my slow cooker to fix these yummy meatballs that are great for sandwiches or appetizers.

  1 package (32 ounces) frozen fully cooked Italian meatballs

  1/2 cup chopped onion

  1/4 cup packed brown sugar

  1 envelope onion soup mix

  1 can (12 ounces) beer *or* nonalcoholic beer

  12 hoagie buns, split

  3 cups (12 ounces) shredded Swiss cheese

1 In a 3-qt. slow cooker, combine the meatballs, onion, brown sugar, soup mix and beer.

2 Cover and cook on low for 3-1/2 to 4-1/2 hours or until heated through.

3 Serve with toothpicks for an appetizer. Or for sandwiches, place six meatballs on each bun bottom. Sprinkle each sandwich with 1/4 cup cheese. Place on baking sheets.

4 Broil 4-6 in. from the heat for 2-3 minutes or until cheese is melted. Replace bun tops.

Yield: 12 servings.

vegetable lentil soup

PREP: 15 MIN. • COOK: 4-1/2 HOURS

Taste of Home Test Kitchen

Here's a healthy soup that's ideal for vegetarians and those watching their weight. Butternut squash and lentils make it filling, while herbs and other veggies round out the flavor.

4 cups vegetable broth

3 cups cubed peeled butternut squash

1 cup dried lentils, rinsed

1 cup chopped carrot

1 cup chopped onion

2 teaspoons minced garlic

1 teaspoon dried oregano

1 teaspoon dried basil

1 can (14-1/2 ounces) Italian diced tomatoes, undrained

1 package (9 ounces) frozen cut green beans

1 In a 5-qt. slow cooker, combine the first eight ingredients. Cover and cook on low for 4 hours or until lentils are tender.

2 Stir in the tomatoes and beans. Cover and cook on high for 30 minutes or until beans are heated through.

Yield: 6 servings.

beef barley soup

PREP: 15 MIN. • COOK: 9 HOURS

Ginny Perkins
Columiana, Ohio

My hubby doesn't usually consider a bowl of soup "dinner," but this hearty, comforting combination, served with corn bread on the side, got a thumbs up even from him!

1-1/2 pounds beef stew meat

1 tablespoon canola oil

1 can (14-1/2 ounces) diced tomatoes

1 cup chopped onion

1 cup diced celery

1 cup sliced fresh carrots

1/2 cup chopped green pepper

4 cups beef broth

2 cups water

1 cup spaghetti sauce

2/3 cup medium pearl barley

1 tablespoon dried parsley flakes

2 teaspoons salt

1-1/2 teaspoons dried basil

3/4 teaspoon pepper

1 In a large skillet, brown meat in oil over medium heat; drain. Meanwhile, in a 5-qt. slow cooker, combine the vegetables, broth, water, spaghetti sauce, barley and seasonings. Stir in beef. Cover and cook on low for 9-10 hours or until vegetables are tender. Skim fat from cooking juices.

Yield: 8 servings (2-1/2 quarts).

creamy ham chowder

PREP: 30 MIN. • COOK: 3-1/2 HOURS

Lee Bremson
Kansas City, Missouri

You'll dig into satisfaction when this thick and creamy chowder is on the menu. It's sure to make friends and family think you labored for hours.

4 cups cubed peeled potatoes

2 tablespoons chopped onion

1/2 cup butter

3/4 cup all-purpose flour

1/4 teaspoon salt

1/4 teaspoon pepper

Pinch ground nutmeg

4 cups chicken broth

4 cups half-and-half cream

2 cups (8 ounces) shredded cheddar cheese

3 cups cubed fully cooked ham

1 package (16 ounces) frozen broccoli cuts, thawed and drained

1 Place potatoes in a large saucepan and cover with water. Bring to a boil. Reduce heat; cover and cook for 10-15 minutes or until tender.

2 Meanwhile, in a large saucepan, cook onion in butter over medium heat for 2 minutes. Stir in the flour, salt, pepper and nutmeg; gradually add broth. Bring to a boil; cook and stir for 2 minutes or until thickened. Stir in cream and cheese.

3 Transfer to a 5-qt. slow cooker. Drain potatoes; add to slow cooker. Stir in ham. Cover and cook on low for 3 hours.

4 Stir in broccoli. Cover and cook 30 minutes longer or until heated through and vegetables are tender.

Yield: 12 servings (about 3-1/2 quarts).

vegetarian split pea soup

PREP: 15 MIN. • COOK: 7 HOURS

Corrie Gamache
Palmyra, Virginia

I adapted this recipe from several I found online. When I was a vegetarian for health reasons, it was a favorite. Even my meat-loving husband asked for seconds!

1 package (16 ounces) dried green split peas, rinsed

1 medium leek (white portion only), chopped

3 celery ribs, chopped

1 medium potato, peeled and chopped

2 medium carrots, chopped

1 garlic clove, minced

1/4 cup minced fresh parsley

4 cans (14-1/2 ounces *each*) vegetable broth

1-1/2 teaspoons ground mustard

1/2 teaspoon pepper

1/2 teaspoon dried oregano

1 bay leaf

1 In a 5-qt. slow cooker, combine all of the ingredients. Cover and cook on low for 7-8 hours or until peas are tender. Discard bay leaf.

Yield: 8 servings (2 quarts).

> **Ground goodness.** Also referred to as dry mustard, ground mustard is made from mustard seeds that have been finely ground. Dry mustard is sold in a spice tin. If a recipe calls for prepared mustard, use yellow or brown mustard, which come in jars or bottles and are commonly served as a condiment.

turkey chili

PREP: 20 MIN. • COOK: 6-1/2 HOURS

Celesta Zanger
Bloomfield Hills, Michigan

I've taken my mother's milder recipe for chili and made it thicker and more robust. It's a favorite, especially in fall and winter.

1 pound lean ground turkey

3/4 cup *each* chopped onion, celery and green pepper

1 can (28 ounces) diced tomatoes, undrained

1 jar (26 ounces) meatless spaghetti sauce

1 can (16 ounces) hot chili beans, undrained

1-1/2 cups water

1/2 cup frozen corn

2 tablespoons chili powder

1 teaspoon ground cumin

1/4 teaspoon pepper

1/8 to 1/4 teaspoon cayenne pepper

1 can (16 ounces) kidney beans, rinsed and drained

1 can (15 ounces) pinto beans, rinsed and drained

Sour cream, optional

1 In a large nonstick skillet, cook the turkey, onion, celery and green pepper over medium heat until meat is no longer pink and vegetables are tender; drain.

2 Transfer to a 5-qt. slow cooker. Add the tomatoes, spaghetti sauce, chili beans, water, corn and seasonings. Cover and cook on high for 1 hour.

3 Reduce heat to low; cook for 5-6 hours. Add kidney and pinto beans; cook 30 minutes longer. Garnish with sour cream if desired.

Yield: 13 servings.

italian
beef on rolls

PREP: 15 MIN. • COOK: 8 HOURS

Jami Hilker
Harrison, Arkansas

This is one of my all-time favorite slow cooker recipes! With 28 grams of protein per serving, it's a great way to meet your daily protein needs!

1 beef sirloin tip roast (2 pounds)

1 can (14-1/2 ounces) diced tomatoes, undrained

1 medium green pepper, chopped

1/2 cup water

1 tablespoon sesame seeds

1-1/2 teaspoons garlic powder

1 teaspoon fennel seed, crushed

1/2 teaspoon salt

1/2 teaspoon pepper

8 hard rolls, split

1 Place the roast in a 3-qt. slow cooker. In a small bowl, combine the tomatoes, green pepper, water and seasonings; pour over roast. Cover and cook on low for 8-9 hours or until meat is tender.

2 Remove roast; cool slightly. Skim fat from cooking juices; shred beef and return to the slow cooker. Serve on rolls.

Yield: 8 servings.

smoked sausage gumbo

PREP: 20 MIN. • COOK: 4 HOURS

Sharon Delaney-Chronis
South Milwaukee, Wisconsin

Serve up the flavors of the bayou! You'll leave the table satisfied, as this dish is chock-full of veggies, seasonings and sausage. Add in even more Cajun flavor by using Andouille sausage.

2 celery ribs, chopped

1 medium onion, chopped

1 medium green pepper, chopped

1 medium carrot, chopped

2 tablespoons olive oil

1/4 cup all-purpose flour

1 cup chicken broth

1 pound smoked kielbasa *or* Polish sausage, cut into 1/2-inch pieces

1 can (14-1/2 ounces) diced tomatoes, undrained

2 teaspoons dried oregano

2 teaspoons dried thyme

1/8 teaspoon cayenne pepper

Hot cooked rice

1 In a large skillet, saute the celery, onion, green pepper and carrot in oil until tender. Stir in flour until blended; gradually add broth. Bring to a boil. Cook and stir for 2 minutes or until thickened.

2 Transfer to a 3-qt. slow cooker. Stir in the sausage, tomatoes, oregano, thyme and cayenne. Cover and cook on low for 4-5 hours or until vegetables are tender. Serve with rice.

Yield: 5 servings.

pulled pork subs

PREP: 15 MIN. • COOK: 5 HOURS

Denise Davis
Porter, Maine

Honey and ground ginger are the flavor boosters behind these no-stress sandwiches that make the most of a bottle of barbecue sauce.

- 1 small onion, finely chopped
- 1 boneless pork shoulder butt roast (2-1/2 pounds)
- 1 bottle (18 ounces) barbecue sauce
- 1/2 cup water
- 1/4 cup honey
- 6 garlic cloves, minced
- 1 teaspoon seasoned salt
- 1 teaspoon ground ginger
- 8 submarine buns, split

1 Place onion and roast in a 5-qt. slow cooker. In a small bowl, combine the barbecue sauce, water, honey, garlic, seasoned salt and ginger; pour over meat. Cover and cook on high for 5-6 hours or until meat is tender.

2 Remove meat; cool slightly. Shred meat with two forks and return to the slow cooker; heat through. Serve on buns. Cut sandwiches in half.

Yield: 16 servings.

sauerkraut sausage soup

PREP: 20 MIN. • COOK: 5 HOURS

Yvonne Kett
Appleton, Wisconsin

My husband and I make our own sauerkraut and grow many of the vegetables in this easy slow cooker soup. It cooks all day and smells delicious when we come home from work.

- 4 cups chicken broth
- 1 pound smoked Polish sausage, cut into 1/2-inch slices
- 1 can (16 ounces) sauerkraut, rinsed and well drained
- 2 cups sliced fresh mushrooms
- 1-1/2 cups cubed peeled potatoes
- 1 can (10-3/4 ounces) condensed cream of mushroom soup, undiluted
- 1-1/4 cups chopped onions
- 2 large carrots, sliced
- 2 celery ribs, chopped
- 2 tablespoons white vinegar
- 2 teaspoons dill weed
- 1 teaspoon sugar
- 1/4 teaspoon pepper

1 In a 5-qt. slow cooker, combine all ingredients. Cover and cook on low for 5-6 hours or until vegetables are tender.

Yield: 10 servings.

beef & vegetable soup

PREP: 20 MIN. • COOK: 8 HOURS

Tammy Landry
Saucier, Mississippi

I've been making this for more than 20 years. The beer makes people stop and wonder what the unique flavor is. Try it, I know you'll love it!

1 pound lean ground beef (90% lean)

1/2 cup chopped sweet onion

1 bottle (12 ounces) beer *or* nonalcoholic beer

1 can (10-1/2 ounces) condensed beef broth, undiluted

1-1/2 cups sliced fresh carrots

1-1/4 cups water

1 cup chopped peeled turnip

1/2 cup sliced celery

1 can (4 ounces) mushroom stems and pieces, drained

1 teaspoon salt

1 teaspoon pepper

1 bay leaf

1/8 teaspoon ground allspice

1 In a large skillet, cook beef and onion over medium heat until meat is no longer pink; drain. Transfer to a 5-qt. slow cooker. Stir in the remaining ingredients. Cover and cook on low for 8-10 hours or until heated through. Discard bay leaf.

Yield: 6 servings.

hearty sausage-chicken chili

PREP: 20 MIN. • COOK: 4 HOURS

Carolyn Etzler
Thurmont, Maryland

The company I work for has an annual Chili Cook-Off, and this unusual recipe of mine was a winner. It combines two other recipes and includes a touch or two of my own.

> 1 pound Italian turkey sausage links, casings removed
>
> 3/4 pound boneless skinless chicken thighs, cut into 3/4-inch pieces
>
> 1 medium onion, chopped
>
> 2 cans (14-1/2 ounces *each*) diced tomatoes with mild green chilies, undrained
>
> 2 cans (8 ounces *each*) tomato sauce
>
> 1 can (16 ounces) kidney beans, rinsed and drained
>
> 1 can (15 ounces) white kidney *or* cannellini beans, rinsed and drained
>
> 1 can (15 ounces) pinto beans, rinsed and drained
>
> 1 can (15 ounces) black beans, rinsed and drained
>
> 1 teaspoon chili powder
>
> 1/2 teaspoon garlic powder
>
> 1/8 teaspoon pepper

1 Crumble the sausage into a large nonstick skillet coated with cooking spray. Add the chicken and onion; cook and stir over medium heat until meat is no longer pink. Drain.

2 Transfer to a 5-qt. slow cooker. Stir in the remaining ingredients. Cover and cook on low for 4 hours.

Yield: 11 servings (2-3/4 quarts).

brats with sauerkraut

PREP: 10 MIN. • COOK: 6 HOURS

Darlene Dixon
Hanover, Minnesota

I've made many variations of this excellent main dish. The bratwurst can be plain, smoked or cheese-flavored, served whole or cut in slices, with a bun or without. It would be popular at a party or potluck.

> 8 uncooked bratwurst links
>
> 1 can (14 ounces) sauerkraut, rinsed and well drained
>
> 2 medium apples, peeled and finely chopped
>
> 3 bacon strips, cooked and crumbled
>
> 1/4 cup packed brown sugar
>
> 1/4 cup finely chopped onion
>
> 1 teaspoon ground mustard
>
> 8 brat buns, split

1 Place the bratwurst in a 5-qt. slow cooker. In a large bowl, combine the sauerkraut, apples, bacon, brown sugar, onion and mustard; spoon over bratwurst. Cover and cook on low for 6-7 hours or until sausage is no longer pink.

2 Place brats in buns; using a slotted spoon, top with sauerkraut mixture.

Yield: 8 servings.

chipotle beef sandwiches

PREP: 25 MIN. • COOK: 7 HOURS

Jessica Ring
Madison, Wisconsin

A jar of chipotle salsa makes it easy to spice up beef sirloin for my mouthwatering sandwiches. Keep this no-stress recipe in mind the next time you have to feed a hungry crowd.

   1 large sweet onion, halved and thinly sliced

   1 beef sirloin tip roast (3 pounds)

   1 jar (16 ounces) chipotle salsa

   1/2 cup beer *or* nonalcoholic beer

   1 envelope beefy onion soup mix

   10 kaiser rolls, split

1 Place onion in a 5-qt. slow cooker. Cut roast in half; place over onion. Combine the salsa, beer and soup mix. Pour over top. Cover and cook on low for 7-8 hours or until meat is tender.

2 Remove roast. Shred meat with two forks and return to the slow cooker; heat through. Using a slotted spoon, spoon shredded meat onto each roll.

Yield: 10 servings.

curried pumpkin soup

PREP: 20 MIN. • COOK: 6 HOURS

Debbie Flocco
Norristown, Pennsylvania

Looking for something new to beat dinnertime doldrums? Try my pumpkin soup! A touch of curry powder lends an aromatic appeal while whipping cream gives the soup its silky texture.

   2-1/2 cups water

   1 can (15 ounces) solid-pack pumpkin

   2 medium tomatoes, quartered

   1 medium potato, peeled and diced

   1 medium onion, chopped

   2 to 3 teaspoons curry powder

   2 teaspoons chicken bouillon granules

   1/2 teaspoon salt

   1/8 teaspoon cayenne pepper

   1/8 teaspoon pepper

   1 cup 2% milk

   1/2 cup heavy whipping cream

1 In a 3-qt. slow cooker, combine the first 10 ingredients. Cover and cook on low for 5-1/2 to 6-1/2 hours or until vegetables are tender.

2 In a blender, process soup in batches until smooth. Return all to slow cooker. Stir in milk and cream. Cook on high for 30 minutes or until heated through.

Yield: 8 servings.

> **Curry powder.** A blend of a variety of ground spices popular in Indian cooking, curry powder imparts a distinctive flavor and rich golden color to recipes and can be found in both mild and hot versions.

baked potato soup

PREP: 35 MIN. • COOK: 6 HOURS

Barbara Bleigh
Colonial Heights, Virginia

The only thing that beats the comforting flavor of this thick and hearty potato soup is possibly the idea that it simmers on its own all day.

2 large onions, chopped

3 tablespoons butter

2 tablespoons all-purpose flour

2 cups water, *divided*

4 cups chicken broth

2 medium potatoes, peeled and diced

1-1/2 cups mashed potato flakes

1/2 pound sliced bacon, cooked and crumbled

3/4 teaspoon pepper

1/2 teaspoon salt

1/2 teaspoon dried basil

1/8 teaspoon dried thyme

1 cup half-and-half cream

1/2 cup shredded cheddar cheese

2 green onions, sliced

1 In a large skillet, saute onions in butter until tender. Stir in flour. Gradually stir in 1 cup water. Bring to a boil; cook and stir for 2 minutes or until thickened. Transfer to a 5-qt. slow cooker.

2 Add the broth, potatoes, potato flakes, bacon, pepper, salt, basil, thyme and remaining water. Cover and cook on low for 6-8 hours or until potatoes are tender. Stir in cream; heat through. Garnish with cheese and green onions.

Yield: 10 servings.

trout chowder

PREP: 15 MIN. • COOK: 1-1/2 HOURS

Linda Kesselring
Corning, New York

This hearty chowder cooks conveniently in a slow cooker so I can spend more time fishing and less in the kitchen. Broccoli adds fresh taste and lively color to the rich cheesy broth.

1 medium onion, chopped

1 tablespoon butter

2 cups whole milk

1 cup ranch salad dressing

1 pound boneless trout fillets, skin removed

1 package (9 ounces) frozen broccoli cuts, thawed

1 cup cubed *or* shredded cheddar cheese

1 cup cubed *or* shredded Monterey Jack cheese

1/4 teaspoon garlic powder

Paprika, optional

1 In a large skillet, saute onion in butter until tender. Transfer to a 3-qt. slow cooker; add the milk, dressing, fish, broccoli, cheeses and garlic powder.

2 Cover and cook on high for 1-1/2 to 2 hours or until soup is bubbly and fish flakes easily with a fork. Sprinkle with the paprika if desired.

Yield: 6 servings.

texican chili

PREP: 25 MIN. • COOK: 9 HOURS

Stacy Law
Cornish, Utah

This flavorful, meaty chili is my favorite...and it's so easy to make in the slow cooker. It's a great way to serve a crowd without last-minute preparation. I got the idea from my mother, who used her slow cooker often for soups and stews.

- 8 bacon strips, diced
- 2-1/2 pounds beef stew meat, cut into 1/2-inch cubes
- 2 cans (one 28 ounces, one 14-1/2 ounces) stewed tomatoes undrained
- 2 cans (8 ounces *each*) tomato sauce
- 1 can (16 ounces) kidney beans, rinsed and drained
- 2 cups sliced carrots
- 1 cup chopped celery
- 3/4 cup chopped onion
- 1/2 cup chopped green pepper
- 1/4 cup minced fresh parsley
- 1 tablespoon chili powder
- 1 teaspoon salt, optional
- 1/2 teaspoon ground cumin
- 1/4 teaspoon pepper

1 In a large skillet, cook bacon until crisp. Remove to paper towels to drain. Brown beef in the drippings over medium heat; drain. Transfer to a 5-qt. slow cooker; add bacon and remaining ingredients. Cover and cook on low for 9-10 hours or until meat is tender, stirring occasionally.

Yield: 16-18 servings.

italian chicken chili

PREP: 20 MIN. • COOK: 6-3/4 HOURS

Genise Krause
Sturgeon Bay, Wisconsin

Though the list of ingredients may seem long, this recipe takes just 20 minutes of prep before it is simmering into a heartwarming main course. Each bite brings variety in taste and texture, not to mention loads of Italian flavor.

1/2 pound bulk Italian sausage

1 teaspoon olive oil

1 pound boneless skinless chicken breasts, cut into 1-inch cubes

1 can (28 ounces) crushed tomatoes

1 can (28 ounces) diced tomatoes, undrained

1 can (15 ounces) white kidney *or* cannellini beans, rinsed and drained

2 celery ribs, chopped

1 cup chopped onion

1 small sweet red pepper, chopped

1/2 cup dry red wine *or* chicken broth

2 tablespoons chili powder

2 teaspoons dried oregano

2 teaspoons minced garlic

1 teaspoon dried thyme

1 medium zucchini, diced

1 cup sliced fresh mushrooms

1/4 cup minced fresh parsley

Shredded Italian cheese blend, optional

1 In a large skillet, cook sausage in oil over medium heat until no longer pink; drain.

2 Transfer to a 5-qt. slow cooker. Stir in the chicken, tomatoes, beans, celery, onion, red pepper, wine or broth, chili powder, oregano, garlic and thyme. Cover and cook on low for 6 hours or until chicken is no longer pink.

3 Stir in the zucchini and mushrooms. Cover and cook on high for 45 minutes or until vegetables are tender. Sprinkle with parsley. Serve with cheese if desired.

Yield: 8 servings (2-3/4 quarts).

savory cheese soup

PREP: 10 MIN. • COOK: 5-3/4 HOURS

Ann Huseby
Lakeville, Minnesota

This comforting soup that yields two servings is a welcome treat on wintry days. It's so satisfying, you might wish there were leftovers!

- 1 can (14-1/2 ounces) chicken broth
- 1/4 cup chopped carrot
- 1/4 cup chopped celery
- 1 tablespoon chopped onion
- 1 tablespoon chopped sweet red pepper
- 2 teaspoons butter
- 1/8 to 1/4 teaspoon pepper
- 2 tablespoons all-purpose flour
- 2 tablespoons cold water
- 1 package (3 ounces) cream cheese, cubed and softened
- 3/4 cup shredded cheddar cheese
- 1/3 cup beer *or* additional chicken broth
- Croutons, crumbled cooked bacon and sliced green onions, optional

1 In a 1-1/2-qt. slow cooker, combine the first seven ingredients. Cover and cook on low for 5 hours or until vegetables are tender.

2 Combine flour and water until smooth; stir into soup. Cover and cook on high for 30 minutes or until thickened.

3 Stir in cream cheese and cheddar cheese until blended. Stir in beer. Cover and cook on low for 15 minutes or until heated through. Top with croutons, bacon and green onions if desired.

Yield: 2 servings.

tangy roast beef sandwiches

PREP: 15 MIN. • COOK: 5 HOURS

Amy Krause
Juneau, Wisconsin

Everyone enjoys these moist, delicious sandwiches. The beef filling can be assembled early in the day to cook until dinnertime.

   1 boneless beef chuck roast (1 pound)

   1 cup water

   1/4 cup chopped onion

   1/4 cup chopped celery

   1 tablespoon butter

   1/3 cup ketchup

   3 tablespoons lemon juice

   1 tablespoon brown sugar

   2 teaspoons red wine vinegar

   1-1/2 teaspoons Worcestershire sauce

   1/8 teaspoon salt

   1/8 teaspoon pepper

   3 sandwich buns, split

1 Place the roast in a 1-1/2-qt. slow cooker; add water. Cover and cook on high for 3 hours or until meat is tender. Remove roast; set aside 1/3 cup cooking juices. Shred meat with two forks and return to the slow cooker.

2 In a small skillet, saute onion and celery in butter. Stir in the ketchup, lemon juice, brown sugar, vinegar, Worcestershire sauce, salt, pepper and reserved cooking juices. Add to slow cooker. Cook on low for 2-3 hours or until heated through and flavors are blended. Serve on buns.

Yield: 3 servings.

home-style chicken soup

PREP: 15 MIN.
COOK: 6-1/4 HOURS

Kathy Rairigh
Milford, Indiana

I've relied on this easily prepared combination of chicken, vegetables, noodles and broth on many occasions. Mom gave me the recipe, and we love it.

- 1 can (14-1/2 ounces) chicken broth
- 1 can (14-1/2 ounces) diced tomatoes, undrained
- 1 cup cubed cooked chicken
- 1 can (8 ounces) mushroom stems and pieces, drained
- 1/4 cup sliced fresh carrot
- 1/4 cup sliced celery
- 1 bay leaf
- 1/8 teaspoon dried thyme
- 3/4 cup cooked egg noodles

1 In a 1-1/2-qt. slow cooker, combine the first eight ingredients. Cover and cook on low for 6 hours. Stir in noodles; cover and cook on high for 15 minutes. Discard bay leaf.

Yield: 4 servings.

hearty minestrone soup

PREP: 25 MIN. • COOK: 6-1/4 HOURS

Bonnie Hosman
Young, Arizona

I picked up this recipe in California in the '80s and have been making it ever since. I love it partly because it's simple to put together and partly because the flavor is so wonderful!

- 2 cans (one 28 ounces, one 14-1/2 ounces) diced tomatoes, undrained
- 2 cups water
- 2 medium carrots, sliced
- 1 medium onion, chopped
- 1 medium zucchini, chopped
- 1 package (3-1/2 ounces) sliced pepperoni
- 2 teaspoons minced garlic
- 2 teaspoons chicken bouillon granules
- 1/2 teaspoon dried basil
- 1/2 teaspoon dried oregano
- 2 cans (16 ounces *each*), kidney beans, rinsed and drained
- 1 package (10 ounces) frozen chopped spinach, thawed and squeezed dry
- 1-1/4 cups cooked elbow macaroni
- Shredded Parmesan cheese

1 In a 5-qt. slow cooker, combine the first 10 ingredients. Cover and cook on low for 6-7 hours or until vegetables are tender.

2 Stir in the beans, spinach and macaroni. Cover and cook 15 minutes longer or until heated through. Sprinkle with cheese.

Yield: 7 servings (2-3/4 quarts).

slow cooker sloppy joes

PREP: 15 MIN. • COOK: 4 HOURS

Joeanne Steras
Garrett, Pennsylvania

Slow cook your way to a crowd-pleasing entree! Ground beef is easily transformed into a classic sandwich filling with just a few pantry staples.

2 pounds ground beef

1 cup chopped green pepper

2/3 cup chopped onion

2 cups ketchup

2 envelopes sloppy joe mix

2 tablespoons brown sugar

1 teaspoon prepared mustard

12 hamburger buns, split

1 In a large skillet, cook beef, pepper and onion over medium heat until meat is no longer pink; drain. Stir in the ketchup, sloppy joe mix, brown sugar and mustard.

2 Transfer to a 3-qt. slow cooker. Cover and cook on low for 4 hours or until flavors are blended. Spoon 1/2 cup onto each bun.

Yield: 12 servings.

makeover hash brown soup

PREP: 15 MIN. • COOK: 6 HOURS

Judith Webb
Blue Springs, Missouri

This rich and creamy soup has all the goodness you'd expect, but it is surprisingly good for you. It's the perfect recipe to chase away chills on a cool autumn day.

2 green onions, chopped

2 teaspoons canola oil

1 package (28 ounces) frozen O'Brien potatoes, thawed

2 cups 2% milk

1 can (10-3/4 ounces) reduced-fat reduced-sodium condensed cream of chicken soup, undiluted

6 turkey bacon strips, diced and cooked

1/2 cup shredded cheddar cheese

1 In a small skillet, saute onions in oil until tender. In a 5-qt. slow cooker, combine the potatoes, milk, soup and onion mixture. Cover and cook on low for 6-7 hours or until heated through. Top each serving with 2 tablespoons bacon and 1 tablespoon cheese.

Yield: 8 servings.

> **Dress it up.** Jazz up individual bowls of soup with a variety of yummy garnishes, such as a sprinkle of nuts, chopped fresh herbs, sliced green onions, slivers of fresh vegetables, croutons, shredded cheese or crumbled bacon.

chicken chili

PREP: 10 MIN. • COOK: 5 HOURS

Taste of Home Test Kitchen

Assemble this midday and your dinner will be ready and waiting for you after work.

1-1/2 pounds boneless skinless chicken breasts, cut into 1/2-inch cubes

1 cup chopped onion

3 tablespoons canola oil

1 can (15 ounces) white kidney *or* cannellini beans, rinsed and drained

1 can (14-1/2 ounces) diced tomatoes, undrained

1 can (14-1/2 ounces) diced tomatoes with mild green chilies, undrained

1 cup frozen corn

1 teaspoon salt

1 teaspoon ground cumin

1 teaspoon minced garlic

1/2 teaspoon celery salt

1/2 teaspoon ground coriander

1/2 teaspoon pepper

Sour cream and shredded cheddar cheese, optional

1 In a large skillet, saute chicken and onion in oil for 5 minutes or until chicken is browned.

2 Transfer to a 5-qt. slow cooker. Stir in the beans, tomatoes, corn and seasonings. Cover and cook on low for 5 hours or until chicken is no longer pink. Garnish with sour cream and cheese if desired.

Yield: 6 servings.

cream of cauliflower soup

PREP: 30 MIN. • COOK: 3-1/2 HOURS

Ruth Worden
Mossena, New York

When a chill is in the air, I like to make soups for the family. Cheese adds flavor and heartiness to this one, which is my own recipe.

  1 large head cauliflower, broken into florets

  2 cups chicken broth

  2 tablespoons reduced-sodium chicken bouillon granules

  2 cups half-and-half cream

  2 cups 2% milk

  1 medium carrot, shredded

  2 bay leaves

  1/4 teaspoon garlic powder

  1/2 cup mashed potato flakes

  2 cups (8 ounces) shredded cheddar cheese

  Paprika

1 In a large saucepan, combine the cauliflower, broth and bouillon. Bring to a boil. Reduce heat; cover and cook for 20 minutes or until tender. Mash cauliflower.

2 Transfer to a 3-qt. slow cooker. Stir in the cream, milk, carrot, bay leaves and garlic powder. Cover and cook on low for 3 hours. Stir in potato flakes.

3 Cook 30 minutes longer or until thickened. Discard bay leaves. Cool slightly.

4 In a blender, process soup in batches until smooth. Return to the slow cooker; stir in cheese. Cook until soup is heated through and cheese is melted. Garnish with paprika.

Yield: 8 servings (2 quarts).

slow-cooked shredded pork

PREP: 15 MIN. • COOK: 6 HOURS

Shirleymae Haefner
O'Fallon, Missouri

The tasty pork filling for these sandwiches requires very little work because it's prepared in the slow cooker. The mild, sweet sauce is appealing, too.

  1 boneless whole pork loin roast
  (2 to 3 pounds)

  1 large onion, thinly sliced

  1 cup beer *or* nonalcoholic beer

  1 cup chili sauce

  2 tablespoons brown sugar

  1 tablespoon prepared horseradish

  8 sandwich rolls, split

1 Place the roast in a 3-qt. slow cooker. Top with onion. Combine the beer, chili sauce, brown sugar and horseradish; pour over pork and onion. Cover and cook on low for 6 to 6-1/2 hours or until meat is tender.

2 Remove pork; shred with two forks. Return meat to cooking juices; heat through. Use a slotted spoon to serve on rolls.

Yield: 8 servings.

slow-cooked potato soup

PREP: 30 MIN. • **COOK: 5 HOURS**

Mary Jo O'Brien
Hastings, Minnesota

I make this thick soup for our annual St. Patrick's Day party, and there's never any leftovers.

  5-1/2 cups cubed peeled potatoes, *divided*

  2-3/4 cups water

  1/3 cup butter, cubed

  1-1/3 cups cubed fully cooked ham

  2 celery ribs, chopped

  2/3 cup chopped onion

  3/4 teaspoon garlic powder

  3/4 teaspoon paprika

  1/8 teaspoon pepper

  1/2 pound process cheese (Velveeta), cubed

  2/3 cup sour cream

  Whole milk, optional

1 Place 4-1/2 cups of the potatoes in a large saucepan and cover with water. Bring to a boil. Reduce heat; cover and cook for 10-15 minutes or until tender. Remove from the heat (do not drain). Mash potatoes; stir in butter.

2 In a 3-qt. slow cooker, combine the ham, celery, onion, garlic powder, paprika, pepper and remaining cubed potatoes. Stir in the mashed potatoes; top with cheese. Cover and cook on low for 5-6 hours or until potatoes and other vegetables are tender. Stir in the sour cream until blended. Thin soup with milk if desired.

Yield: 6 servings.

halibut chowder

PREP: 20 MIN. • **COOK: 5-1/2 HOURS**

Donna Goutermont
Juneau, Alaska

Try this great way to mix up dinner standbys. Mashed potato flakes thicken this easy chowder, and you can vary the chili powder and cayenne to suit your taste.

  2 cups water

  2 cups 2% milk

  2 medium potatoes, cubed

  1 large onion, chopped

  1 cup mashed potato flakes

  1 can (8 ounces) tomato sauce

  2 garlic cloves, minced

  1 teaspoon celery salt

  1 teaspoon dried parsley flakes

  1/2 teaspoon ground mustard

  1/4 teaspoon chili powder

  1/4 teaspoon cayenne pepper

  1 pound halibut fillets, cut into chunks

  1 tablespoon butter

1 In a 3-qt. slow cooker, combine the first 12 ingredients. Cover and cook on low for 5 hours or until potatoes are tender.

2 Add halibut and butter. Cover and cook 30-45 minutes longer or until fish flakes easily with a fork.

Yield: 6 servings.

Go fish! If your family's not wild about fish, Halibut Chowder is a good recipe to start out with since halibut is a milder-tasting fish. Cod, haddock, sole, flounder and walleye are also pleasantly mild and have a delicate texture.

veggie meatball soup

PREP: 20 MIN. • COOK: 6 HOURS

Penny Fagan
Mobile, Alabama

Loaded with veggies, meatballs and spices, this meal-in-one soup is hearty enough to warm up any cold winter day. It's a recipe you'll make again and again!

1 package (12 ounces) frozen fully cooked Italian meatballs

1 can (28 ounces) diced tomatoes, undrained

3 cups beef broth

2 cups shredded cabbage

1 can (16 ounces) kidney beans, rinsed and drained

1 medium zucchini, sliced

1 cup fresh green beans, cut into 1-inch pieces

1 cup water

2 medium carrots, sliced

1 teaspoon dried basil

1/2 teaspoon minced garlic

1/4 teaspoon salt

1/8 teaspoon dried oregano

1/8 teaspoon pepper

1 cup uncooked elbow macaroni

1/4 cup minced fresh parsley

Grated Parmesan cheese, optional

1 In a 5-qt. slow cooker, combine the first 14 ingredients. Cover and cook on low for 5-1/2 to 6 hours or until vegetables are almost tender.

2 Stir in the macaroni and parsley; cook 30 minutes longer or until macaroni is tender. Serve with cheese if desired.

Yield: 6 servings (2-1/2 quarts).

chunky chicken soup

PREP: 15 MIN. • COOK: 4-1/2 HOURS

Nancy Clow
Mallorytown, Ontario

I am a stay-at-home mom who relies on my slow cooker for easy, nutritious meals with minimal cleanup and prep time. I knew this recipe was a hit when I didn't have any leftovers and my husband asked me to make it again.

1-1/2 pounds boneless skinless chicken breasts, cut into 2-inch strips

2 teaspoons canola oil

2/3 cup finely chopped onion

2 medium carrots, chopped

2 celery ribs, chopped

1 cup frozen corn

2 cans (10-3/4 ounces *each*) condensed cream of potato soup, undiluted

1-1/2 cups chicken broth

1 teaspoon dill weed

1 cup frozen peas

1/2 cup half-and-half cream

1 In a large skillet over medium-high heat, brown chicken in oil or until no longer pink. With a slotted spoon, transfer to a 5-qt. slow cooker. Add the onion, carrots, celery and corn. In a large bowl, whisk the soup, broth and dill until blended; stir into slow cooker. Cover and cook on low for 4 hours or until vegetables are tender. Stir in peas and cream.

2 Cover and cook 30 minutes longer or until heated through.

Yield: 7 servings.

two-bean chili

PREP: 40 MIN. • COOK: 8 HOURS

Ronald Johnson
Elmhurst, Illinois

The first time I had this chili at a Super Bowl party, I was on my second bowl before I realized it had no meat! It's so chock-full of ingredients and flavor that it's hard to believe this is a low-fat recipe. Enjoy!

1/2 pound sliced fresh mushrooms

1 large green pepper, chopped

1 large sweet red pepper, chopped

2 celery ribs, chopped

1 medium onion, chopped

1 jalapeno pepper, seeded and chopped

1 tablespoon olive oil

4 garlic cloves, minced

2 teaspoons ground cumin

1 teaspoon dried oregano

1 can (28 ounces) diced tomatoes, undrained

1 can (16 ounces) red beans, rinsed and drained

1 can (15 ounces) black beans, rinsed and drained

1 large carrot, chopped

1/2 cup water

1/2 cup barbecue sauce

1/4 cup chili powder

1 teaspoon Liquid Smoke, optional

OPTIONAL TOPPINGS:

Reduced-fat sour cream, hot pepper sauce, shredded cheddar cheese, chopped onion *and/or* crushed baked tortilla chip scoops

1 In a large skillet over medium heat, cook and stir the mushrooms, peppers, celery, onion and jalapeno in oil until onion is lightly browned. Add the garlic, cumin and oregano; cook and stir 1 minute longer.

2 Transfer to a 5-qt. slow cooker. Stir in the tomatoes, beans, carrot, water, barbecue sauce, chili powder and Liquid Smoke if desired. Cover and cook on low for 8 hours or until vegetables are tender. Serve with sour cream, pepper sauce, cheese, onion and/or chips if desired.

Yield: 6 servings (2 quarts).

EDITOR'S NOTE: When cutting hot peppers, disposable gloves are recommended. Avoid touching your face.

Great toppings. The toppings for chili make it a fun dish to eat. Set out bowls of toppings and let your group mix-and-match to create their own unique bowl of chili. Here's a few suggestions for the toppings: jalapeno pepper rings, crushed tortillas, sliced ripe olives, sliced green onions, shredded cheese, chopped red pepper, sour cream, minced fresh cilantro or chopped tomatoes.

tex-mex beef barbecues

PREP: 20 MIN. • COOK: 5 HOURS

Lynda Zuniga
Crystal City, Texas

I recently took this dish to a potluck, and guests loved it! The recipe came from my mom, and it tastes equally good with ground beef.

1 fresh beef brisket (3-1/2 pounds)

1 jar (18 ounces) hickory smoke-flavored barbecue sauce

1/2 cup finely chopped onion

1 envelope chili seasoning

1 tablespoon Worcestershire sauce

1 teaspoon minced garlic

1 teaspoon lemon juice

14 hamburger buns, split

1 Cut brisket in half; place in a 5-qt. slow cooker. In a small bowl, combine the barbecue sauce, onion, chili seasoning, Worcestershire sauce, garlic and lemon juice. Pour over beef. Cover and cook on high for 5-6 hours or until meat is tender.

2 Remove beef; cool slightly. Shred and return to the slow cooker. Heat through. Serve on buns.

Yield: 14 servings.

EDITOR'S NOTE: This is a fresh beef brisket, not corned beef.

roundup chili

PREP: 35 MIN. • COOK: 6 HOURS

Linda Stemen
Monroeville, Indiana

Two types of meat make this not-too-spicy chili a hearty meal. It's great for casual gatherings.

2 pounds lean ground beef (90% lean)

1 beef flank steak (1-1/2 pounds), cubed

1 medium onion, chopped

1 celery rib, chopped

1 can (29 ounces) tomato sauce

2 cans (14-1/2 ounces *each*) diced tomatoes, undrained

1 can (16 ounces) kidney beans, rinsed and drained

1 can (15 ounces) pinto beans, rinsed and drained

1 can (4 ounces) chopped green chilies

2 to 3 tablespoons chili powder

3 teaspoons ground cumin

2 teaspoons salt

2 teaspoons pepper

1/2 teaspoon ground mustard

1/2 teaspoon paprika

1/2 teaspoon cayenne pepper

1/4 teaspoon garlic powder

Hot pepper sauce, shredded cheddar cheese and additional chopped onion, optional

1 In a large skillet, cook the ground beef, flank steak, onion and celery over medium heat until meat is no longer pink; drain.

2 Transfer to a 6-qt. slow cooker. Stir in the tomato sauce, tomatoes, beans, chilies and seasonings. Cover and cook on low for 6-8 hours until steak is tender.

3 Serve with the hot pepper sauce, cheese and onion if desired.

Yield: 12 servings (3 quarts).

white bean chicken chili

PREP: 35 MIN. • COOK: 3 HOURS

Kristine Bowles
Rio Rancho, New Mexico

My sister shared this chili recipe with me. I often double it and add one extra can of beans, then serve with cheddar biscuits or warmed tortillas. The jalapeno adds just enough heat to notice but not too much for my children.

3/4 pound boneless skinless chicken breasts, cubed

1/2 teaspoon salt

1/4 teaspoon pepper

1 medium onion, chopped

1 jalapeno pepper, seeded and chopped

2 teaspoons dried oregano

1 teaspoon ground cumin

2 tablespoons olive oil

4 garlic cloves, minced

2 cans (15 ounces *each*) white kidney *or* cannellini beans, rinsed and drained, *divided*

3 cups chicken broth, *divided*

1-1/2 cups (6 ounces) shredded cheddar cheese

Sour cream and minced fresh cilantro, optional

1 Sprinkle chicken with salt and pepper. In a large skillet over medium heat, cook the chicken, onion, jalapeno, oregano and cumin in oil for 3-4 minutes or until chicken is browned and vegetables are crisp-tender. Add garlic; cook 1 minute longer.

2 Transfer to a 3-qt. slow cooker. In a small bowl, mash 1 cup of beans; add 1/2 cup broth and stir until blended. Add to the slow cooker with the remaining beans and broth. Cover and cook on low for 3 to 3-1/2 hours or until heated through.

3 Stir before serving. Sprinkle with cheese. Top with sour cream and cilantro if desired.

Yield: 6 servings.

special southwestern soup

PREP: 10 MIN. • COOK: 3 HOURS

Taste of Home Test Kitchen

This recipe offers all of the savory comfort families crave along with the time-saving convenience today's cooks can't do without. Feel free to stir in any leftover taco meat from last night's dinner. You can also leave out the chicken for an incredible meat-free specialty.

1-1/2 pounds boneless skinless chicken breasts, cubed

2 teaspoons canola oil

1/2 cup water

1 envelope reduced-sodium taco seasoning

Dash red pepper flakes

1 can (32 ounces) tomato juice

1 jar (16 ounces) salsa

Dash red pepper sauce

1 can (15 ounces) kidney beans, rinsed and drained

1 can (15 ounces) black beans, rinsed and drained

1 package (10 ounces) frozen corn, thawed

6 tablespoons cheddar cheese

6 tablespoons sour cream

2 tablespoons minced fresh cilantro

1 In a large nonstick skillet, saute chicken in oil until no longer pink. Add water and taco seasoning; simmer, uncovered, until chicken is well coated.

2 Transfer to a 5-qt. slow cooker. Stir in the red pepper flakes, tomato juice, salsa, red pepper sauce, beans and corn. Cover and cook on low for 3-4 hours or until heated through. Serve with cheese, sour cream and cilantro.

Yield: 6 servings.

healthy tomato soup

PREP: 5 MIN. • COOK: 5 HOURS

Heather Campbell
Lawrence, Kansas

To trim the sodium, I like to season this slow cooker soup with spices and herbs rather than salt. It's good with sandwiches and for dipping bread.

> 1 can (46 ounces) tomato juice
>
> 1 can (8 ounces) tomato sauce
>
> 1/2 cup water
>
> 1/2 cup chopped onion
>
> 1 celery rib with leaves, chopped
>
> 2 tablespoons sugar
>
> 1/2 teaspoon dried basil
>
> 3 to 5 whole cloves
>
> 1 bay leaf

1 In a 3-qt. slow cooker, combine all of the ingredients. Cover and cook on low for 5-6 hours or until heated through. Discard cloves and bay leaf.

Yield: 6 servings.

cincinnati chili

PREP: 25 MIN. • COOK: 5-1/2 HOURS

Joyce Alm
Thorp, Washington

The chocolate in this recipe threw me off at first, but now it's the only way I make chili. You'll find layers of delicious flavor in this heartwarming dish. It's well worth the time it takes.

> 3 pounds ground beef
>
> 1-1/2 cups chopped onions
>
> 1-1/2 teaspoons minced garlic
>
> 2 cans (16 ounces *each*) kidney beans, rinsed and drained
>
> 2 cans (15 ounces *each*) tomato sauce
>
> 2 cups beef broth
>
> 1/4 cup chili powder
>
> 1/4 cup red wine vinegar
>
> 1/4 cup Worcestershire sauce
>
> 1 ounce unsweetened chocolate, coarsely chopped
>
> 1-1/2 teaspoons ground cinnamon
>
> 1-1/2 teaspoons ground cumin
>
> 1 teaspoon salt
>
> 1 teaspoon dried oregano
>
> 1/2 teaspoon pepper
>
> 1/8 teaspoon ground cloves
>
> Hot cooked spaghetti
>
> Shredded cheddar cheese and sliced green onions, optional

1 In a Dutch oven, cook beef and onions over medium heat until meat is no longer pink. Add garlic; cook 1 minute longer. Drain.

2 In a 5-qt. slow cooker, combine the beans, tomato sauce, broth, chili powder, vinegar, Worcestershire sauce, chocolate, cinnamon, cumin, salt, oregano, pepper and cloves. Stir in beef mixture. Cover and cook on low for 5-1/2 to 6 hours or until heated through.

3 Serve with spaghetti. Garnish with cheese and green onions if desired.

Yield: 10 servings.

slow-cooked white chili

PREP: 25 MIN. • COOK: 5 HOURS

Lori Weber
Wentzville, Missouri

This satisfying slow-simmered chili features chicken, two kinds of beans and crunchy corn. It's easy and tastes great. It's a family favorite that we enjoy with corn bread.

3/4 pound boneless skinless chicken breasts, cubed

1 medium onion, chopped

1 tablespoon canola oil

1 garlic clove, minced

1-1/2 cups water

1 can (15 ounces) white kidney *or* cannellini beans, rinsed and drained

1 can (15 ounces) garbanzo beans *or* chickpeas, rinsed and drained

1 can (11 ounces) whole kernel white corn, drained, *or* 1-1/4 cups frozen shoepeg corn

1 can (4 ounces) chopped green chilies

1 to 2 teaspoons chicken bouillon granules

1 teaspoon ground cumin

1 In a large skillet, saute chicken and onion in oil until onion is tender. Add garlic; cook 1 minute longer. Transfer to a 3-qt. slow cooker. Stir in the remaining ingredients. Cover and cook on low for 5-6 hours or until chicken is no longer pink.

Yield: 8 servings (2 quarts).

vegetable beef soup

PREP: 15 MIN. • COOK: 8 HOURS

Carol Calhoun
Sioux Falls, South Dakota

Convenient frozen veggies and hash browns make this meaty soup a snap to mix up. Simply brown the ground beef, then stir everything together to simmer all day. It's wonderful served with warm bread and a green salad.

1 pound ground beef

1 can (46 ounces) tomato juice

1 package (16 ounces) frozen mixed vegetables, thawed

2 cups frozen cubed hash brown potatoes, thawed

1 envelope onion soup mix

1 In a large skillet, cook beef over medium heat until no longer pink; drain. Transfer to a 5-qt. slow cooker. Stir in the tomato juice, mixed vegetables, potatoes and soup mix. Cover and cook on low for 8-9 hours or until heated through.

Yield: 10 servings.

slow cooker vegetable soup

PREP: 15 MIN. • COOK: 8 HOURS

Heather Thurmeier
Pense, Saskatchewan

What a treat to come home from work and have this savory soup ready to ladle into bowls. It's a nice traditional beef soup with old-fashioned goodness. We pair it with crusty rolls topped with melted mozzarella cheese.

> 1 pound round steak, cut into 1/2-inch cubes
>
> 1 can (14-1/2 ounces) diced tomatoes, undrained
>
> 2 medium potatoes, peeled and cubed
>
> 2 medium onions, diced
>
> 3 celery ribs, sliced
>
> 2 carrots, sliced
>
> 3 beef bouillon cubes
>
> 1/2 teaspoon dried basil
>
> 1/2 teaspoon dried oregano
>
> 1/2 teaspoon salt
>
> 1/4 teaspoon pepper
>
> 3 cups water
>
> 1-1/2 cups frozen mixed vegetables

1 In a 3-qt. slow cooker, combine the first 12 ingredients. Cover and cook on high for 6 hours. Add vegetables; cover and cook 2 hours longer or until meat and vegetables are tender.

Yield: 10 servings (about 2-1/2 quarts).

Savory substitute. One bouillon cube dissolved in 1 cup of water is equal to 1 cup of beef broth. So, it's okay to use 3 cups of beef broth instead of the 3 beef bouillon cubes and 3 cups of water in the Slow Cooker Vegetable Soup.

---

shredded french dip

PREP: 5 MIN. • COOK: 6 HOURS

Carla Kimball
Callaway, Nebraska

A chuck roast slow-simmered in a beefy broth is delicious shredded and spooned onto rolls. I serve the cooking juices in individual cups for dipping.

> 1 boneless beef chuck roast (3 pounds), trimmed
>
> 1 can (10-1/2 ounces) condensed French onion soup, undiluted
>
> 1 can (10-1/2 ounces) condensed beef consomme, undiluted
>
> 1 can (10-1/2 ounces) condensed beef broth, undiluted
>
> 1 teaspoon beef bouillon granules
>
> 8 to 10 French *or* Italian rolls, split

1 Cut roast in half and place in a 3-qt. slow cooker. Combine the soup, consomme, broth and bouillon; pour over roast. Cover and cook on low for 6-8 hours or until meat is tender.

2 Remove meat and shred with two forks. Serve on rolls. Skim fat from cooking juices and serve as a dipping sauce.

Yield: 10 servings.

veggie-sausage cheese soup

PREP: 55 MIN. • COOK: 7 HOURS

Richard Grant
Hudson, New Hampshire

I took this soup to a potluck at work, where it was well received...and was the only dish prepared by a guy! The great combination of textures and flavors had everyone asking for the recipe.

2 medium onions, finely chopped

1 *each* medium green and sweet red pepper, chopped

2 celery ribs, chopped

1 tablespoon olive oil

4 garlic cloves, minced

1 pound smoked kielbasa *or* Polish sausage, cut into 1/4-inch slices

2 medium potatoes, diced

1 can (14-3/4 ounces) cream-style corn

1 can (14-1/2 ounces) chicken broth

1 can (10-3/4 ounces) condensed cream of mushroom soup, undiluted

2 medium carrots, sliced

1 cup whole kernel corn

1 cup sliced fresh mushrooms

1 tablespoon Worcestershire sauce

1 tablespoon Dijon mustard

1 tablespoon dried basil

1 tablespoon dried parsley flakes

1/2 teaspoon pepper

2 cups (8 ounces) shredded sharp cheddar cheese

1 can (12 ounces) evaporated milk

1 In a large skillet, saute the onions, peppers and celery in oil until tender. Add garlic; cook 1 minute longer.

2 Transfer to a 5-qt. slow cooker. Stir in the sausage, potatoes, cream-style corn, broth, soup, carrots, corn, mushrooms, Worcestershire sauce, Dijon mustard and seasonings. Cover and cook on low for 6-1/2 to 7-1/2 hours or until vegetables are tender.

3 Stir in cheese and milk. Cook on low 30 minutes longer or until cheese is melted. Stir until blended.

Yield: 16 servings (4 quarts).

italian sausage sandwiches

PREP: 10 MIN. • COOK: 4 HOURS

Taste of Home Test Kitchen

Need a different type of sandwich for a party? Try this recipe, and everyone will be complimenting you on these great-tasting sandwiches.

2 jars (26 ounces *each*) meatless spaghetti sauce

2 medium green peppers, cut into strips

2 medium onions, thinly sliced

1/2 teaspoon garlic powder

1/2 teaspoon fennel seed, crushed

2 packages (20 ounces *each*) Italian turkey sausage links

10 sandwich buns, split

1 In a 3-qt. slow cooker, combine the spaghetti sauce, green peppers, onions, garlic powder and fennel seed. Cover and cook on low for 4 hours or until vegetables are tender.

2 Grill sausages according to package directions. Serve on buns with sauce.

Yield: 10 servings.

zippy steak chili

PREP: 15 MIN. • COOK: 6 HOURS

Denise Habib
Poolesville, Maryland

Looking for a thick, chunky chili with a little extra-special kick for the big football game? Try this recipe. It was given to me by a co-worker originally from Texas. I've made it on numerous occasions, and the gang always enjoys it.

- 1 pound beef top sirloin steak, cut into 1/2-inch cubes
- 1/2 cup chopped onion
- 2 tablespoons canola oil
- 2 tablespoons chili powder
- 1 teaspoon garlic powder
- 1 teaspoon ground cumin
- 1 teaspoon dried oregano
- 1 teaspoon pepper
- 2 cans (10 ounces *each*) diced tomatoes and green chilies, undrained
- 1 can (15-1/2 ounces) chili starter
- Shredded cheddar cheese, chopped onion and sour cream, optional

1 In a large skillet, cook steak and onion in oil over medium heat until meat is no longer pink. Sprinkle with seasonings.

2 In a 5-qt. slow cooker, combine tomatoes and chili starter. Stir in beef mixture. Cover and cook on low for 6-8 hours or until meat is tender. Serve with cheese, onion and sour cream if desired.

Yield: 5 servings.

italian chili

PREP: 20 MIN. • COOK: 6-1/2 HOURS

Taste of Home Test Kitchen

By adding Italian seasoning and fresh veggies, we put an Italian spin on traditional Southwestern-style chili and created this hearty slow-simmered dish.

1 pound ground beef

1/2 pound bulk Italian sausage

1 can (28 ounces) diced tomatoes

1 can (8 ounces) tomato sauce

1 cup chopped onion

1 cup chopped sweet red pepper

1 cup water

1/2 cup chopped celery

1/4 cup beef broth

1 tablespoon chili powder

1 tablespoon Italian seasoning

1 teaspoon sugar

1 teaspoon minced garlic

1/2 teaspoon salt

1 can (16 ounces) kidney beans, rinsed and drained

1 cup sliced fresh mushrooms

1 cup diced zucchini

3 tablespoons minced fresh parsley

Shredded part-skim mozzarella cheese, optional

1 In a large skillet, cook beef and sausage over medium heat until no longer pink. Meanwhile, in a 3-qt. slow cooker, combine the tomatoes, tomato sauce, onion, red pepper, water, celery, broth, chili powder, Italian seasoning, sugar, garlic and salt.

2 Drain beef mixture; add to the slow cooker. Cover and cook on low for 6 hours or until vegetables are tender.

3 Add the beans, mushrooms, zucchini and parsley. Cover and cook on high for 30 minutes or until vegetables are tender. Sprinkle with cheese if desired.

Yield: 6 servings.

vegetable bean soup

PREP: 30 MIN. • COOK: 6 HOURS

Belinda Moran
Woodbury, Tennessee

Kitchen staples and canned goods help me get this heartwarming soup on the table with very little preparation. Feel free to change the ingredients according to your tastes by adding a few of your favorite vegetables, or swap out some of the beans with the variety you like best.

2 cans (14-1/2 ounces *each*) petite diced tomatoes

1 can (16 ounces) kidney beans, rinsed and drained

1 can (15-1/4 ounces) whole kernel corn, drained

1 can (15 ounces) garbanzo beans *or* chickpeas, rinsed and drained

1 can (15 ounces) black beans, rinsed and drained

1 can (10 ounces) diced tomatoes and green chilies

1 can (8 ounces) tomato sauce

1 cup chopped green pepper

1 cup chopped zucchini

3/4 cup water

1/2 cup chopped onion

1/2 cup chopped celery

2 tablespoons chili powder

4 teaspoons dried oregano

2 garlic cloves, minced

1 teaspoon ground cumin

1 teaspoon pepper

1/2 teaspoon salt

2 bay leaves

1 In a 5-qt. slow cooker, combine all ingredients. Cover and cook on low for 6-8 hours or until vegetables are tender. Discard bay leaves before serving.

Yield: 7 servings.

hearty goose soup

PREP: 15 MIN. • COOK: 5 HOURS

Loretta Fenrich
Barney Lake, Washington

After my son went goose hunting, I had to cook what he brought home. So I got ingredients together and came up with this chunky soup. It's chock-full of pasta and vegetables.

2-1/4 cups cubed uncooked goose

1 pound red potatoes, cubed

1 large onion, chopped

1 *each* medium green, sweet yellow and red pepper, chopped

2 medium carrots, cut into 1/2-inch slices

1 cup water

3 garlic cloves, minced

2 teaspoons dried basil

Salt and pepper to taste

1 can (15 ounces) tomato sauce

1 can (14-1/2 ounces) Italian stewed tomatoes

2 cups uncooked elbow macaroni

1 In a 5-qt. slow cooker, combine the goose, potatoes, onion, peppers, carrots, water, garlic, basil, salt and pepper. Cover and cook on high for 4 hours or until meat is tender.

2 Stir in tomato sauce and tomatoes; cook 1 hour longer. Just before serving, cook macaroni according to package directions; drain. Stir into the soup.

Yield: 13 servings (about 3 quarts).

ham barbecue

PREP: 10 MIN. • COOK: 4 HOURS

Jennifer Middlekauff
New Holland, Pennsylvania

We have used this recipe countless times for family gatherings and birthday parties. The sandwiches are so easy to make, and they taste great. In fact, I usually double the recipe so I'm sure to have leftovers.

- 2 pounds thinly sliced deli ham
- 1 cup water
- 1 cup ketchup
- 1/4 cup packed brown sugar
- 1/4 cup Worcestershire sauce
- 2 tablespoons white vinegar
- 2 teaspoons prepared mustard
- 12 hamburger buns, split and toasted

1 Place the ham in a greased 3-qt. slow cooker. In a large bowl, combine the water, ketchup, brown sugar, Worcestershire sauce, vinegar and mustard; pour over ham and stir well. Cover and cook on low for 4-5 hours or until heated through. Serve on buns.

Yield: 12 servings.

colony mountain chili

PREP: 25 MIN. • COOK: 6 HOURS

Marjorie O'Dell
Bow, Washington

My husband created this chili for a local cooking contest, and it won the People's Choice award. It's loaded with beef, Italian sausage, tomatoes and beans and seasoned with chili powder, cumin and red pepper flakes for zip.

1 pound beef top sirloin steak, cut into 3/4-inch cubes

4 Italian sausage links, casings removed and cut into 3/4-inch slices

2 tablespoons olive oil, *divided*

1 medium onion, chopped

2 green onions, thinly sliced

3 garlic cloves, minced

2 teaspoons beef bouillon granules

1 cup boiling water

1 can (6 ounces) tomato paste

3 tablespoons chili powder

2 tablespoons brown sugar

2 tablespoons Worcestershire sauce

2 teaspoons ground cumin

1 to 2 teaspoons crushed red pepper flakes

1 teaspoon salt

1/2 teaspoon pepper

3 cans (14-1/2 ounces *each*) stewed tomatoes, cut up

2 cans (15 ounces *each*) pinto beans, rinsed and drained

Shredded cheddar cheese

1 In a large skillet, brown the beef and sausage in 1 tablespoon oil; drain. Transfer meat to a 5-qt. slow cooker. In the same skillet, saute onion and green onions in remaining oil until tender. Add garlic; cook 1 minute longer. Transfer to slow cooker.

2 In a small bowl, dissolve bouillon in water. Stir in the tomato paste, chili powder, brown sugar, Worcestershire sauce and seasonings until blended; add to slow cooker. Stir in tomatoes and beans. Cover and cook on high for 6-8 hours or until the meat is tender. Serve with cheese if desired.

Yield: 10 servings.

spicy two-bean chili

PREP: 20 MIN. • COOK: 8 HOURS

Lesley Pew
Lynn, Massachusetts

Chili fans will get a kick out of this nontraditional recipe. Tomatoes with green chilies, lime juice and kidney and black beans give it an original twist. It's wonderful ladled over rice.

2 pounds ground beef

3 large onions, chopped

6 garlic cloves, minced

2 cans (16 ounces *each*) kidney beans, rinsed and drained

2 cans (15 ounces *each*) black beans, rinsed and drained

2 cans (10 ounces *each*) diced tomatoes and green chilies, undrained

1 can (14-1/2 ounces) chicken broth

1/2 cup lime juice

6 tablespoons cornmeal

1/4 cup chili powder

4 teaspoons dried oregano

3 teaspoons ground cumin

2 teaspoons salt

2 teaspoons rubbed sage

1/2 teaspoon white pepper

1/2 teaspoon paprika

1/2 teaspoon pepper

Hot cooked rice

Shredded cheddar cheese

1 In a Dutch oven, cook beef and onions over medium heat until meat is no longer pink. Add garlic; cook 1 minute longer; drain.

2 Transfer to a 5-qt. slow cooker. Stir in the beans, tomatoes, broth, lime juice, cornmeal and seasonings. Cover and cook on low for 8 hours or until heated through. Serve with rice; sprinkle with cheese.

Yield: 11 servings.

seasoned pork sandwiches

PREP: 20 MIN. • COOK: 5 HOURS

Jacque Thompson
Houston, Texas

This is one of those dishes that my husband never seems to get tired of. The bonus for me is that it's easy to make and even easier to clean up!

1 boneless whole pork loin roast (2 to 3 pounds)

1 tablespoon fajita seasoning mix

1/4 teaspoon garlic powder

1/2 cup Italian salad dressing

1/4 cup Worcestershire sauce

8 sandwich rolls, split

1 Cut roast in half; place in a 5-qt. slow cooker. Sprinkle with fajita seasoning and garlic powder. Pour salad dressing and Worcestershire sauce over meat. Cover and cook on low for 5-6 hours or until meat is tender.

2 Remove roast; shred meat with two forks. Return to cooking juices; heat through. Using a slotted spoon, serve pork on rolls.

Yield: 8 servings.

vegetable barley soup

PREP: 25 MIN. • COOK: 8-1/4 HOURS

Mary Tallman
Arbor Vitae, Wisconsin

You'll love this delicious vegetarian soup that's brimming with veggies and barley. The great news is it's good for you, too!

1 large sweet potato, peeled and cubed

1-1/2 cups fresh baby carrots, halved

1-1/2 cups frozen cut green beans

1-1/2 cups frozen corn

3 celery ribs, thinly sliced

1 small onion, chopped

1/2 cup chopped green pepper

2 garlic cloves, minced

6 cups water

2 cans (14-1/2 ounces *each*) vegetable broth

1 cup medium pearl barley

1 bay leaf

1-3/4 teaspoons salt

1/2 teaspoon fennel seed, crushed

1/4 teaspoon pepper

1 can (14-1/2 ounces) Italian diced tomatoes, undrained

1 In a 5-qt. slow cooker, combine the first eight ingredients. Stir in the water, broth, barley, bay leaf and seasonings. Cover and cook on low for 8-9 hours or until barley and vegetables are tender.

2 Stir in tomatoes; cover and cook on high for 15-20 minutes or until heated through. Discard bay leaf before serving.

Yield: 12 servings (about 3-1/2 quarts).

slow 'n' easy chili

PREP: 10 MIN. • COOK: 6 HOURS

Ginny Puckett
Lutz, Florida

What's nice about this recipe is that you can add any extras (like chopped bell peppers or sliced fresh mushrooms) to make your own specialty. I only get the best reviews when I serve this chili.

1/2 pound ground beef, cooked and drained

1/2 pound bulk pork sausage, cooked and drained

1 can (28 ounces) crushed tomatoes

1 can (16 ounces) chili beans, undrained

1 can (10-3/4 ounces) condensed tomato soup, undiluted

1 large onion, chopped

2 envelopes chili seasoning

Shredded cheddar cheese, optional

1 In a 3-qt. slow cooker, combine the first seven ingredients. Cover and cook on low for 6-8 hours or until thickened and heated through, stirring occasionally. Garnish with cheese if desired.

6-8 servings.

barbecue chicken sandwiches

PREP: 20 MIN. • COOK: 5 HOURS

Lynn Ireland
Lebanon, Wisconsin

I love to use my slow cooker. In fact, I have three of them in different sizes! These saucy chicken sandwiches are real crowd-pleasers.

- 3 pounds boneless skinless chicken thighs
- 1 cup ketchup
- 1 small onion, chopped
- 1/4 cup water
- 1/4 cup cider vinegar
- 2 tablespoons Worcestershire sauce
- 1 tablespoon brown sugar
- 1 garlic clove, minced
- 1 bay leaf
- 2 teaspoons paprika
- 1 teaspoon dried oregano
- 1 teaspoon chili powder
- 1/2 teaspoon salt
- 1/2 teaspoon pepper
- 10 kaiser rolls, split

1 Place chicken in a 5-qt. slow cooker. In a small bowl, combine the ketchup, onion, water, vinegar, Worcestershire sauce, brown sugar, garlic, bay leaf and seasonings. Pour over chicken. Cover and cook on low for 5 hours or until meat is tender.

2 Discard bay leaf. Remove chicken; shred with two forks and return to slow cooker. Heat through. Serve on rolls.

Yield: 10 servings.

beef vegetable soup

PREP: 10 MIN. • COOK: 4 HOURS

Colleen Jubl
Dayton, Ohio

Here's a slow-cooked meal-in-one just perfect for chilly winter nights. It's nice to come home to a hearty soup that's ready to eat. It goes well with a fruit salad and bread.

- 1 pound lean ground beef (90% lean)
- 1 medium onion, chopped
- 2 garlic cloves, minced
- 4 cups spicy hot V8 juice
- 2 cups coleslaw mix
- 1 can (14-1/2 ounces) Italian stewed tomatoes
- 1 package (10 ounces) frozen corn
- 1 package (9 ounces) frozen cut green beans
- 2 tablespoons Worcestershire sauce
- 1 teaspoon dried basil
- 1/4 teaspoon pepper

1 In a large nonstick skillet, cook beef and onion over medium heat until meat is no longer pink. Add garlic; cook 1 minute longer. Drain. Transfer to a 5-qt. slow cooker. Stir in the remaining ingredients. Cover and cook on high for 4-5 hours or until heated through.

Yield: 9 servings.

> **Ground beef.** Ground beef is usually labeled using the cut of meat that it is ground from, such as ground chuck or ground round. (Ground beef comes from a combination of beef cuts.) Ground beef can also be labeled according to its fat content or the percentage of lean meat to fat, such as 85% or 90% lean. The higher the percentage, the leaner the meat.

all-day soup

PREP: 25 MIN. • COOK: 8 HOURS

Cathy Logan
Sparks, Nevada

I start this soup in the morning, and by evening, dinner's ready to go! My family loves all of the hearty vegetable and steak pieces, smothered in a zesty tomato broth.

 1 beef flank steak (1-1/2 pounds), cut into 1/2-inch cubes

 1 medium onion, chopped

 1 tablespoon olive oil

 5 medium carrots, thinly sliced

 4 cups shredded cabbage

 4 medium red potatoes, diced

 2 celery ribs, diced

 2 cans (14-1/2 ounces *each*) diced tomatoes, undrained

 2 cans (14-1/2 ounces *each*) beef broth

 1 can (10-3/4 ounces) condensed tomato soup, undiluted

 1 tablespoon sugar

 2 teaspoons Italian seasoning

 1 teaspoon dried parsley flakes

1 In a large skillet, brown steak and onion in oil; drain. Transfer to a 5-qt. slow cooker.

Stir in the remaining ingredients. Cover and cook on low for 8-10 hours or until meat is tender.

Yield: 8 servings.

italian meatball 'n' bean soup

PREP: 30 MIN. • COOK: 5 HOURS

Amanda Bowyer
Caldwell, Idaho

This is a taste sensation the whole family will love.

 1 egg

 3 tablespoons 2% milk

 1/3 cup seasoned bread crumbs

 1 pound bulk Italian sausage

 1/2 pound ground turkey

 2 cans (14-1/2 ounces *each*) diced tomatoes

 1 can (15 ounces) white kidney *or* cannellini beans, rinsed and drained

 1 can (15 ounces) black beans, rinsed and drained

 1 can (8 ounces) tomato sauce

 1 cup water

 2 green onions, thinly sliced

 1 teaspoon Italian seasoning

 1 teaspoon dried minced garlic

 1/2 teaspoon crushed red pepper flakes

1 In a large bowl, combine the egg, milk, and bread crumbs. Crumble sausage and turkey over mixture and mix well. Shape into 1-in. balls. In a large skillet, brown meatballs in batches; drain.

2 Transfer meatballs to a 3-qt. slow cooker. Stir in the remaining ingredients. Cover and cook on low for 5 hours or until meat is no longer pink.

Yield: 6 servings.

beef barbecue

PREP: 5 MIN. • COOK: 6-1/4 HOURS

Karen Walker
Sterling, Virginia

We like to keep our freezer stocked with plenty of beef roasts. When we're not in the mood for pot roast, I fix these satisfying sandwiches instead. The meat cooks in a tasty sauce while I'm at work. Then I just slice it thinly and serve it on rolls.

  1 boneless beef chuck roast (3 pounds)

  1 cup barbecue sauce

  1/2 cup apricot preserves

  1/3 cup chopped green *or* sweet red pepper

  1 small onion, chopped

  1 tablespoon Dijon mustard

  2 teaspoons brown sugar

 12 sandwich rolls, split

1 Cut the roast into quarters; place in a greased 5-qt. slow cooker. In a large bowl, combine the barbecue sauce, preserves, green pepper, onion, mustard and brown sugar; pour over roast. Cover and cook on low for 6-8 hours or until meat is tender.

2 Remove roast and thinly slice; return meat to slow cooker and stir gently. Cover and cook 15-30 minutes longer. Skim fat from sauce. Serve beef and sauce on rolls.

Yield: 12 servings.

p. 110

beef

p. 70

p. 74

p. 130

smoked beef brisket

PREP: 10 MIN. • COOK: 8 HOURS

Dana Cebolski
Bessemer, Michigan

I give a sensational smoky taste to tender slices of this slow-cooked beef brisket. It's one of my family's favorites any time of the year.

1 fresh beef brisket (2-1/2 pounds)

1 tablespoon Liquid Smoke, optional

1 teaspoon salt

1/2 teaspoon pepper

1/2 cup chopped onion

1/2 cup ketchup

2 teaspoons Dijon mustard

1/2 teaspoon celery seed

1 Cut the brisket in half; rub with Liquid Smoke if desired, salt and pepper. Place in a 3-qt. slow cooker. Top with onion. Combine the ketchup, mustard and celery seed; spread over meat.

2 Cover and cook on low for 8-9 hours. Remove brisket and keep warm.

3 Transfer cooking juices to a blender; cover and process until smooth. Serve with brisket. To serve brisket, thinly slice across the grain.

Yield: 6 servings.

EDITOR'S NOTE: This is a fresh beef brisket, not corned beef.

melt-in-your-mouth pot roast

PREP: 10 MIN. • COOK: 6 HOURS

Jeannie Klugh
Lancaster, Pennsylvania

Slow-simmered and seasoned with rosemary, mustard and thyme, this tender and tasty pot roast is so easy to make and always a hit. I sometimes substitute burgundy or brandy plus a half cup of water for the broth...the aroma is wonderful!

1 pound medium red potatoes, quartered

1 cup fresh baby carrots

1 boneless beef chuck roast (3 to 4 pounds)

1/4 cup Dijon mustard

2 teaspoons dried rosemary, crushed

1 teaspoon garlic salt

1/2 teaspoon dried thyme

1/2 teaspoon pepper

1/3 cup chopped onion

1-1/2 cups beef broth

1 Place potatoes and carrots in a 5-qt. slow cooker. Cut roast in half. In a small bowl, combine the mustard, rosemary, garlic salt, thyme and pepper; rub over roast.

2 Place in slow cooker; top with onion and broth. Cover and cook on low for 6-8 hours or until meat and vegetables are tender.

Yield: 6-8 servings.

traditional beef stew

PREP: 15 MIN. • COOK: 8 HOURS

Rosana Pape
Hamilton, Indiana

The aroma of this classic beef stew is irresistible, making it impossible not to dig in the moment you walk through the door.

- 1 pound beef stew meat, cut into 1-inch cubes
- 1 pound fresh baby carrots
- 2 medium potatoes, cut into chunks
- 2 medium onions, cut into wedges
- 1 cup drained diced tomatoes
- 1 cup beef broth
- 1 celery rib, cut into 1/2-inch pieces
- 2 tablespoons quick-cooking tapioca
- 1 teaspoon Worcestershire sauce
- 1/4 teaspoon salt
- 1/4 teaspoon pepper

1 In a 3-qt. slow cooker, combine all the ingredients.

2 Cover and cook on low for 8-10 hours or until meat and vegetables are tender.

Yield: 4 servings.

herbed beef with noodles

PREP: 25 MIN. • COOK: 5 HOURS

Roslyn Hurst
Belmont, California

Just a handful of ingredients and a sprinkling of spices go into this hearty dish. Although it's very simple, it's wonderful and full of subtle and creamy flavors.

- 2 pounds boneless beef top round steak
- 1/2 teaspoon salt
- 1/2 teaspoon pepper, *divided*
- 2 teaspoons canola oil
- 1 can (10-3/4 ounces) reduced-fat reduced-sodium condensed cream of celery soup, undiluted
- 1 medium onion, chopped
- 1 tablespoon fat-free milk
- 1 teaspoon dried oregano
- 1/2 teaspoon dried thyme
- 6 cups cooked wide egg noodles
- Chopped celery leaves, optional

1 Cut steak into serving-size pieces; sprinkle with salt and 1/4 teaspoon pepper. In a large nonstick skillet coated with cooking spray, brown meat in oil on both sides. Transfer to a 3-qt. slow cooker.

2 In a small bowl, combine the soup, onion, milk, oregano, thyme and remaining pepper. Pour over meat. Cover and cook on low for 5-6 hours or until meat is tender.

3 Serve with noodles. Sprinkle with celery leaves if desired.

Yield: 8 servings.

chuck roast dinner

PREP: 10 MIN. • COOK: 6 HOURS

Cindy Miller
Estes Park, Colorado

A tasty tomato sauce nicely coats this combo of beef, potatoes and carrots. My dad gave me the recipe. It was one of our favorites when we would go hiking all day, and it takes only minutes to throw together!

>   1 boneless beef chuck roast (3 pounds), cut into serving-size pieces
>
>   3 medium potatoes, peeled and cut into chunks
>
>   4 medium carrots, cut into chunks
>
>   2 cans (11-1/2 ounces *each*) tomato juice
>
>   1/4 cup Worcestershire sauce
>
>   3 tablespoons quick-cooking tapioca

1 In a 5-qt. slow cooker, combine all ingredients. Cover and cook on high for 6-8 hours or until meat is tender.

Yield: 8-10 servings.

slow cooker beef stew

PREP: 20 MIN. • COOK: 6 HOURS

Donna Wenger
Little Rock, Arkansas

I work long hours and try to find recipes for hearty meals that will be ready when I get home. Everyone who tries this really enjoys the rich taste and tender meat.

>   2 pounds beef top round steak, cut into 1-inch cubes
>
>   8 medium carrots, cut into 1-inch pieces
>
>   1 pound small red potatoes, quartered
>
>   1/2 pound sliced fresh mushrooms
>
>   1 medium sweet red pepper, chopped
>
>   1 can (14-1/2 ounces) diced tomatoes, undrained
>
>   1/4 cup all-purpose flour
>
>   1 can (6 ounces) tomato paste
>
>   3/4 cup beef broth
>
>   1/3 cup dry red wine *or* additional beef broth
>
>   1-1/2 teaspoons salt
>
>   1 teaspoon minced garlic
>
>   1 teaspoon pepper
>
>   1/2 teaspoon dried thyme

1 In a large skillet, brown beef on all sides. In a 5-qt. slow cooker, combine the carrots, potatoes, mushrooms and red pepper. Pour tomatoes over the top.

2 In a small bowl, whisk the flour, tomato paste and broth until smooth. Stir in the wine, salt, garlic, pepper and thyme; pour into slow cooker. Top with beef.

3 Cover and cook on low for 6-8 hours or until meat is tender.

Yield: 6 servings.

stamp-of-approval spaghetti sauce

PREP: 30 MIN. • COOK: 8 HOURS

Melissa Taylor
Higley, Arizona

My father is very opinionated—especially about food, and this succulent recipe received his almost unreachable stamp of approval. I have yet to hear a disagreement from anyone who has tried it!

2 pounds ground beef

3/4 pound bulk Italian sausage

4 medium onions, finely chopped

8 garlic cloves, minced

4 cans (14-1/2 ounces *each*) diced tomatoes, undrained

4 cans (6 ounces *each*) tomato paste

1/2 cup water

1/4 cup sugar

1/4 cup Worcestershire sauce

1 tablespoon canola oil

1/4 cup minced fresh parsley

2 tablespoons minced fresh basil *or* 2 teaspoons dried basil

1 tablespoon minced fresh oregano *or* 1 teaspoon dried oregano

4 bay leaves

1 teaspoon rubbed sage

1/2 teaspoon salt

1/2 teaspoon dried marjoram

1/2 teaspoon pepper

Hot cooked spaghetti

1 In a Dutch oven, cook the beef, sausage and onions over medium heat until meat is no longer pink. Add garlic; cook 1 minute longer. Drain.

2 Transfer to a 5-qt. slow cooker. Stir in the tomatoes, tomato paste, water, sugar, Worcestershire sauce, oil and seasonings. Cover and cook on low for 8 hours. Discard bay leaves. Serve with spaghetti.

Yield: 12 servings (3 quarts).

slow cooker fajitas

PREP: 25 MIN. • COOK: 8 HOURS

Katie Urso
Seneca, Illinois

I love fajitas like those that are served in Mexican restaurants, but when I prepared them at home, the meat was always chewy. Then I tried this recipe in my slow cooker, and my husband and I savored every last bite. Fresh cilantro gives these fajitas the extra punch that makes them taste truly authentic.

1 *each* medium green, sweet red and yellow pepper, cut into 1/2-inch strips

1 sweet onion, cut into 1/2-inch strips

2 pounds beef top sirloin steaks, cut into thin strips

3/4 cup water

2 tablespoons red wine vinegar

1 tablespoon lime juice

1 teaspoon ground cumin

1 teaspoon chili powder

1/2 teaspoon salt

1/2 teaspoon garlic powder

1/2 teaspoon pepper

1/2 teaspoon cayenne pepper

8 flour tortillas (8 inches), warmed

1/2 cup salsa

1/2 cup shredded reduced-fat cheddar cheese

8 teaspoons minced fresh cilantro

1 Place peppers and onion in a 5-qt. slow cooker. Top with beef. Combine the water, vinegar, lime juice and seasonings; pour over meat. Cover and cook on low for 8-9 hours or until tender.

2 Using a slotted spoon, place about 3/4 cup meat mixture down the center of each tortilla. Top with 1 tablespoon salsa, 1 tablespoon cheese and 1 teaspoon cilantro; roll up.

Yield: 8 servings.

gone-all day stew

PREP: 25 MIN. • COOK: 4 HOURS

Patricia Kile
Elizabethtown, Pennsylvania

This healthy stew is one of my husband's favorite meals. I always use fresh mushrooms, and I toss low-sodium bouillon into the slow cooker...there is no need to dissolve first in liquid. No additional salt is necessary.

1/4 cup all-purpose flour

1 boneless beef chuck roast (2 pounds), cut into 1-inch cubes

2 tablespoons canola oil

1 can (10-3/4 ounces) condensed tomato soup, undiluted

1 cup water *or* red wine

2 teaspoons beef bouillon granules

3 teaspoons Italian seasoning

1 bay leaf

1/2 teaspoon coarsely ground pepper

6 medium onions, quartered

4 medium potatoes, cut into 1-1/2-inch chunks

3 medium carrots, cut into 1-inch slices

12 large fresh mushrooms

1/2 cup celery, cut into 1-inch slices

Hot cooked egg noodles, optional

1 Place flour in a large resealable plastic bag. Add beef, a few pieces at a time, and shake to coat.

2 In a large skillet, brown meat in oil in batches; drain. Transfer to a 5-qt. slow cooker. Combine the tomato soup, water, bouillon and seasonings; pour over beef. Add the onions, potatoes, carrots, mushrooms and celery. Cover and cook on low for 4-5 hours or until meat is tender. Discard bay leaf before serving. Serve with egg noodles if desired.

Yield: 8 servings.

tender beef brisket

PREP: 15 MIN. • COOK: 8 HOURS

Jenni Arnold
Woodbury, Tennessee

Brisket can be difficult to cook, but this recipe always turns out great. I live in the country and have a 60-mile commute to work, so I use the slow cooker often. It's a great way to get a good meal on the table for my family after a long day.

1 fresh beef brisket (4 pounds)

1 can (15 ounces) tomato sauce

1 can (12 ounces) beer *or* nonalcoholic beer

1 cup chopped green pepper

2/3 cup chopped onion

2 tablespoons brown sugar

2 tablespoons balsamic vinegar

2 tablespoons Worcestershire sauce

2 teaspoons prepared mustard

1 teaspoon salt

1 teaspoon garlic powder

1/2 teaspoon pepper

1 Cut brisket into thirds; place in a 5-qt. slow cooker. In a large bowl, combine the remaining ingredients; pour over beef.

2 Cover and cook on low for 8-9 hours or until meat is tender.

3 Thinly slice meat across the grain. If desired, thicken pan juices.

Yield: 10 servings.

EDITOR'S NOTE: This is a fresh beef brisket, not corned beef.

mushroom pepper steak

PREP: 15 MIN. • COOK: 6-1/4 HOURS

Katie Goble
Valparaiso, Indiana

Round steak is slow-simmered until tender and smothered with a gravy that's packed with colorful peppers in this yummy recipe.

- 2 pounds beef top round steak
- 2 cups *each* sliced green, sweet red and yellow peppers (1/2-inch strips)
- 1 can (7 ounces) mushroom stems and pieces, drained
- 2 medium onions, quartered and sliced
- 1/2 cup water
- 1 teaspoon salt
- 1/2 teaspoon pepper
- 1 can (15 ounces) tomato sauce
- 1/4 cup cornstarch
- 1/4 cup cold water
- Hot mashed potatoes

1 Cut steak into serving-size pieces. Place in a 5-qt. slow cooker. Add the peppers, mushrooms, onions, water, salt and pepper. Pour tomato sauce over the top.

2 Cover and cook on low for 6 to 6-1/2 hours or until meat is tender.

3 Using a slotted spoon, remove beef and vegetables; keep warm. In a small bowl, combine cornstarch and cold water until smooth. Gradually stir into cooking juices; cover and cook on high for 15 minutes or until thickened. Serve with beef, vegetables and mashed potatoes.

Yield: 8 servings.

slow-cooked spaghetti sauce

PREP: 15 MIN. • COOK: 6 HOURS

David Shields
Barberton, Ohio

When I wanted a versatile tomato sauce that could be used for different types of dishes, I tried making my own. The result was this thick sauce that's great not only with pasta, but also on pizza.

- 1 pound ground beef
- 4 cans (14-1/2 ounces *each*) diced tomatoes, undrained
- 6 cans (6 ounces *each*) tomato paste
- 1 cup beef broth
- 1/4 cup packed brown sugar
- 3 tablespoons minced fresh marjoram *or* 1 tablespoon dried marjoram
- 2 tablespoons garlic powder
- 2 tablespoons minced fresh basil *or* 2 teaspoons dried basil
- 2 tablespoons minced fresh oregano *or* 2 teaspoons dried oregano
- 2 tablespoons minced fresh parsley
- 1 teaspoon salt
- 1 bay leaf
- Hot cooked spaghetti

1 In a large skillet, cook beef over medium heat until no longer pink; drain.

2 Transfer to a 5-qt. slow cooker. Stir in the tomatoes, tomato paste, broth, brown sugar and seasonings. Cover and cook on low for 6-8 hours or until bubbly. Discard bay leaf. Serve with spaghetti.

Yield: 12-14 servings.

slow-cooked beef brisket

PREP: 10 MIN. • COOK: 8-1/2 HOURS

Anna Stodolak
Volant, Pennsylvania

When my husband and I were both working full-time, we loved this recipe's long cook time. The beef brisket tastes so good after simmering all day in the slow cooker, and the cinnamon and chili sauce add a unique touch to the gravy.

1 large onion, sliced

1 fresh beef brisket (3 to 4 pounds), cut in half

1/4 teaspoon pepper

1 jar (4-1/2 ounces) sliced mushrooms, drained

3/4 cup beef broth

1/2 cup chili sauce

1/4 cup packed brown sugar

2 garlic cloves, minced

1/4 cup all-purpose flour

1/4 cup cold water

Place onion in a 5-qt. slow cooker. Rub brisket with pepper; place over onion. Top with mushrooms. In a bowl, combine the broth, chili sauce, brown sugar and garlic; pour over brisket. Cover and cook on low for 8-9 hours or until meat is tender.

1 Remove brisket and keep warm. In a small bowl, combine flour and water until smooth; stir into cooking juices. Cover and cook on high for 30 minutes or until thickened. Slice brisket; serve with gravy.

Yield: 6-8 servings.

EDITOR'S NOTE: This is a fresh beef brisket, not corned beef.

sweet-sour meatballs

PREP: 10 MIN. • COOK: 5 HOURS

Lisa Stepanski
Munnsville, New York

For fix-it-and-forget-it convenience on busy week-days, I pop frozen meatballs in the slow cooker before leaving my house. Hours later, I come home to the heartwarming aroma of this Asian-style specialty all ready to serve! How great is that?

16 frozen fully cooked homestyle meatballs (1/2 ounce *each*) , thawed

1/2 cup sugar

2 tablespoons plus 2 teaspoons cornstarch

1/3 cup white vinegar

1 tablespoon reduced-sodium soy sauce

1/2 medium green pepper, cut into 1-inch pieces

1 can (8 ounces) pineapple chunks, undrained

Hot cooked rice, optional

1 Place meatballs in a 1-1/2-qt. slow cooker. In a small bowl, combine the sugar, cornstarch, vinegar and soy sauce; pour over meatballs. Add green pepper. Cover and cook on low for 4-1/2 hours.

2 Stir in pineapple; cover and cook 30 minutes longer. Serve with rice if desired.

Yield: 2 servings.

slow cooker chuck roast

PREP: 20 MIN. • COOK: 4 HOURS

Linnea Rein
Topeka, Kansas

This fork-tender roast is fairly quick for a slow cooker recipe and is perfect to prepare for a busy weekend afternoon.

 1 boneless beef chuck roast (4 pounds), trimmed and cut in half
 1 can (8 ounces) tomato sauce
 1/2 cup chopped onion
 1/4 cup water
 1/4 cup cider vinegar
 1/4 cup ketchup
 2 teaspoons Worcestershire sauce
 1 teaspoon paprika
 1 teaspoon prepared mustard
 1/2 teaspoon beef bouillon granules
 1/4 teaspoon garlic powder
 1/4 cup cornstarch
 6 tablespoons cold water
 Dash salt and pepper

1 Place roast in a 5-qt. slow cooker. Combine the tomato sauce, onion, water, vinegar, ketchup, Worcestershire sauce, paprika, mustard, bouillon and garlic powder; pour over meat. Cover and cook on low for 4-5 hours or until meat is tender.

2 Remove meat and keep warm. Skim fat from cooking juices if necessary; transfer to a large saucepan. Combine cornstarch and cold water until smooth; stir into cooking juices. Bring to a boil; cook and stir for 2 minutes or until thickened. Season with salt and pepper. Serve with roast.

Yield: 10 servings.

zippy beef fajitas

PREP: 20 MIN. • COOK: 6 HOURS

Laurie Sadowski
St. Catharines, Ontario

This is a flavorful and fast way to prepare steak filling for fajitas. The yummy flavor comes from aromatic ingredients like garlic and gingerroot. There's even a can of cola in the recipe.

 1 beef flank steak (1-1/2 pounds)
 2 teaspoons ground ginger
 2 teaspoons crushed red pepper flakes
 3/4 teaspoon garlic powder
 1/4 teaspoon pepper
 1 medium sweet red pepper, cut into strips
 1 medium green pepper, cut into strips
 1 can (12 ounces) cola
 5 green onions, chopped
 1/3 cup soy sauce
 2 tablespoons minced fresh gingerroot
 2 tablespoons tomato paste
 1 garlic clove, minced
 6 flour tortillas (8 inches), warmed

1 Cut steak in half lengthwise. In a small bowl, combine the ground ginger, pepper flakes, garlic powder and pepper; rub over steak. Transfer to a 3-qt. slow cooker; add red and green peppers. Combine the cola, green onions, soy sauce, gingerroot, tomato paste and garlic; pour over top.

2 Cover and cook on low 6-7 hours or until meat is tender.

3 Shred meat with two forks and return to the slow cooker; heat through. Using a slotted spoon, place about 1 cupful of beef mixture off center on each tortilla. Fold sides over filling.

Yield: 6 servings.

roast beef and gravy

PREP: 15 MIN. • COOK: 8 HOURS

Abby Metzger
Larchwood, Iowa

This is by far the simplest way to make roast beef and gravy. On busy days, I can put this main dish in the slow cooker and forget about it. My family likes it with mashed potatoes and fruit salad.

> 1 boneless beef chuck roast (3 pounds)
>
> 2 cans (10-3/4 ounces *each*) condensed cream of mushroom soup, undiluted

1/3 cup sherry *or* beef broth

1 envelope onion soup mix

1 Cut roast in half; place in a 3-qt. slow cooker. In a large bowl, combine the remaining ingredients; pour over roast.

2 Cover and cook on low for 8-9 hours or until meat is tender.

Yield: 8-10 servings.

mushroom-beef spaghetti sauce

PREP: 20 MIN. • COOK: 6 HOURS

Meg Fisher
Marietta, Georgia

I got the recipe for this sauce in a recipe exchange and wish I could credit the person who gave it to me. My children love it! I added mushrooms, but if you'd like it even chunkier, add some bell pepper and other veggies, too.

1 pound lean ground beef (90% lean)

1/2 pound sliced fresh mushrooms

1 small onion, chopped

2 cans (14-1/2 ounces *each*) diced tomatoes, undrained

1 can (12 ounces) tomato paste

1 can (8 ounces) tomato sauce

1 cup reduced-sodium beef broth

2 tablespoons dried parsley flakes

1 tablespoon brown sugar

1 teaspoon dried basil

1 teaspoon dried oregano

1 teaspoon salt

1/4 teaspoon pepper

Hot cooked spaghetti

Shredded Parmesan cheese, optional

1 In a large nonstick skillet, cook the beef, mushrooms and onion over medium heat until meat is no longer pink; drain. Transfer to a 3-qt. slow cooker.

2 Stir in the tomatoes, tomato paste, tomato sauce, broth, parsley, brown sugar, basil, oregano, salt and pepper. Cover and cook on low for 6-8 hours. Serve with spaghetti. Sprinkle with cheese if desired.

Yield: 12 servings (1-1/2 quarts).

home-style stew

PREP: 20 MIN. • COOK: 6 HOURS

Marie Shanks
Terre Haute, Indiana

My husband and I work full time and have three daughters, so good, quick meals are important. This stew tastes wonderful!

2 packages (16 ounces *each*) frozen vegetables for stew

1-1/2 pounds beef stew meat, cut into 1-inch cubes

1 can (10-3/4 ounces) condensed cream of mushroom soup, undiluted

1 can (10-3/4 ounces) condensed tomato soup, undiluted

1 envelope reduced-sodium onion soup mix

1 Place the vegetables in a 5-qt. slow cooker. In a large nonstick skillet coated with cooking spray, brown beef on all sides.

2 Transfer to slow cooker. Combine the remaining ingredients; pour over top.

3 Cover and cook on low for 6-7 hours or until beef is tender.

Yield: 5 servings.

burgundy pot roast

PREP: 20 MIN. • COOK: 5 HOURS

Debbie Daly
Buckingham, Illinois

I make this regularly, as it's one of my husband's favorite meals. I'm always asked for the recipe. You'll love how this delicious pot roast seems to melt-in-your-mouth.

1 boneless beef chuck roast (3 to 4 pounds)

1 can (28 ounces) diced tomatoes, drained

3/4 cup chopped onion

3/4 cup burgundy wine *or* beef broth

1-1/2 teaspoons salt

1 teaspoon dried basil

1/2 teaspoon dried oregano

1 garlic clove, minced

1/4 teaspoon pepper

1/4 cup cornstarch

1/2 cup cold water

1 Cut roast in half. Place in a 5-qt. slow cooker. Add the tomatoes, onion, wine, salt, basil, oregano, garlic and pepper. Cover and cook on low for 5 to 5-1/2 hours.

2 Remove meat to a serving platter; keep warm. Skim fat from cooking juices; transfer to a small saucepan. Combine cornstarch and water until smooth. Gradually stir into pan. Bring to a boil; cook and stir for 2 minutes or until thickened. Serve with meat.

Yield: 8 servings.

slow-cooked stew

PREP: 20 MIN. • COOK: 9 HOURS

Diane Delaney
Harrisburg, Pennsylvania

You can't beat this combination of tender beef and colorful vegetables in a savory sauce. It's an easy meal that looks like you fussed all day.

4 cups reduced-sodium V8 juice

3 tablespoons quick-cooking tapioca

1 tablespoon sugar

1/4 teaspoon pepper

2 cups frozen cut green beans

2 cups fresh baby carrots, halved lengthwise

2 celery ribs, thinly sliced

1 small onion, chopped

1-1/2 pounds beef stew meat, cut into 1-inch cubes

Hot cooked noodles

1 In a large bowl, combine the V8, tapioca, sugar and pepper; let stand for 15 minutes.

2 In a 5-qt. slow cooker, combine the beans, carrots, celery and onion. Top with beef. Add V8 mixture. Cover and cook on low for 9-10 hours or until beef is tender. Serve over noodles.

Yield: 10 servings.

hearty short ribs

PREP: 15 MIN. • COOK: 6 HOURS

Helena Ivy
St. Louis, Missouri

The whole family will love these ribs! The meat is so tender, it will simply fall off the bone, and the gravy is perfect with either mashed potatoes or rice.

1 large onion, sliced

4 pounds bone-in beef short ribs

1/2 pound sliced fresh mushrooms

1 can (10-3/4 ounces) condensed cream of mushroom soup, undiluted

1/2 cup water

1 envelope brown gravy mix

1 teaspoon minced garlic

1/2 teaspoon dried thyme

1 tablespoon cornstarch

2 tablespoons cold water

Hot mashed potatoes

1 Place onion in a 5-qt. slow cooker; top with ribs. Combine the mushrooms, soup, 1/2 cup water, gravy mix, garlic and thyme; pour over ribs. Cover and cook on low for 6 to 6-1/2 hours or until meat is tender.

2 Remove meat to serving platter; keep warm. Skim fat from cooking juices; transfer to a small saucepan. Bring to a boil.

3 Combine cornstarch and cold water until smooth. Gradually stir into pan. Bring to a boil. Cook and stir for 2 minutes or until thickened. Serve with meat and mashed potatoes.

Yield: 6 servings.

italian pot roast

PREP: 30 MIN. • COOK: 6 HOURS

Karen Burdell
Lafayette, Colorado

I'm always collecting recipes from newspapers and magazines, and this one just sounded too good not to try! You'll love the slow cooker convenience and the blend of healthful ingredients and aromatic spices.

6 whole peppercorns

4 whole cloves

3 whole allspice

1 cinnamon stick (3 inches)

1 boneless beef chuck roast (2 pounds)

2 teaspoons olive oil

2 celery ribs, sliced

2 medium carrots, sliced

1 large onion, chopped

4 garlic cloves, minced

1 cup sherry *or* reduced-sodium beef broth

1 can (28 ounces) crushed tomatoes

1/4 teaspoon salt

Hot cooked egg noodles, optional

1 Place the peppercorns, cloves, allspice and cinnamon stick on a double thickness of cheesecloth; bring up corners of cloth and tie with string to form a bag. Set aside.

2 In a large skillet, brown meat in oil on all sides; transfer to a 4-qt. slow cooker. Top with celery, carrots and spice bag.

3 In the same pan, saute onion in drippings until tender. Add garlic; cook 1 minute longer. Add sherry, stirring to loosen browned bits from pan. Bring to a boil; cook and stir until liquid is reduced to 2/3 cup. Stir in tomatoes and salt; pour over vegetables.

4 Cover and cook on low for 6-7 hours or until meat and vegetables are tender. Remove meat to a serving platter; keep warm. Discard spice bag. Skim fat from vegetable mixture; serve with beef and noodles if desired.

Yield: 8 servings.

Reheating pot roast. Using a slow cooker to cook a pot roast at a low heat yields tender and juicy meat. After the beef is refrigerated then reheated, it can become dry or tough. To help retain the moisture when reheating, simply slice the meat and place it in a baking dish. Pour the leftover pan juices over the meat, adding extra beef broth if needed to cover. Cover and bake at 325° only until heated through.

2 Transfer to a 5-qt. slow cooker. Stir in the remaining ingredients.

3 Cover and cook on high for 3-4 hours or until heated through.

Yield: 8-10 servings.

steak 'n' gravy

PREP: 15 MIN. • COOK: 4-1/2 HOURS

Betty Janway
Ruston, Louisiana

Slow cooking in a zesty tomato sauce for hours helps the round steak become nice and tender. This gently spiced steak with gravy makes a satisfying meal served over rice or mashed potatoes.

  1 pound beef top round steak

  1 tablespoon canola oil

  1-1/2 cups water

  1 can (8 ounces) no-salt-added tomato sauce

  1 teaspoon ground cumin

  1 teaspoon garlic powder

  1/2 teaspoon salt-free seasoning blend

  1/4 teaspoon pepper

  2 tablespoons all-purpose flour

  1/4 cup cold water

  2 cups mashed potatoes

1 Cut beef into 1-in cubes; brown in oil in a skillet. Transfer to a 3-qt. slow cooker. Cover with water; add tomato sauce and seasonings. Cover and cook on low for 8 hours, or on high for 4 hours, or until meat is tender.

2 In a small bowl, combine flour and cold water; stir into liquid in slow cooker. Cover and cook on high 30 minutes longer or until gravy is thickened. Serve with potatoes.

Yield: 4 servings.

hearty beans with beef

PREP: 5 MIN. • COOK: 3 HOURS

Jan Biehl
Leesburg, Indiana

My husband raved about this sweet bean dish after tasting it at a party, so I knew I had to get the recipe. It's perfect for get-togethers because you can mix it up a day early and toss it in the slow cooker a few hours before your guests arrive.

  1 pound ground beef

  1 medium onion, chopped

  1 can (16 ounces) baked beans, undrained

  1 can (15-1/2 ounces) butter beans, rinsed and drained

  1/2 cup ketchup

  1/3 cup packed brown sugar

  1 tablespoon barbecue sauce

  1/4 teaspoon Worcestershire sauce

1 In a large skillet, cook beef and onion over medium heat until meat is no longer pink; drain.

slow-cooked meat loaf

PREP: 15 MIN. • COOK: 5 HOURS

Ginger Cortese
Hollsopple, Pennsylvania

My husband and I both work late, so it's great to come home to this classic dish with mashed potatoes and a veggie side. It reminds me of a supper my mom would serve.

1 can (10-3/4 ounces) condensed cream of celery soup, undiluted

1-1/4 cups water

1 egg

1/4 cup dry bread crumbs

2 tablespoons grated Parmesan cheese

1-1/2 teaspoons dried parsley flakes

1/2 teaspoon garlic powder

1/4 teaspoon onion powder

1/8 teaspoon salt, optional

1/8 teaspoon pepper

1/2 pound lean ground beef (90% lean)

Hot mashed potatoes, optional

1 In a small bowl, combine soup and water until blended. Pour half into a 1-1/2-qt. slow cooker. Cover and refrigerate remaining soup mixture.

2 In a bowl, combine the egg, bread crumbs, cheese, parsley, garlic powder, onion powder, salt if desired and pepper. Crumble beef over mixture and mix well. Shape into a loaf; place in slow cooker. Cover and cook on low for 5 hours or until meat is no longer pink and a meat thermometer reads 160°.

3 For gravy, place reserved soup mixture in a small saucepan; cook over low heat until heated through. Serve with meat loaf and mashed potatoes if desired.

Yield: 2 servings.

german-style short ribs

PREP: 15 MIN. • COOK: 8 HOURS

Bregitte Rugman
Shanty Bay, Ontario

Our whole family is excited when I plug in the slow cooker to make these fall-off-the-bone tender ribs. We like them served over rice or egg noodles. My husband, Mark, and I have eight children whom I homeschool, so easy recipes are a must in our active household.

3/4 cup dry red wine *or* beef broth

1/2 cup mango chutney

3 tablespoons quick-cooking tapioca

1/4 cup water

3 tablespoons brown sugar

3 tablespoons cider vinegar

1 tablespoon Worcestershire sauce

1/2 teaspoon salt

1/2 teaspoon ground mustard

1/2 teaspoon chili powder

1/2 teaspoon pepper

4 pounds bone-in beef short ribs

2 medium onions, sliced

Hot cooked egg noodles

In a 5-qt. slow cooker, combine the first 11 ingredients. Add ribs and turn to coat. Top with onions.

1 Cover and cook on low for 8-10 hours or until meat is tender.

2 Remove ribs from slow cooker. Skim fat from cooking juices; serve with ribs and noodles.

Yield: 8 servings.

burgundy beef stew

PREP: 25 MIN. • COOK: 8 HOURS

Mindy Ilar
St. Albans, West Virginia

This stew brims with home-cooked comfort. I dress up the dish with sirloin, turkey bacon and herbs, making it special enough for company.

- 1/2 cup all-purpose flour
- 1 pound beef top sirloin steak, cut into 1/2-inch pieces
- 3 turkey bacon strips, diced
- 8 small red potatoes, halved
- 2 medium carrots, cut into 1-inch pieces
- 1 cup sliced fresh mushrooms
- 3/4 cup frozen pearl onions, thawed
- 3 garlic cloves, minced
- 1 bay leaf
- 1 teaspoon dried marjoram
- 1/2 teaspoon salt
- 1/2 teaspoon dried thyme
- 1/4 teaspoon pepper
- 1/2 cup reduced-sodium beef broth
- 1 cup Burgundy wine *or* additional reduced-sodium beef broth
- 6 cups hot cooked egg noodles

1 Place flour in a large resealable plastic bag. Add beef, a few pieces at a time, and shake to coat.

2 In a large skillet coated with cooking spray, brown beef and bacon in batches on all sides.

3 Place beef and bacon in a 5-qt. slow cooker. Stir in the vegetables, garlic, seasonings, broth and wine or additional broth.

4 Cover and cook on low for 8-9 hours or until meat is tender.

5 Discard bay leaf. Thicken cooking juices if desired. Serve with noodles.

Yield: 6 servings.

flavorful pot roast

PREP: 10 MIN. • COOK: 7 HOURS

Arlene Butler
Ogden, Utah

I use my slow cooker to prepare this tender pot roast. Convenient packages of dressing and gravy mixes combine to make a delicious sauce.

- 2 boneless beef chuck roasts (2-1/2 pounds *each*)
- 1 envelope ranch salad dressing mix
- 1 envelope Italian salad dressing mix
- 1 envelope brown gravy mix
- 1/2 cup water

1 Place the chuck roasts in a 5-qt. slow cooker. In a small bowl, combine the salad dressing and gravy mixes; stir in water. Pour over meat. Cover and cook on low for 7-8 hours or until tender. If desired, thicken cooking juices for gravy.

Yield: 12-15 servings.

> **Doneness test.** Pot roasts are done when a long-handled fork can be easily inserted into the thickest part of the roast. If the pot roast is cooked until it falls apart, the meat is actually overcooked and will be stringy, tough and dry.

chunky pasta sauce

PREP: 15 MIN. • COOK: 6 HOURS

Christy Hinrichs
Parkville, Missouri

Your kitchen will smell heavenly when it's time to dish up this hearty meal. With beef, pork and lots of veggies over pasta, this dish has it all. Add the extra 1/2 cup water if you want your sauce a bit thinner.

- 1 pound ground beef
- 1/2 pound ground pork
- 2 cans (28 ounces *each*) diced tomatoes
- 1/2 to 1 cup water
- 1 can (6 ounces) tomato paste
- 1 medium onion, cut into wedges
- 1 medium sweet red pepper, cut into 1-inch pieces
- 1 cup chopped carrots
- 2 tablespoons sugar
- 2 teaspoons minced garlic
- 1 teaspoon salt
- 1 teaspoon dried basil
- 1 teaspoon dried oregano
- 1 teaspoon pepper
- 6 cups cooked bow tie pasta

1 In a large skillet, cook beef and pork over medium heat until no longer pink; drain.

2 Transfer to a 3-qt. slow cooker. Stir in the tomatoes, water, tomato paste, vegetables, sugar, garlic and seasonings. Cover and cook on low for 6-7 hours or until vegetables are tender. Serve with pasta.

Yield: 8 servings.

brisket with cranberry gravy

PREP: 15 MIN. • COOK: 5-1/2 HOURS

Noelle LaBrecque
Round Rock, Texas

With just a few minutes of hands-on work, this tender beef brisket simmers into a delectable entree. The meat and gravy are great for sandwiches and leftovers the next day.

1 medium onion, sliced

1 fresh beef brisket (3 pounds), halved

1 can (14 ounces) jellied cranberry sauce

1/2 cup thawed cranberry juice concentrate

2 tablespoons cornstarch

1/4 cup water

1 Place onion in a 5-qt. slow cooker; top with brisket. Combine the cranberry sauce and juice concentrate; pour over beef.

2 Cover and cook on low for 5-1/2 to 6 hours or until meat is tender.

3 Remove brisket and keep warm. Strain cooking juices, discarding onion; skim fat.

4 In a small saucepan, combine cornstarch and water until smooth; stir in the cooking juices. Bring to a boil over medium heat, stirring constantly. Cook and stir for 2 minutes or until thickened. Thinly slice brisket across the grain; serve with gravy.

Yield: 12 servings.

EDITOR'S NOTE: This is a fresh beef brisket, not corned beef.

italian roast with alfredo potatoes

PREP: 10 MIN.
COOK: 7 HOURS 20 MIN.

Taste of Home Test Kitchen

This hearty meal is a great way to start the week. Since most of the work is done by the slow cooker, you'll have very little to do. Just boil the potatoes and smash them with Alfredo sauce, butter and pepper. They go great with the roast and gravy.

1 boneless beef chuck roast (4 pounds), trimmed

1 envelope brown gravy mix

1 envelope Italian salad dressing mix

1/2 cup water

1 medium sweet red pepper, cut into 1-inch pieces

1 cup chopped green pepper

2/3 cup chopped onion

8 medium red potatoes, quartered

2 tablespoons cornstarch

1/4 cup cold water

3/4 cup refrigerated Alfredo sauce

2 tablespoons butter

1/4 teaspoon pepper

1 tablespoon minced chives

1 Cut roast in half; place in a 5-qt. slow cooker. In a small bowl, combine the gravy mix, dressing mix and water; pour over roast. Top with peppers and onion. Cover and cook on low for 7-8 hours or until meat is tender.

2 Place potatoes in a large saucepan; cover with water. Bring to a boil. Reduce heat; cover and simmer for 15-20 minutes or until tender. Meanwhile, remove roast and cut a portion of the meat into cubes, measuring 3 cups; cover and save for another use. Slice the remaining beef and keep warm.

3 Skim fat from cooking juices if necessary; pour into a large saucepan. Combine cornstarch and cold water until smooth; stir into cooking juices. Bring to a boil; cook and stir for 2 minutes or until thickened.

4 Drain potatoes; mash with Alfredo sauce, butter and pepper. Sprinkle with chives. Serve with sliced beef and gravy.

Yield: 4 servings plus leftovers.

Family-pleasing dinner. To round out the meal, serve Italian Roast with Alfredo Potatoes alongside buttermilk biscuits and steamed broccoli spears. For dessert, serve an Italian cream cake, tiramisu or spumoni ice cream. It is guaranteed to be a home-style meal your clan will love!

beef 'n' chili beans

PREP: 15 MIN. • COOK: 6 HOURS

Anita Hudson
Savoy, Texas

I took this dish to the last church meal we had, and it was a hit! Several of the ladies requested the recipe. I have to admit it is so easy to make.

3 pounds beef stew meat, cut into 1-inch cubes

2 tablespoons brown sugar

1-1/2 teaspoons ground mustard

1 teaspoon salt

1 teaspoon paprika

1/2 teaspoon chili powder

1/4 teaspoon pepper

1 large onion, chopped

2 cans (10 ounces *each*) diced tomatoes and green chilies, undrained

1 can (16 ounces) Ranch Style beans (pinto beans in seasoned tomato sauce)

1 can (15-1/4 ounces) whole kernel corn, drained

1 Place the beef in a 3-qt. slow cooker. Combine the brown sugar, mustard, salt, paprika, chili powder and pepper; sprinkle over beef and toss to coat. Top with onion, tomatoes, beans and corn.

2 Cover and cook on low for 6-8 hours or until meat is tender.

Yield: 6-8 servings.

slow-cooked pot roast

PREP: 10 MIN. • COOK: 6-1/2 HOURS

Vera Carroll
Medford, Massachusetts

I like to serve my fork-tender pot roast with sauteed tarragon carrots and rosemary-roasted red potatoes. This homey meal suits all tastes.

1 large sweet onion, chopped

1 cup sliced baby portobello mushrooms

1 beef rump roast *or* bottom round roast (3 pounds)

1/2 teaspoon salt

1/4 teaspoon pepper

1 cup dry red wine *or* beef broth

1 tablespoon brown sugar

1 tablespoon Dijon mustard

1 teaspoon Worcestershire sauce

2 tablespoons cornstarch

2 tablespoons cold water

1 Place onion and mushrooms in a 5-qt. slow cooker. Rub roast with salt and pepper; cut in half and place over onion mixture. In a small bowl, combine the wine, brown sugar, mustard and Worcestershire sauce; pour over roast.

2 Cover and cook on low for 6-7 hours or until meat is tender.

3 Mix cornstarch and water until smooth; stir into cooking juices. Cover and cook on high for 30 minutes or until gravy is thickened.

Yield: 6 servings.

beef burgundy

PREP: 10 MIN. • COOK: 5-1/2 HOURS

Mary Jo Miller
Mansfield, Ohio

For this recipe, I trim the meat, cut up the vegetables and store them in separate containers the night before. The next day, I can toss all of the ingredients into the slow cooker in minutes. Shortly before dinnertime, I cook the noodles and bake some cheesy garlic toast to complete the meal.

> 1-1/2 pounds beef stew meat, cut into 1-inch cubes
>
> 1/2 pound whole fresh mushrooms, halved
>
> 4 medium carrots, chopped
>
> 1 can (10-3/4 ounces) condensed golden mushroom soup, undiluted

1 large onion, cut into thin wedges

1/2 cup Burgundy wine *or* beef broth

1/4 cup quick-cooking tapioca

1/2 teaspoon salt

1/4 teaspoon dried thyme

1/4 teaspoon pepper

Hot cooked egg noodles

1 In a 5-qt. slow cooker, combine the first 10 ingredients.

2 Cover and cook on low for 5-1/2 to 6-1/2 hours or until meat is tender. Serve with noodles.

Yield: 6 servings.

pizza in a pot

PREP: 15 MIN. • COOK: 3 HOURS

Dianna Cline
Philippi, West Virginia

With warm breadsticks or garlic toast on the side, this is one dinner I know my family will always eagerly eat.

- 1-1/2 pounds ground beef
- 1 medium green pepper, chopped
- 1 medium onion, chopped
- 1 can (15 ounces) tomato sauce
- 1 jar (14 ounces) pizza sauce
- 2 tablespoons tomato paste
- 3 cups spiral pasta, cooked and drained
- 2 packages (3-1/2 ounces *each*) sliced pepperoni
- 2 cups (8 ounces) shredded part-skim mozzarella cheese

1 In a large skillet, cook the beef, green pepper and onion over medium heat until meat is no longer pink; drain. Stir in the tomato sauce, pizza sauce and tomato paste.

2 In a 5-qt. slow cooker, layer the pasta, beef mixture, pepperoni and cheese. Cover and cook on low for 3-4 hours or until heated through.

Yield: 8 servings.

bavarian pot roast

PREP: 10 MIN. • COOK: 7 HOURS

Patricia Gasmund
Rockford, Illinois

I grew up eating pot roast but disliked it until I got this recipe and changed a few ingredients. My 7-year-old especially loves the seasoned apple gravy.

- 1 beef top round roast (2 pounds)
- 1 cup unsweetened apple juice
- 1/2 cup tomato sauce
- 1 small onion, chopped
- 1 tablespoon white vinegar
- 1-1/2 teaspoons minced fresh gingerroot
- 1 teaspoon salt
- 1 teaspoon ground cinnamon
- 2 tablespoons cornstarch
- 1/4 cup water

1 In a large skillet coated with cooking spray, brown roast on all sides; drain. Transfer to a 3-qt. slow cooker.

2 In a small bowl, combine the juice, tomato sauce, onion, vinegar, ginger, salt and cinnamon; pour over roast. Cover and cook on low for 6 hours.

3 In a small bowl, combine cornstarch and water until smooth; stir into cooking juices until well combined.

4 Cover and cook 1 hour longer or until the meat is tender and gravy begins to thicken.

Yield: 6 servings.

slow-cooked rump roast

PREP: 10 MIN. • COOK: 10-1/2 HOURS

Mimi Walker
Palmyra, Pennsylvania

I enjoy a good pot roast, but I was tired of the same old thing...so I started experimenting. Cooking the beef in horseradish sauce gives it a tangy flavor. Even my children love this roast with its tender veggies and gravy.

1 beef rump roast *or* bottom round roast (3 to 3-1/2 pounds)

2 tablespoons canola oil

4 medium carrots, halved lengthwise and cut into 2-inch pieces

3 medium potatoes, peeled and cut into chunks

2 small onions, sliced

1/2 cup water

6 to 8 tablespoons horseradish sauce

1/4 cup red wine vinegar

1/4 cup Worcestershire sauce

2 garlic cloves, minced

1-1/2 to 2 teaspoons celery salt

3 tablespoons cornstarch

1/3 cup cold water

1 Cut roast in half. In a large skillet, brown meat on all sides in oil over medium-high heat; drain. Place carrots and potatoes in a 5-qt. slow cooker. Top with meat and onions. Combine the water, horseradish sauce, vinegar, Worcestershire sauce, garlic and celery salt. Pour over meat. Cover and cook on low for 10-12 hours or until meat and vegetables are tender.

2 Combine cornstarch and cold water until smooth; stir into slow cooker. Cover and cook on high for 30 minutes or until gravy is thickened.

Yield: 6-8 servings.

seasoned short ribs

PREP: 15 MIN. • COOK: 6 HOURS

Taste of Home Test Kitchen

These juicy, barbecue-style short ribs are sure to be popular with your family. Line your broiler pan with foil for easy cleanup.

1-1/2 cups tomato juice

1/2 cup maple syrup

1/4 cup chopped onion

3 tablespoons cider vinegar

1 tablespoon Worcestershire sauce

1 tablespoon Dijon mustard

2 teaspoons minced garlic

1/4 teaspoon ground cinnamon

1/4 teaspoon ground cloves

4 pounds bone-in beef short ribs

1 teaspoon pepper

1 tablespoon cornstarch

2 tablespoons cold water

1 In a small bowl, combine the first nine ingredients; set aside. Cut ribs into serving-size pieces; place on a broiler pan. Sprinkle with pepper.

2 Broil 4-6 in. from the heat for 3-5 minutes on each side or until browned; drain on paper towels. Place ribs in a 5-qt. slow cooker; top with tomato juice mixture.

3 Cover and cook on low for 6-7 hours or until meat is tender.

4 In a small bowl, combine cornstarch and cold water until smooth. Pour 1 cup cooking liquid into a small saucepan; skim off fat. Bring to a boil; stir in cornstarch mixture. Return to a boil; cook and stir for 2 minutes or until thickened. Serve over ribs.

Yield: 4 servings.

hearty beef vegetable stew

PREP: 20 MIN. • COOK: 5 HOURS

Angela Nelson
Ruther Glen, Virginia

*I received this wonderful recipe from a co-worker.
It's awesome! It is a hit with everyone, including
our two young children. And it's good for you, too.*

  1-1/2 pounds lean boneless beef chuck roast,
  cut into 1-inch cubes

  2 teaspoons canola oil

  1-1/2 pounds red potatoes, cut
  into 1-inch cubes

  3 medium carrots, cut into 1-inch slices

  1 medium onion, chopped

  1/2 cup chopped celery

  1 can (28 ounces) crushed tomatoes,
  undrained

  3 tablespoons quick-cooking tapioca

  2 tablespoons dried basil

  1 tablespoon sugar

  1/2 teaspoon salt

  1/8 teaspoon pepper

1 In a large nonstick skillet, brown meat in
oil over medium heat. Meanwhile, place
the potatoes, carrots, onion and celery in a
5-qt. slow cooker. Drain meat; add to slow
cooker. Combine the tomatoes, tapioca,
basil, sugar, salt and pepper; pour over the
top.

2 Cover and cook on high for 5-6 hours or
until meat and vegetables are tender.

Yield: 6 servings.

smothered round steak

PREP: 20 MIN. • COOK: 7 HOURS

Kathy Garrett
Camden, West Virginia

Try less expensive round steak and gravy served over egg noodles for a hearty meal. Meaty and chock full of veggies, this slow cooker creation will take the worry out of "what's-for-supper" any weeknight.

1/3 cup all-purpose flour

1 teaspoon salt

1/4 teaspoon pepper

1-1/2 pounds beef top round steak, cut into 1-1/2-inch strips

1 large onion, sliced

1 large green pepper, sliced

1 can (14-1/2 ounces) diced tomatoes, undrained

1 jar (4 ounces) sliced mushrooms, drained

3 tablespoons soy sauce

2 tablespoons molasses

Hot cooked egg noodles, optional

1 In a large resealable plastic bag, combine the flour, salt and pepper. Add beef and shake to coat. Transfer to a 3-qt. slow cooker. Add the onion, green pepper, tomatoes, mushrooms, soy sauce and molasses.

2 Cover and cook on low for 7-8 hours or until meat is tender. Serve with noodles if desired.

Yield: 4 servings.

texas-style beef brisket

PREP: 25 MIN. + MARINATING
COOK: 6-1/2 HOURS

Vivian Warner
Elkhart, Kansas

A friend tried this recipe and liked it, so I thought I would try it too. When my husband told me how much he enjoyed it, I knew I'd be making it often.

3 tablespoons Worcestershire sauce

1 tablespoon chili powder

2 bay leaves

2 garlic cloves, minced

1 teaspoon celery salt

1 teaspoon pepper

1 teaspoon Liquid Smoke, optional

1 fresh beef brisket (6 pounds)

1/2 cup beef broth

BARBECUE SAUCE:

1 medium onion, chopped

2 tablespoons canola oil

2 garlic cloves, minced

1 cup ketchup

1/2 cup molasses

1/4 cup cider vinegar

2 teaspoons chili powder

1/2 teaspoon ground mustard

1 In a large resealable plastic bag, combine the Worcestershire sauce, chili powder, bay leaves, garlic, celery salt, pepper and Liquid Smoke if desired. Cut brisket in half; add to bag. Seal bag and turn to coat. Refrigerate overnight.

2 Transfer beef to a 5 – or 6-qt. slow cooker; add broth. Cover and cook on low for 6-8 hours or until tender.

3 For sauce, in a small saucepan, saute onion in oil until tender. Add garlic; cook 1 minute longer. Stir in the remaining ingredients; heat through.

4 Remove brisket from the slow cooker; discard bay leaves. Place 1 cup cooking juices in a measuring cup; skim fat. Add to the barbecue sauce. Discard remaining juices.

5 Return brisket to the slow cooker; top with sauce mixture. Cover and cook on high for 30 minutes to allow flavors to blend. Thinly slice across the grain; serve with sauce.

Yield: 12 servings.

EDITOR'S NOTE: This is a fresh beef brisket, not corned beef.

beef brisket in beer

PREP: 15 MIN. • COOK: 8 HOURS

Eunice Stoen
Decorah, Iowa

One bite of this super-tender brisket, and you'll want to curl up and relax for the evening! With its pleasant gravy, this entree is perfect served with a side of mashed potatoes.

  1 fresh beef brisket (2-1/2 to 3 pounds)

  2 teaspoons Liquid Smoke, optional

  1 teaspoon celery salt

  1/2 teaspoon pepper

  1/4 teaspoon salt

  1 large onion, sliced

  1 can (12 ounces) beer *or* nonalcoholic beer

  2 teaspoons Worcestershire sauce

  2 tablespoons cornstarch

  1/4 cup cold water

1 Cut brisket in half; rub with Liquid Smoke if desired, celery salt, pepper and salt. Place in a 3-qt. slow cooker. Top with onion. Combine beer and Worcestershire sauce; pour over meat.

2 Cover and cook on low for 8-9 hours or until tender.

3 Remove brisket and keep warm. Strain cooking juices; transfer to a small saucepan. Combine cornstarch and water until smooth; stir into juices. Bring to a boil; cook and stir for 2 minutes or until thickened. Thinly slice beef across the grain; serve with gravy.

Yield: 6 servings.

EDITOR'S NOTE: This is a fresh beef brisket, not corned beef.

slow-cooked beef 'n' veggies

PREP: 15 MIN. + MARINATING
COOK: 8 HOURS

LaDonna Reed
Ponca City, Oklahoma

My husband and I came up with this soothing slow cooker recipe. It's simple, has lots of flavor and is low in fat.

  1 boneless beef top round steak (1/2 pound), cut into two pieces

  Dash seasoned salt, optional

  Dash pepper

  Dash garlic powder

  1 cup Italian salad dressing

  1/2 cup water

  1 tablespoon browning sauce

  2 medium carrots, cut into 2-inch pieces

  2 medium red potatoes, cubed

  1 small onion, sliced

  1/2 small green pepper, cut into small chunks

1 Sprinkle one side of steak with seasoned salt if desired and pepper; sprinkle other side with garlic powder. Place in a large resealable plastic bag; seal bag and refrigerate for 2-3 hours or overnight.

2 In a 3-qt. slow cooker, combine the salad dressing, water and browning sauce. Add carrots and potatoes; toss to coat. Add steak and coat with sauce. Top with onion and green pepper.

3 Cover and cook on low for 8-9 hours or until meat is tender.

Yield: 2 servings.

loaded vegetable beef stew

PREP: 40 MIN. • COOK: 8-1/2 HOURS

Kari Caven
Post Falls, Idaho

I first had this dish during a trip to Argentina. It inspired me to recreate it at home. It turned out so well, I wrote "Yum!" on the recipe card!

8 bacon strips, diced

3 pounds beef stew meat, cut into 1-inch cubes

6 medium carrots, cut into 1-inch pieces

6 medium tomatoes, peeled and cut into wedges

4 medium potatoes, peeled and cubed

3 cups cubed peeled butternut squash

2 medium green peppers, chopped

2 teaspoons dried thyme

2 garlic cloves, minced

2 cans (14-1/2 ounces *each*) beef broth

6 cups chopped cabbage

1/2 teaspoon pepper

1 In a large skillet, cook bacon over medium heat until crisp. Using a slotted spoon, remove to paper towels to drain. In the drippings, brown beef in batches. Refrigerate the bacon until serving.

2 In a 5-qt. slow cooker, combine the carrots, tomatoes, potatoes, squash, green peppers, thyme and garlic. Top with beef. Pour broth over the top. Cover and cook on low for 8 hours.

3 Stir in cabbage and pepper. Cover and cook on high for 30 minutes or until cabbage is tender. Sprinkle each serving with bacon.

Yield: 12 servings (1-1/3 cups each).

double-onion beef brisket

PREP: 25 MIN. • COOK: 6 HOURS

Elaine Sweet
Dallas, Texas

It's the slow cooking of this brisket that makes it so tender. Chili sauce, cider vinegar and brown sugar give it a wonderfully sweet-tangy flavor.

1 fresh beef brisket (4 pounds)

1-1/2 teaspoons kosher salt

1-1/2 teaspoons coarsely ground pepper

2 tablespoons olive oil

3 medium onions, halved and sliced

3 celery ribs, chopped

1 cup chili sauce

1/4 cup packed brown sugar

1/4 cup cider vinegar

1 envelope onion soup mix

1 Cut brisket in half; sprinkle all sides with salt and pepper. In a large skillet, brown brisket in oil; remove and set aside. In the same skillet, cook and stir onions on low heat for 8-10 minutes or until caramelized.

2 Place half of the onions in a 5-qt. slow cooker; top with celery and brisket. Combine the chili sauce, brown sugar, vinegar and soup mix. Pour over brisket; top with remaining onions.

3 Cover and cook on low for 6-7 hours or until meat is tender. Let stand for 5 minutes before slicing. Skim fat from cooking juices and serve with meat.

Yield: 10 servings.

EDITOR'S NOTE: This is a fresh beef brisket, not corned beef.

...ew

8 HOURS

...with great taste and
...ring it with warm
...or French bread for a

...(90% lean)

...s spaghetti sauce

...ozen mixed

...tomatoes and

...ef bouillon granules

1 teaspoon pepper

1 In a large skillet, cook beef and onion over medium heat until meat is no longer pink; drain. Transfer to a 5-qt. slow cooker. Stir in the remaining ingredients. Cover and cook on low for 8 hours or until the vegetables are tender.

Yield: 12 servings.

beef stroganoff

PREP: 25 MIN. • COOK: 7 HOURS

Lisa VanEgmond
Annapolis, Illinois

A favorite traditional dinner becomes fuss-free in the slow cooker with this convenient recipe. Tender sirloin steak in delicious gravy is served over noodles for a home-style meal your whole family will request time and again.

3 to 4 pounds beef top sirloin steak, cubed
2 cans (14-1/2 ounces *each*) chicken broth
1 pound sliced fresh mushrooms
1 can (12 ounces) regular cola
1/2 cup chopped onion
1 envelope onion soup mix
1 to 2 teaspoons garlic powder
2 teaspoons dried parsley flakes
1/2 teaspoon pepper
2 envelopes country gravy mix
2 cups (16 ounces) sour cream
Hot cooked noodles

1 In a 5-qt. slow cooker, combine the first nine ingredients. cover and cook on low for 7-8 hours or until beef is tender.

2 With a slotted spoon, remove beef and mushrooms. Place gravy mix in a large saucepan; gradually whisk in cooking liquid. Bring to a boil; cook and stir for 2 minutes or until thickened. Remove from the heat; stir in sour cream. Add beef and mushrooms to the gravy. Serve with noodles.

Yield: 12-16 servings.

coffee-flavored beef roast

PREP: 35 MIN. • COOK: 6 HOURS

Jean Collier
Hanford, California

Coming home to a complete meal like this is simply wonderful. My recipe takes very little preparation.

6 medium red potatoes, cut into wedges

6 medium carrots, cut into 1-inch lengths

2 beef sirloin tip roasts (2 to 3 pounds *each*)

1 teaspoon salt, *divided*

1/2 teaspoon pepper, *divided*

2 teaspoons canola oil

1 medium onion, halved and sliced

2 cups whole fresh mushrooms, quartered

2 garlic cloves, minced

1-1/2 cups brewed coffee

1 teaspoon chili powder

3 tablespoons cornstarch

1/4 cup cold water

1 Place potatoes and carrots in a 5-qt. slow cooker. Sprinkle beef with half of the salt and pepper. In a large skillet, brown beef in oil on all sides. Transfer to slow cooker.

2 In the same skillet, saute onion and mushrooms in the drippings for 2 minutes. Add garlic; cook 1 minute longer. Stir in the coffee, chili powder and remaining salt and pepper. Pour over meat.

3 Cover and cook on low for 6-8 hours or until meat is tender.

4 Remove meat and vegetables to a serving platter; keep warm. Skim fat from cooking juices; transfer to a small saucepan. Bring liquid to a boil.

5 Combine cornstarch and water until smooth; gradually stir into the pan. Bring to a boil; cook and stir for 2 minutes or until thickened. Serve with meat and vegetables.

Yield: 8 servings (2 cups gravy).

burgundy beef

PREP: 20 MIN. • COOK: 8 HOURS

Lora Snyder
Columbus, Massachusetts

On chilly days, it's a pleasure to smell the aroma of this savory pot roast bubbling in the slow cooker. The tender beef, vegetables and tasty gravy are truly mouthwatering over a bed of noodles.

1/2 pound sliced fresh mushrooms

1/2 pound fresh baby carrots

1 medium green pepper, julienned

1 boneless beef chuck roast (2-1/2 pounds)

1 can (10-3/4 ounces) condensed golden mushroom soup, undiluted

1/4 cup Burgundy wine *or* beef broth

1 tablespoon Worcestershire sauce

1 envelope onion soup mix

1/4 teaspoon pepper

2 to 3 tablespoons cornstarch

2 tablespoons cold water

Hot cooked wide egg noodles

1 In a 5-qt. slow cooker, combine the mushrooms, carrots and green pepper; place roast on top. In a large bowl, combine the soup, wine, Worcestershire sauce, soup mix and pepper; pour over roast. Cover and cook on low for 8-9 hours or until meat is tender.

2 Transfer roast and vegetables to a serving platter; keep warm. Strain cooking juices and skim fat; place in a large saucepan.

3 Combine cornstarch and cold water until smooth; gradually stir into cooking juices. Bring to a boil; cook and stir for 2 minutes or until thickened. Serve with the beef, vegetables and noodles.

Yield: 6-8 servings.

pot roast with mushroom gravy

PREP: 20 MIN. • COOK: 8 HOURS

Tyler Sherman
Madison, Wisconsin

You just can't beat the comforting goodness of a pot roast...especially one that simmers extra slowly in its own juices during the day. Hearty vegetables like potatoes, carrots, mushrooms, celery and onion make it a great meal-in-one.

- 1 pound small red potatoes, halved
- 2 cups fresh baby carrots
- 1 package (8 ounces) sliced fresh mushrooms
- 1 medium onion, cut into six wedges
- 2 celery ribs, cut into 1-inch pieces
- 1 boneless beef chuck roast (3 pounds)
- 1 can (14-1/2 ounces) reduced-sodium beef broth
- 1 can (10-1/2 ounces) mushroom gravy
- 1 package (1-1/2 ounces) beef stew seasoning mix

1 Place the potatoes, carrots, mushrooms, onion and celery in a 5-qt. slow cooker. Cut roast in half; place over vegetables. In a small bowl, combine the broth, gravy and seasoning mix; pour over roast.

2 Cover and cook on low for 8-9 hours or until meat is tender.

Yield: 8 servings.

mushroom 'n' steak stroganoff

PREP: 15 MIN. • COOK: 6-1/4 HOURS

Marilyn Shehane
Colorado Springs, Colorado

I rely on this recipe when we have family visiting. I put it in the slow cooker in the morning and when we get home from sightseeing all day, it's ready!

- 2 tablespoons all-purpose flour
- 1/2 teaspoon garlic powder
- 1/2 teaspoon pepper
- 1/4 teaspoon paprika
- 1-3/4 pounds beef top round steak, cut into 1-1/2-inch strips
- 1 can (10-3/4 ounces) condensed cream of mushroom soup, undiluted
- 1/2 cup water
- 1/4 cup onion mushroom soup mix
- 2 jars (4-1/2 ounces *each*) sliced mushrooms, drained
- 1/2 cup sour cream
- 1 tablespoon minced fresh parsley
- Hot cooked egg noodles, optional

1 In a large resealable plastic bag, combine the flour, garlic powder, pepper and paprika. Add beef strips and shake to coat.

2 Transfer to a 3-qt. slow cooker. In a small bowl, combine the soup, water and soup mix; pour over beef. Cover and cook on low for 6-7 hours or until meat is tender.

3 Stir in the mushrooms, sour cream, and parsley. Cover and cook 15 minutes longer or until sauce is thickened. Serve with noodles if desired.

Yield: 6 servings.

meat loaf from the slow cooker

PREP: 25 MIN. • COOK: 3 HOURS

Laura Burgess
Mount Vernon, South Dakota

This is one of my personal favorites. I'm often asked for the recipe. A dinnertime classic gets lightened up and easier to make, but keeps its tried-and-true flavor.

> 1/2 cup tomato sauce
>
> 1/2 cup egg substitute
>
> 1/4 cup ketchup
>
> 1 teaspoon Worcestershire sauce
>
> 1 small onion, chopped
>
> 1/3 cup crushed saltines (about 10 crackers)
>
> 3/4 teaspoon minced garlic
>
> 1/2 teaspoon seasoned salt
>
> 1/8 teaspoon seasoned pepper
>
> 1-1/2 pounds lean ground beef (90% lean)
>
> 1/2 pound reduced-fat bulk pork sausage
>
> SAUCE:
>
> 1/2 cup ketchup
>
> 3 tablespoons brown sugar
>
> 3/4 teaspoon ground mustard
>
> 1/4 teaspoon ground nutmeg

1 Cut three 25-in. x 3-in. strips of heavy-duty foil; crisscross so they resemble spokes of a wheel. Place strips on the bottom and up the sides of an oval 5-qt. slow cooker. Coat strips with cooking spray.

2 In a large bowl, combine the first nine ingredients. Crumble beef and sausage over mixture and mix well (mixture will be moist). Shape into a loaf. Place meat loaf in the center of the strips.

3 In a small bowl, combine sauce ingredients. Spoon over meat loaf. Cover and cook on low 3-4 hours or until a meat thermometer reads 160°. Using foil strips as handles, remove the meat loaf to a platter.

Yield: 8 servings.

southwestern beef stew

PREP: 30 MIN. • COOK: 8 HOURS

Regina Stock
Topeka, Kansas

This zippy stew seasoned with picante sauce is great on cold winter evenings. The preparation is so easy...it's ready in minutes after a long and busy day at work.

> 2 pounds beef stew meat, cut into 1-inch cubes
>
> 1 jar (16 ounces) picante sauce
>
> 2 medium potatoes, peeled and cut into 1/2-inch cubes
>
> 4 medium carrots, cut into 1/2-inch slices
>
> 1 large onion, chopped
>
> 1 teaspoon chili powder
>
> 1/4 teaspoon salt
>
> 1/4 teaspoon ground cumin
>
> 1 tablespoon cornstarch
>
> 1/4 cup cold water

1 In a large nonstick skillet coated with cooking spray, brown beef on all sides; drain. Transfer to a 3-qt. slow cooker. Stir in the picante sauce, potatoes, carrots, onion, chili powder, salt and cumin.

2 Cover and cook on low for 8-9 hours or until meat and vegetables are tender.

3 In a small bowl, combine cornstarch and water until smooth; stir into stew. Cover and cook on high for 15 minutes or until gravy is thickened.

Yield: 7 servings.

corned beef supper

PREP: 25 MIN. • COOK: 4 HOURS

Dawn Fagerstrom
Warren, Minnesota

What better way to celebrate St. Patrick's Day than with this hearty one-pot meal for two? I often fix it for the holiday, but it's good any time of the year.

1 small onion, sliced

4 small carrots, cut into chunks

2 medium potatoes, cut into chunks

1 corned beef brisket with spice packet (1 pound)

1/3 cup unsweetened apple juice

2 whole cloves

1 tablespoon brown sugar

1/2 teaspoon grated orange peel

1/2 teaspoon prepared mustard

2 cabbage wedges

1 Place onion in a 3-qt. slow cooker. Top with carrots, potatoes and brisket. Combine the apple juice, cloves, brown sugar, orange peel, mustard and contents of spice packet; pour over brisket. Cover and cook on high for 3-1/2 to 4 hours.

2 Add cabbage; cover and cook 30 minutes longer or until meat and vegetables are tender. Strain and discard cloves; serve pan juices with corned beef and vegetables.

Yield: 2 servings.

cider mushroom brisket

PREP: 10 MIN. • **COOK: 6 HOURS**

Colleen Weston
Denver, Colorado

Apple juice and gingersnaps give an autumn feel to this tender, slow-cooked brisket. It's quick to prep, and the mouthwatering aroma will linger for hours.

　1 fresh beef brisket (6 pounds)

　2 jars (12 ounces *each*) mushroom gravy

　1 cup apple cider *or* juice

　1 envelope onion mushroom soup mix

　6 gingersnap cookies, crushed

1 Cut brisket into thirds; place in a 5- or 6-qt. slow cooker. In a large bowl, combine the gravy, cider, soup mix and cookie crumbs; pour over beef.

2 Cover and cook on low for 6-8 hours or until meat is tender.

3 Thinly slice meat across the grain. Skim fat from cooking juices; thicken if desired.

Yield: 12 servings.

EDITOR'S NOTE: This is a fresh beef brisket, not corned beef.

butternut beef stew

PREP: 30 MIN. • COOK: 7 HOURS

Erin Lembke
Monroe, Washington

I tweaked this recipe I found in a magazine to suit my taste for sweet and spicy. I found that pureeing the tomatoes added a thicker consistency without using flour.

1-1/4 pounds beef stew meat, cut into 1-inch cubes

1 tablespoon canola oil

1-1/2 cups cubed peeled butternut squash

1 cup chopped cabbage

1/2 cup coarsely chopped sweet red pepper

1 celery rib with leaves, chopped

1 can (10 ounces) diced tomatoes and green chilies

1/4 cup packed brown sugar

1 can (14-1/2 ounces) beef broth

1 tablespoon adobo sauce

1 teaspoon dried oregano

1/4 teaspoon salt

1/8 teaspoon pepper

1 In a large skillet, brown meat in oil on all sides; drain. Transfer to a 3-qt. slow cooker. Stir in the squash, cabbage, red pepper and celery.

2 In a blender, combine tomatoes and brown sugar. Cover and process until blended. Pour over vegetables. Combine the broth, adobo sauce, oregano, salt and pepper; add to slow cooker.

3 Cover and cook on low for 7-8 hours or until meat and vegetables are tender. If desired, thicken pan juices.

Yield: 4 servings.

flank steak fajitas

PREP: 20 MIN. • COOK: 6 HOURS

Twila Burkholder
Middleburg, Pennsylvania

The beef comes out juicy and flavorful when I use the slow cooker to create these tempting fajitas. I like to serve them with a side of Spanish rice.

1 beef flank steak (1-1/2 pounds)

1 medium onion, sliced

1 cup tomato juice

1 jalapeno pepper, seeded and chopped

2 garlic cloves, minced

1 tablespoon minced fresh cilantro

1 teaspoon ground cumin

1 teaspoon chili powder

1/4 teaspoon salt

1 medium green pepper, julienned

1 medium sweet red pepper, julienned

6 flour tortillas (8 inches), warmed

Shredded cheddar cheese, sour cream and guacamole, optional

1 Thinly slice steak across the grain into strips; place in a 5-qt. slow cooker. Add the onion, tomato juice, jalapeno, garlic, cilantro, cumin, chili powder and salt. Cover and cook on low for 5 hours.

2 Add green and red peppers. Cover and cook 1 hour longer or until meat and vegetables are tender.

3 Using a slotted spoon, spoon meat mixture down the center of each tortilla. Sprinkle with cheese if desired. Fold sides of tortilla over filling. Serve with sour cream and guacamole if desired.

Yield: 6 servings.

EDITOR'S NOTE: When cutting hot peppers, disposable gloves are recommended. Avoid touching your face.

celebration roast

PREP: 15 MIN. • COOK: 7 HOURS

Cindy Morris
Coyle, Oklahoma

This tender beef with its peppery brown gravy is sure to be a new favorite when served over noodles. It's an easy way to feed a large group a hearty, satisfying meal.

2 beef top round roasts *or* beef sirloin tip roasts (3 to 4 pounds *each*)

2 small onions, halved and thinly sliced

3 teaspoons garlic pepper blend

2 teaspoons dried basil

1 teaspoon salt

2 packages (16 ounces *each*) bow tie pasta

CRACKED PEPPER GRAVY:

1/2 cup butter, cubed

1/2 cup all-purpose flour

2 teaspoons coarsely ground pepper

1 teaspoon salt

5 cups milk

2 to 4 tablespoons browning sauce, optional

1 Cut each roast in half; place two halves in a 5-qt. slow cooker. Place the remaining halves in another 5-qt. slow cooker. Top each with half of the onions, pepper blend, basil and salt.

2 Cover and cook on low for 7-8 hours or until meat is tender.

3 Cook pasta according to package directions. Meanwhile, in a large saucepan, melt butter. Stir in the flour, pepper and salt until blended; gradually add milk. Bring to a boil; cook and stir for 2 minutes or until thickened. Stir in browning sauce if desired.

4 Drain pasta; serve with beef and gravy.

Yield: 16 servings.

hungarian goulash

PREP: 15 MIN. • COOK: 8 HOURS

Jackie Kohn
Duluth, Minnesota

A great family dish, this recipe boasts a rich creamy sauce certain to satisfy goulash lovers. I enjoy sharing recipes with friends and family, and this one's great for potluck suppers, too. Garnish with fresh parsley for flavor and color.

2 pounds beef top round steak, cut into 1-inch cubes

1 cup chopped onion

2 tablespoons all-purpose flour

1-1/2 teaspoons paprika

1 teaspoon garlic salt

1/2 teaspoon pepper

1 can (14-1/2 ounces) diced tomatoes, undrained

1 bay leaf

1 cup (8 ounces) sour cream

Hot cooked noodles

Minced fresh parsley, optional

1 Place beef and onion in a 3-qt. slow cooker. Combine the flour, paprika, garlic salt and pepper; sprinkle over beef and stir to coat. Stir in tomatoes. Add bay leaf.

2 Cover and cook on low for 8-10 hours or until meat is tender.

3 Discard bay leaf. Just before serving, stir in sour cream; heat through. Serve with noodles. Sprinkle with parsley if desired.

Yield: 6-8 servings.

slow-cooked swiss steak

PREP: 10 MIN. • COOK: 6 HOURS

Sarah Burks
Wathena, Kansas

*This is a favorite for me to make, because I can flour
and season the steaks and refrigerate them overnight.
The next morning, I just put all the ingredients in the
slow cooker, and I have an effortless entree waiting for
us when I arrive home from work.*

   2 tablespoons all-purpose flour

   1/2 teaspoon salt

   1/4 teaspoon pepper

1-1/2 pounds beef round steak, cut into
six pieces

1 medium onion, cut into 1/4-inch slices

1 celery rib, cut into 1/2-inch slices

2 cans (8 ounces *each*) tomato sauce

1 In a large resealable plastic bag, combine
the flour, salt and pepper. Add the steak;
seal bag and toss to coat.

2 Place the onion in a greased 3-qt. slow
cooker. Top with the steak, celery and
tomato sauce. Cover and cook on low for
6-8 hours or until meat is tender.

Yield: 6 servings.

fabulous fajitas

PREP: 20 MIN. • COOK: 3-1/2 HOURS

Janie Reitz
Rochester, Minnesota

I've enjoyed cooking since I was a girl growing up in the Southwest. When friends ask me for new recipes to try, I suggest these fajitas. It's wonderful to put the beef in the slow cooker before church and come home to a delicious main dish.

1-1/2 pounds beef top sirloin steak, cut into thin strips

2 tablespoons canola oil

2 tablespoons lemon juice

1 garlic clove, minced

1-1/2 teaspoons ground cumin

1 teaspoon seasoned salt

1/2 teaspoon chili powder

1/4 to 1/2 teaspoon crushed red pepper flakes

1 large green pepper, julienned

1 large onion, julienned

6 to 8 flour tortillas (8 inches)

Shredded cheddar cheese, salsa, sour cream, lettuce and tomatoes, optional

1 In a skillet, brown steak in oil over medium heat. Place steak and drippings in a 3-qt. slow cooker. Stir in the lemon juice, garlic, cumin, salt, chili powder and red pepper flakes.

2 Cover and cook on high for 2-1/2 to 3 hours or until meat is almost tender. Add green pepper and onion; cover and cook for 1 hour or until meat and vegetables are tender.

3 Warm tortillas according to package directions; spoon beef and vegetables down the center of tortillas. Top each with cheese, salsa, sour cream, lettuce and tomatoes if desired.

Yield: 6-8 servings.

mushroom round steak

PREP: 20 MIN. • COOK: 6 HOURS

Lois Hedke
South Rockwood, Michigan

This two-serving recipe is light on ingredients and big on taste. This is our favorite "quickie." All you need is a salad to make it a meal.

1/2 medium green pepper, cut into 1/2-inch pieces

1/4 cup sliced onion

1 beef top round steak (10 ounces), cut into two pieces

2/3 cup condensed cream of mushroom soup, undiluted

1/3 cup water

1-1/2 cups uncooked egg noodles

1 Place green pepper and onion in a 1-1/2-qt. slow cooker; top with beef. In a small bowl, combine soup and water; pour over meat. Cover and cook on low for 6-7 hours or until meat is tender.

2 Cook the noodles according to the package directions; drain. Serve with round steak and gravy.

Yield: 2 servings.

picante beef roast

PREP: 15 MIN. • COOK: 8 HOURS

Margaret Thiel
Levittown, Pennsylvania

Before putting this roast in the slow cooker, be sure to trim the fat from it to avoid greasy gravy. If your roast weighs 3 or more pounds, cut it in half to ensure even cooking.

> 1 beef rump roast *or* bottom round roast (3 pounds), trimmed and halved
>
> 1 jar (16 ounces) picante sauce
>
> 1 can (15 ounces) tomato sauce
>
> 1 envelope taco seasoning
>
> 3 tablespoons cornstarch
>
> 1/4 cup water

1 Cut roast in half; place in a 5-qt. slow cooker. In a large bowl, combine the picante sauce, tomato sauce and taco seasoning; pour over roast.

2 Cover and cook on low for 8-9 hours or until meat is tender.

3 Remove meat to a serving platter; keep warm. Skim fat from cooking juices; transfer 3 cups to a small saucepan. Bring liquid to a boil.

4 Combine cornstarch and water until smooth. Gradually stir into pan. Bring to a boil; cook and stir for 2 minutes or until thickened. Slice roast; serve with gravy.

Yield: 8 servings.

spicy goulash

PREP: 25 MIN. • COOK: 5-1/2 HOURS

Melissa Polk
West Lafayette, Indiana

Ground cumin, chili powder and a can of Mexican diced tomatoes jazz up my goulash recipe. Even the elbow macaroni is prepared in the slow cooker.

> 1 pound lean ground beef (90% lean)
>
> 4 cans (14-1/2 ounces *each*) Mexican diced tomatoes, undrained
>
> 2 cans (16 ounces *each*) kidney beans, rinsed and drained
>
> 2 cups water
>
> 1 medium onion, chopped
>
> 1 medium green pepper, chopped
>
> 1/4 cup red wine vinegar
>
> 2 tablespoons chili powder
>
> 1 tablespoon Worcestershire sauce
>
> 2 teaspoons beef bouillon granules
>
> 1 teaspoon dried basil
>
> 1 teaspoon dried parsley flakes
>
> 1 teaspoon ground cumin
>
> 1/4 teaspoon pepper
>
> 2 cups uncooked elbow macaroni

1 In a large skillet, cook beef over medium heat until no longer pink; drain. Transfer to a 5-qt. slow cooker. Stir in the tomatoes, beans, water, onion, green pepper, vinegar, chili powder, Worcestershire sauce, bouillon and seasonings.

2 Cover and cook on low for 5-6 hours or until heated through.

3 Stir in the macaroni; cover and cook 30 minutes longer or until the macaroni is tender.

Yield: 12 servings.

1/4 teaspoon pepper

1 envelope onion soup mix

2 cups water

1 tablespoon white vinegar

1 bay leaf

1/2 small head cabbage, cut into wedges

3 tablespoons butter

2 tablespoons all-purpose flour

1 tablespoon dried minced onion

2 tablespoons prepared horseradish

1 Place the carrots, onion and celery in a 5-qt. slow cooker. Cut roast in half. Place roast over vegetables; sprinkle with 1/2 teaspoon salt and pepper. Add the soup mix, water, vinegar and bay leaf. Cover and cook on low for 7-9 hours or until beef is tender.

2 Remove beef and keep warm; discard bay leaf. Add cabbage. Cover and cook on high for 30-40 minutes or until cabbage is tender.

3 Meanwhile, melt butter in a small saucepan; stir in flour and onion. Skim fat from cooking liquid in slow cooker. Add 1-1/2 cups cooking liquid to the saucepan. Stir in horseradish and remaining salt; bring to a boil. Cook and stir for 2 minutes or until thickened and bubbly. Serve with roast and vegetables.

Yield: 6-8 servings.

Flavorful pot roast. The horseradish gravy in this recipe tenderizes the meat while giving it some bite. For another taste twist, sprinkle chopped onion, Worcestershire sauce and a bay leaf on your beef. A mixture of onion soup mix, mushrooms and coffee also makes a great topping.

hearty new england dinner

PREP: 20 MIN. • COOK: 7-1/2 HOURS

Claire McCombs
San Diego, California

This favorite slow-cooker recipe came from a friend. At first, my husband was a bit skeptical about a roast that wasn't fixed in the oven, but he loves the old-fashioned goodness of this version. The horseradish in the gravy adds zip.

2 medium carrots, sliced

1 medium onion, sliced

1 celery rib, sliced

1 boneless beef chuck roast (about 3 pounds)

1 teaspoon salt, *divided*

tender beef over noodles

PREP: 15 MIN. • COOK: 5-1/2 HOURS

Olivia Gust
Salem, Oregon

I dress up thrifty stew meat with noodles and a slightly sweet red sauce for this satisfying main dish. It goes great with a salad and garlic bread.

1/2 to 3/4 pound beef stew meat

1/3 cup chopped onion

1 teaspoon canola oil

1 cup water, *divided*

1/3 cup ketchup

1 tablespoon brown sugar

1 tablespoon Worcestershire sauce

1/2 teaspoon paprika

1/4 teaspoon ground mustard

3 tablespoons all-purpose flour

1 cup uncooked egg noodles

Minced fresh parsley, optional

1 In a small skillet, brown beef and onion in oil; drain. Transfer to a 1-1/2-qt. slow cooker.

2 In a small bowl, combine 1/2 cup water, ketchup, brown sugar, Worcestershire sauce, paprika and mustard; pour over meat. Cover and cook on low for 5 hours or until meat is tender.

3 Combine flour and remaining water until smooth; stir into meat mixture. Cover and cook 30 minutes longer or until thickened.

4 Meanwhile, cook noodles according to package directions; drain. Stir in parsley if desired. Serve with beef.

Yield: 2 servings.

beef barley stew

PREP: 20 MIN. • COOK: 6 HOURS

Barb Smith
Regina, Saskatchewan

On cool days, which we get plenty of here, I like to get out my slow cooker and make up a batch of this comforting stew. Trying to appeal to the 10 picky eaters in our large household is not too easy, but with this recipe, everyone asks for seconds.

1-1/2 pounds beef stew meat, cut into 1-inch pieces

1 medium onion, chopped

2 tablespoons canola oil

4 cups water

1 can (15 ounces) tomato sauce

5 medium carrots, cut into 1/2-inch pieces

1 celery rib, thinly sliced

2 teaspoons salt

1/2 teaspoon dried oregano

1/2 teaspoon paprika

1/4 teaspoon pepper

2 cups fresh *or* frozen green beans, thawed

2 cups fresh *or* frozen corn, thawed

3/4 cup medium pearl barley

1 In a large skillet, brown beef and onion in oil until meat is no longer pink; drain. Transfer to a 5-qt. slow cooker. Add water, tomato sauce, carrots, celery, salt, oregano, paprika and pepper.

2 Cover and cook on low for 4-5 hours. Add the beans, corn and barley; cover and cook on low 2 hours longer or until barley, beef and vegetables are tender.

Yield: 6-8 servings.

swiss steak supper

PREP: 20 MIN. • COOK: 5-1/2 HOURS

Kathleen Romaniuk
Chomedey, Quebec

To save a step, I keep peppered seasoned salt on hand to use instead of the seasoned salt and pepper in this satisfying dish.

- 1-1/2 pounds beef top round steak
- 1/2 teaspoon seasoned salt
- 1/4 teaspoon coarsely ground pepper
- 1 tablespoon canola oil
- 3 medium potatoes
- 1-1/2 cups fresh baby carrots
- 1 medium onion, sliced
- 1 can (14-1/2 ounces) Italian diced tomatoes
- 1 jar (12 ounces) home-style beef gravy
- 1 tablespoon minced fresh parsley

1 Cut steak into six serving-size pieces; flatten to 1/4-in. thickness. Rub with seasoned salt and pepper. In a large skillet, brown beef in oil on both sides; drain.

2 Cut each potato into eight wedges. In a 5-qt. slow cooker, layer the potatoes, carrots, beef and onion. Combine tomatoes and gravy; pour over the top.

3 Cover and cook on low for 5-1/2 to 6 hours or until meat and vegetables are tender. Sprinkle with parsley.

Yield: 6 servings.

steak strips with dumplings

PREP: 25 MIN. • COOK: 5 HOURS

John Smalldridge
Princeton, Idaho

I love to spend a day down by the lake and come home to this slow-cooked specialty that's ready to eat! While it's handy to make on warm summer days, it's great for chilly winter nights, too.

> 3/4 pound beef top round steak, cut into 1/2-inch strips
>
> 1/4 teaspoon pepper
>
> 2 teaspoons canola oil
>
> 2/3 cup condensed cream of chicken soup, undiluted
>
> 1/2 cup beef broth
>
> 4 large fresh mushrooms, sliced
>
> 1/4 cup *each* chopped onion, green pepper and celery

DUMPLINGS:

> 1/2 cup all-purpose flour
>
> 3/4 teaspoon baking powder
>
> 1/4 teaspoon salt
>
> 2 tablespoons beaten egg
>
> 3 tablespoons 2% milk
>
> 1/2 teaspoon dried parsley flakes

1 Sprinkle steak with pepper. In a small skillet, brown steak in oil over medium-high heat. Transfer to a 1-1/2-qt. slow cooker. Combine the soup, broth and vegetables; pour over steak. Cover and cook on low for 4-5 hours.

2 For dumplings, in a small bowl, combine the flour, baking powder and salt. Stir in egg and milk just until blended. Drop by tablespoonfuls onto meat mixture. Sprinkle with parsley.

3 Cover and cook on high for 1 hour or until a toothpick inserted in a dumpling comes out clean (do not lift the cover while cooking).

Yield: 2 servings.

tangy pot roast

PREP: 15 MIN. • COOK: 7 HOURS

Paula Beach
Milton, New York

This super-tender roast gets its special flavor from zippy Catalina dressing. Made in a slow cooker, it takes the edge off a busy day.

   3 medium potatoes, thinly sliced

   1-1/3 cups thinly sliced fresh carrots

   2/3 cup sliced onion

   1 boneless beef chuck roast (3 pounds)

   1 teaspoon salt

   1/2 teaspoon pepper

   1/2 cup Catalina salad dressing

   1/4 cup dry red wine *or* beef broth

1 Place the potatoes, carrots and onion in a 5-qt. slow cooker. Cut roast in half; rub with salt and pepper. Place over vegetables. In a small bowl, combine salad dressing and red wine; pour over roast.

2 Cover and cook on low for 7-8 hours or until meat is tender.

3 Skim fat from cooking juices; thicken juices if desired.

Yield: 6 servings.

meatball tortellini

PREP: 10 MIN. • COOK: 3 HOURS

Tracie Bergeron
Chauvin, Louisiana

I combined some favorite staples from our freezer and pantry to come up with this easy dish. It has few ingredients and little preparation.

   1 package (16 ounces) frozen California-blend vegetables, thawed

   1 package frozen fully cooked Italian meatballs (12 ounces), thawed

   2 cups uncooked dried cheese tortellini

   2 cans (10-3/4 ounces *each*) condensed cream of mushroom soup, undiluted

   2-1/4 cups water

   1 teaspoon Creole seasoning

1 In a 3-qt. slow cooker, combine the vegetables, meatballs and tortellini. In a large bowl, whisk the soup, water and Creole seasoning. Pour over vegetable-meatball mixture; stir well. Cover and cook on low for 3-4 hours or until the tortellini and vegetables are tender.

Yield: 6-8 servings.

EDITOR'S NOTE: The following spices may be substituted for 1 teaspoon Creole seasoning: 1/4 teaspoon each salt, garlic powder and paprika; and a pinch each of dried thyme, ground cumin and cayenne pepper.

Eliminate extras. Use up leftover meatballs by stuffing them into cooked jumbo pasta shells. Pour spaghetti sauce in a baking dish with the shells and shredded mozzarella cheese. Warm in a 350° oven for about a half hour.

1. In a large skillet, cook the beef, onion and green pepper until beef is browned and vegetables are tender; drain. Add the next eight ingredients; bring to a boil. Reduce heat; cover and simmer for 10 minutes. Combine cheeses.

2. In a 5-qt. slow cooker, layer about 3/4 cup beef mixture, one tortilla and about 1/3 cup cheese. Repeat layers. Cover and cook on low for 5-7 hours or until heated through.

Yield: 4 servings.

slow cooker enchiladas

PREP: 30 MIN. • COOK: 5 HOURS

Mary Luebbert
Benton, Kansas

When you're craving Southwestern food but won't have time to prepare it in the evening, rely on this recipe. I simply fill the slow cooker in the morning, then come home to a sensational supper.

1 pound ground beef

1 cup chopped onion

1/2 cup chopped green pepper

1 can (16 ounces) pinto *or* kidney beans, rinsed and drained

1 can (15 ounces) black beans, rinsed and drained

1 can (10 ounces) diced tomatoes and green chilies, undrained

1/3 cup water

1 teaspoon chili powder

1/2 teaspoon ground cumin

1/2 teaspoon salt

1/4 teaspoon pepper

1 cup (4 ounces) shredded sharp cheddar cheese

1 cup (4 ounces) shredded Monterey Jack cheese

6 flour tortillas (6 inches)

zesty beef stew

PREP: 10 MIN. • COOK: 3-1/2 HOURS

Margaret Turza
South Bend, Indiana

Assembly couldn't be simpler for this hearty no-fuss stew! I created this dish when I didn't have some of my usual ingredients for vegetable beef soup. My husband said it was the best I ever made!

1 pound beef stew meat, cut into 1-inch cubes

1 package (16 ounces) frozen mixed vegetables, thawed

1 can (15 ounces) pinto beans, rinsed and drained

1-1/2 cups water

1 can (8 ounces) pizza sauce

2 tablespoons medium pearl barley

1 tablespoon dried minced onion

2 teaspoons beef bouillon granules

1/4 teaspoon crushed red pepper flakes

1. In a 3-qt. slow cooker, combine all the ingredients. Cover and cook on low for 3-1/2 to 4-1/2 hours or until meat is tender.

Yield: 6 servings.

sweet 'n' tangy pot roast

PREP: 10 MIN. • COOK: 9-1/2 HOURS

Carol Mulligan
Honeoye Falls, New York

I fixed this roast the first time I cooked for my husband-to-be more than 20 years ago. For dessert, I spooned chocolate pudding over marshmallows. He thought he'd died and gone to heaven!

> 1 boneless beef chuck roast (3 pounds)
> 1/2 teaspoon salt
> 1/2 teaspoon pepper
> 1 cup water
> 1 cup ketchup
> 1/4 cup red wine *or* beef broth
> 1 envelope brown gravy mix
> 2 teaspoons Dijon mustard

> 1 teaspoon Worcestershire sauce
> 1/8 teaspoon garlic powder
> 3 tablespoons cornstarch
> 1/4 cup cold water

1 Cut roast in half and place in a 5-qt. slow cooker. Sprinkle with salt and pepper. In a bowl, combine the water, ketchup, wine or broth, gravy mix, mustard, Worcestershire sauce and garlic powder; pour over meat.

2 Cover and cook on low for 9-10 hours or until meat is tender.

3 Combine cornstarch and cold water until smooth. Stir into slow cooker. Cover and cook on high for 30 minutes or until gravy is thickened. Remove meat from slow cooker. Slice and serve with gravy.

Yield: 8 servings.

meat sauce for spaghetti

PREP: 30 MIN. • COOK: 8 HOURS

Mary Tallman
Arbor Vitae, Wisconsin

Here's a thick, hearty sauce that turns ordinary spaghetti and garlic bread into a filling feast. When I'm in a hurry, I make this slow cooker recipe in an electric frying pan instead.

- 1 pound ground beef
- 1 pound bulk Italian sausage
- 1 can (28 ounces) crushed tomatoes, undrained
- 1 medium green pepper, chopped
- 1 medium onion, chopped
- 1 cup finely chopped carrots
- 1 cup water
- 1 can (8 ounces) tomato sauce
- 1 can (6 ounces) tomato paste
- 1 tablespoon brown sugar
- 1 tablespoon Italian seasoning
- 2 garlic cloves, minced
- 1/2 teaspoon salt
- 1/4 teaspoon pepper
- Hot cooked spaghetti

1 In a large skillet, cook beef and sausage over medium heat until no longer pink; drain.

2 Transfer to a 5-qt. slow cooker. Stir in the tomatoes, green pepper, onion, carrots, water, tomato sauce, tomato paste, brown sugar, Italian seasoning, garlic, salt and pepper. Cover and cook on low for 8-10 hours or until bubbly. Serve with spaghetti.

Yield: 9 servings.

rosemary pot roast

PREP: 15 MIN. • COOK: 8 HOURS

Marcia Schroeder
River Edge, New Jersey

Come home to a comforting, ready-to-eat entree with this slow-cooker favorite. A neighbor shared the recipe with me. It's so easy and fills the house with a wonderful aroma. I've served it often...guests always want the recipe.

1 boneless beef chuck steak (3/4 inch thick and 3/4 pound)

1 to 2 teaspoons canola oil

1/4 cup beef broth

1/4 cup tomato sauce

1/4 cup dry red wine *or* additional beef broth

2 tablespoons chopped onion

1 garlic clove, minced

1-1/2 teaspoons dried parsley flakes

1/4 teaspoon minced fresh rosemary

1/8 teaspoon salt

1/8 teaspoon pepper

1-1/2 teaspoons cornstarch

1 tablespoon water

1 In a large skillet, brown beef in oil on both sides. Transfer to a 1-1/2-qt. slow cooker. In a small bowl, combine the broth, tomato sauce, wine, onion, garlic, parsley, rosemary, salt and pepper; pour over beef. Cover and cook on low for 8 hours or until meat is tender.

2 Remove beef and keep warm. In a small saucepan, combine cornstarch and water until smooth; stir in cooking juices. Bring to a boil; cook and stir for 2 minutes or until thickened. Serve with beef.

Yield: 2 servings.

p. 147

pork

p. 136

p. 135

p. 154

slow-cooked sweet 'n' sour pork

PREP: 20 MIN. • COOK: 6-1/2 HOURS

Martha Nickerson
Hancock, Maine

A co-worker gave me this recipe more than 20 years ago, and my family still enjoys this satisfying entree.

2 tablespoons plus 1-1/2 teaspoons paprika

1-1/2 pounds boneless pork loin roast, cut into 1-inch strips

1 tablespoon canola oil

1 can (20 ounces) unsweetened pineapple chunks

1 medium onion, chopped

1 medium green pepper, chopped

1/4 cup cider vinegar

3 tablespoons brown sugar

3 tablespoons reduced-sodium soy sauce

1 tablespoon Worcestershire sauce

1/2 teaspoon salt

2 tablespoons cornstarch

1/4 cup cold water

Hot cooked rice, optional

1 Place paprika in a large resealable plastic bag. Add pork, a few pieces at a time, and shake to coat. In a nonstick skillet, brown pork in oil in batches over medium-high heat. Transfer to a 3-qt. slow cooker.

2 Drain pineapple, reserving juice; refrigerate the pineapple. Add the pineapple juice, onion, green pepper, vinegar, brown sugar, soy sauce, Worcestershire sauce and salt to slow cooker; mix well. Cover and cook on low for 6-8 hours or until the meat is tender.

3 Combine cornstarch and water until smooth; stir into pork mixture. Add pineapple. Cover and cook 30 minutes longer or until sauce is thickened. Serve over rice if desired.

Yield: 6 servings.

tuscan pork stew

PREP: 15 MIN. • COOK: 8-1/2 HOURS

Penny Hawkins
Mebane, North Carolina

Tender chunks of pork slowly cook in a nicely seasoned, wine-infused sauce. Add some crushed red pepper flakes for a little added kick.

  1 boneless whole pork loin roast (1-1/2 pounds), cut into 1-inch cubes

  2 tablespoons olive oil

  2 cans (14-1/2 ounces *each*) Italian diced tomatoes, undrained

  2 cups reduced-sodium chicken broth

  2 cups frozen pepper stir-fry vegetable blend, thawed

  1/2 cup dry red wine *or* additional reduced-sodium chicken broth

  1/4 cup orange marmalade

  2 garlic cloves, minced

  1 teaspoon dried oregano

  1/2 teaspoon fennel seed

  1/2 teaspoon pepper

  1/8 teaspoon crushed red pepper flakes, optional

  2 tablespoons cornstarch

  2 tablespoons cold water

  Hot cooked fettuccine, optional

1 In a large skillet, brown pork in oil until no longer pink; drain. Place pork in a 5-qt. slow cooker.

2 In a large bowl, combine the tomatoes, broth, vegetable blend, wine, marmalade, garlic, oregano, fennel seed, pepper and pepper flakes if desired; pour over pork. Cover and cook on low for 8 hours or until meat is tender.

3 Mix cornstarch and water until smooth; stir into stew. Cover and cook on high for 30 minutes or until gravy is thickened. Serve with fettuccine if desired.

Yield: 8 servings.

slow cooker pork chops

PREP: 15 MIN. • COOK: 3 HOURS

Sue Bingham
Madisonville, Tennessee

Everyone will enjoy these fork-tender pork chops with a creamy, light gravy. I like to serve mine with mashed potatoes and coleslaw or a salad.

3/4 cup all-purpose flour, *divided*

1/2 teaspoon ground mustard

1/2 teaspoon garlic pepper blend

1/4 teaspoon seasoned salt

4 boneless pork loin chops (1/2 inch thick and 4 ounces *each*)

2 tablespoons canola oil

1 can (14-1/2 ounces) chicken broth

1 In a large resealable plastic bag, combine 1/2 cup flour, mustard, pepper blend and seasoned salt. Add chops, one at a time, and shake to coat. In a large skillet, brown meat in oil on each side.

2 Transfer to a 5-qt. slow cooker. Place remaining flour in a small bowl; whisk in broth until smooth. Pour over chops. Cover and cook on low for 3 to 3-1/2 hours or until meat is tender.

3 Remove pork to a serving plate and keep warm. Whisk pan juices until smooth; serve with pork.

Yield: 4 servings.

potato sausage supper

PREP: 15 MIN. • COOK: 6 HOURS

Patricia Ginn
Delphi, Indiana

I fix this comforting meal-in-one dish at least once a month. I often bring the hearty layered casserole to family reunions and always return with an empty slow cooker.

4 medium potatoes, peeled and sliced

1 pound smoked kielbasa *or* Polish sausage, cut into 1/2-inch slices

2 medium onions, sliced and separated into rings

1 can (10-3/4 ounces) condensed cheddar cheese soup, undiluted

1 can (10-3/4 ounces) condensed cream of celery soup, undiluted

1 package (10 ounces) frozen peas, thawed

1 In a greased 5-qt. slow cooker; layer a third of each of the potatoes, sausage, onions and cheddar cheese soup. Repeat layers twice.

2 Pour celery soup over the top. Cover and cook on low for 5-1/2 hours or until the potatoes are tender. Add the peas and cook 30 minutes longer.

Yield: 6-8 servings.

peachy spareribs

PREP: 10 MIN. • COOK: 5-3/4 HOURS

Jeanne Brino
Woodbury, Minnesota

Canned peaches make a delightful addition to the sauce I use to flavor my spareribs. Served over rice, these sweet-tangy ribs make a sensational meal any time of the year.

4 pounds pork spareribs

1 can (15-1/4 ounces) sliced peaches, undrained

1/2 cup packed brown sugar

1/4 cup ketchup

1/4 cup white vinegar

2 tablespoons soy sauce

1 garlic clove, minced

1 teaspoon salt

1 teaspoon pepper

2 tablespoons cornstarch

2 tablespoons cold water

Hot cooked rice

1 Cut ribs into serving-size pieces. In a large skillet, brown ribs on all sides; drain.

2 Transfer to a 5-qt. slow cooker. Combine peaches, brown sugar, ketchup, vinegar, soy sauce, garlic, salt and pepper; pour over ribs. Cover and cook on low for 5-1/2 to 6 hours or until meat is tender.

3 Remove pork and peaches to a serving platter; keep warm. Skim fat from cooking juices; transfer to a small saucepan. Bring liquid to a boil. Combine cornstarch and water until smooth. Gradually stir into the pan. Bring to a boil; cook and stir for 2 minutes or until thickened. Serve with pork and rice.

Yield: 8 servings.

pork chops with sauerkraut

PREP: 15 MIN. • COOK: 3 HOURS

Stephanie Miller
Omaha, Nebraska

I pair tender pork chops with tangy sauerkraut in this filling main dish. It's so quick and easy to put together.

4 bone-in center-cut pork loin chops (1/2 inch thick and 8 ounces *each*)

2 tablespoons canola oil

1 jar (32 ounces) sauerkraut, undrained

3/4 cup packed brown sugar

1 medium green pepper, sliced

1 medium onion, sliced

1 In a large skillet over medium heat, brown pork chops in oil for 3-4 minutes on each side; drain. In a 5-qt. slow cooker, combine the sauerkraut and brown sugar. Top with the pork chops, green pepper and onion.

2 Cover and cook on low for 3 to 3-1/2 hours or until meat is tender. Serve with a slotted spoon.

Yield: 4 servings.

robust italian sausage & pasta

PREP: 15 MIN. • COOK: 6-1/2 HOURS

LaDonna Reed
Ponca City, Oklahoma

Sit back, relax and let the slow cooker do the hard work for you with this savory main dish. Since you don't cook the pasta separately, there's one less pot to wash after supper.

4 Italian sausage links (4 ounces *each*), halved

1 jar (25.6 ounces) Italian sausage spaghetti sauce

1 can (10 ounces) diced tomatoes and green chilies, undrained

1 large green pepper, julienned

1 medium onion, diced

2 garlic cloves, minced

1 teaspoon Italian seasoning

2 cups uncooked spiral pasta

1 In a large nonstick skillet, brown sausage links. Transfer to a 3-qt. slow cooker. Add the spaghetti sauce, tomatoes, green pepper, onion, garlic and Italian seasoning.

2 Cover and cook on low for 6 hours. Stir in pasta. Cover and cook on high for 30-40 minutes or until pasta is tender.

Yield: 4 servings.

Swift switch. Change the flavor by using diced tomatoes with roasted garlic for a milder sauce or diced tomatoes with jalapeno peppers for added heat.

slow-cooked pork roast

PREP: 20 MIN.
COOK: 6 HOURS + STANDING

Marion Lowery
Medford, Oregon

This pork roast makes a wonderful summer meal, as the oven never needs heating. It's so tender, that it just falls apart when served.

2 cans (8 ounces *each*) unsweetened crushed pineapple, undrained

1 cup barbecue sauce

2 tablespoons unsweetened apple juice

1 tablespoon minced fresh rosemary
or 1 teaspoon dried rosemary, crushed

1 teaspoon minced garlic

2 teaspoons grated lemon peel

1 teaspoon Liquid Smoke, optional

1/2 teaspoon salt

1/4 teaspoon pepper

1 boneless pork loin roast (3 to 4 pounds)

1 In a large saucepan, combine the first nine ingredients. Bring to a boil. Reduce heat; simmer, uncovered, for 3 minutes.

2 Meanwhile, cut roast in half. In a nonstick skillet coated with cooking spray, brown pork roast.

3 Place roast halves in a 5-qt. slow cooker. Pour sauce over the roast and turn to coat. Cook on low for 6-7 hours or until the meat is tender. Let stand for 15 minutes before carving the roast.

Yield: 12 servings.

saucy pork chops

PREP: 5 MIN. • COOK: 4 HOURS

Sharon Polk
Lapeer, Michigan

I serve these tender chops a couple of times a month because we love them. The tangy sauce is delicious over mashed potatoes, rice or noodles.

  8 boneless pork chops (1/2 inch thick)

  2 tablespoons canola oil

  1/4 teaspoon salt

  1/8 teaspoon pepper

  2 cans (10-3/4 ounces *each*) condensed cream of chicken soup, undiluted

  1 medium onion, chopped

  1/2 cup ketchup

  2 tablespoons Worcestershire sauce

  Mashed potatoes *or* hot cooked rice

1 In a large skillet, cook pork chops in oil until lightly browned on each side. Sprinkle with salt and pepper. Transfer to a 3-qt. slow cooker.

2 In a large bowl, combine the soup, onion, ketchup and Worcestershire sauce; pour over chops. Cover and cook on high for 4-5 hours or until meat is tender. Serve with potatoes or rice.

Yield: 8 servings.

three beans and sausage

PREP: 15 MIN. • COOK: 4 HOURS

Judy Sumner
Riverton, Utah

For a stick-to-your ribs meal, try this hearty combination of beans and smoked sausage. Because it calls for several canned items, it's easy to prepare and let cook for the afternoon. It's also inexpensive to serve.

  1-1/2 pounds smoked sausage, cut into 1-inch pieces

  1 can (16 ounces) kidney beans, rinsed and drained

  1 can (15-1/2 ounces) great northern beans, rinsed and drained

  1 can (15 ounces) black beans, rinsed and drained

  1 cup chopped onion

  1 cup water

  1 can (8 ounces) tomato sauce

  2/3 cup chopped celery

  1 teaspoon chicken bouillon granules

  1 teaspoon minced garlic

  1 bay leaf

  1/2 teaspoon pepper

  1/4 teaspoon dried oregano, optional

  1/4 teaspoon dried thyme, optional

  Hot cooked rice

1 In a 5-qt. slow cooker, combine the first 12 ingredients. Sprinkle with oregano and thyme if desired. Cover and cook on low for 4 to 4-1/2 hours or until heated through. Discard bay leaf. Serve with rice.

Yield: 8 servings.

sesame pork ribs

PREP: 15 MIN. • COOK: 5 HOURS

Sandy Alexander
Fayetteville, North Carolina

No one ever believes how little effort it takes to make these juicy ribs. The flavor of the lightly sweet and tangy sauce penetrates through the meat as the ribs simmer for hours.

3/4 cup packed brown sugar

1/2 cup soy sauce

1/2 cup ketchup

1/4 cup honey

2 tablespoons white wine vinegar

3 garlic cloves, minced

1 teaspoon salt

1 teaspoon ground ginger

1/4 to 1/2 teaspoon crushed red pepper flakes

5 pounds country-style pork ribs

1 medium onion, sliced

2 tablespoons sesame seeds, toasted

2 tablespoons chopped green onions

1 In a large bowl, combine the first nine ingredients. Add ribs and turn to coat. Place the onion in a 5-qt. slow cooker; top with ribs and sauce. Cover and cook on low for 5-6 hours or until meat is tender.

2 Place ribs on a serving platter; sprinkle with sesame seeds and green onions.

Yield: 6 servings.

sweet sausage 'n' beans

PREP: 10 MIN. • COOK: 4 HOURS

Taste of Home Test Kitchen

We found our inspiration for this convenient small-batch recipe across the pond! This slow cooker version of a traditional French dish called cassoulet is sweet, saucy and chock-full of beans, smoked sausage and vegetables.

1/4 cup thinly sliced carrot

1/4 cup chopped onion

1 cup frozen lima beans, thawed

1 cup frozen cut green beans, thawed

1/2 pound smoked sausage, cut into 1/4-inch slices

3/4 cup baked beans

1/4 cup ketchup

2 tablespoons brown sugar

1-1/2 teaspoons cider vinegar

1/2 teaspoon prepared mustard

1 In a 1-1/2-qt. slow cooker, layer the carrot, onion, lima beans, green beans, sausage and baked beans. In a small bowl, combine the ketchup, brown sugar, vinegar and mustard; pour over beans. Cover and cook on high for 4 hours or until vegetables are tender. Stir before serving.

Yield: 3 servings.

slow cooker cranberry pork

PREP: 10 MIN. • COOK: 6 HOURS

Joyce Turley
Slaughters, Kentucky

You can put this roast in the slow cooker and then forget about it, knowing it will be moist and tender when you get home after a long day at work or a busy day running errands. The fruity sauce complements the meat very well.

1 boneless rolled pork loin roast
(3 to 4 pounds), halved

2 tablespoons canola oil

1 can (14 ounces) whole-berry cranberry sauce

3/4 cup sugar

3/4 cup cranberry juice

1 teaspoon ground mustard

1 teaspoon pepper

1/4 teaspoon ground cloves

1/4 cup cornstarch

1/4 cup cold water

Salt to taste

1 In a Dutch oven, brown roast in oil on all sides over medium-high heat. Transfer to a 5-qt. slow cooker. Combine the cranberry sauce, sugar, cranberry juice, mustard, pepper and cloves; pour over roast.

2 Cover and cook on low for 6-8 hours or until the meat is tender. Remove roast and keep warm.

3 In a saucepan, combine cornstarch, water and salt until smooth; stir in cooking juices. Bring to a boil; cook and stir for 2 minutes or until thickened. Serve with roast.

Yield: 9-12 servings.

glazed pork roast

PREP: 30 MIN. • COOK: 4 HOURS

Radelle Knappenberger
Oviedo, Florida

This light recipe is always popular with adults and children alike. It's an excellent "take-along" meal for potlucks.

1 boneless whole pork loin roast (4 pounds), trimmed

1 tablespoon olive oil

1 tablespoon butter, melted

2/3 cup thawed orange juice concentrate

1/3 cup water

3 garlic cloves, minced

1-1/2 teaspoons salt

1/2 teaspoon pepper

GLAZE:

1/4 cup packed brown sugar

2 tablespoons balsamic vinegar

1 tablespoon thawed orange juice concentrate

1 garlic clove, minced

1 can (11 ounces) mandarin oranges, drained, optional

1 Cut roast in half. In a large skillet, brown roast halves in oil and butter on all sides.

2 Transfer to a 5-qt. slow cooker. Add the orange juice concentrate, water, garlic, salt and pepper. Cover and cook on low for 4-6 hours or until a meat thermometer reads 160° and meat is tender.

3 For glaze, in a small saucepan, combine the brown sugar, vinegar, orange juice concentrate and garlic. Bring to a boil. Reduce heat; simmer, uncovered, for 3-5 minutes or until reduced to about 1/4 cup. Brush over the roast. Garnish with the oranges if desired.

Yield: 16 servings.

spicy sausage hash browns

PREP: 15 MIN. • COOK: 5 HOURS

Angela Sheridan
Opdyke, Illinois

I love to develop my own recipes and often have people request them. Family members and friends from church tend to be my favorite and most honest critics.

1 tube (16 ounces) bulk spicy pork sausage

1 package (30 ounces) frozen shredded hash brown potatoes, thawed

2 cups (16 ounces) sour cream

1 jar (16 ounces) double-cheddar cheese sauce

2 cans (4 ounces *each*) chopped green chilies

1/2 teaspoon crushed red pepper flakes

1 In a large skillet, cook sausage over medium heat until no longer pink; drain. In a 4-qt. slow cooker, combine all ingredients. Cover and cook on low for 5-6 hours or until heated through.

Yield: 9 servings.

country pork chop supper

PREP: 10 MIN. • COOK: 5 HOURS

Sandy Mullen
Gage, Oklahoma

It doesn't get much easier than this quick and hearty all-in-one slow cooker meal. And it doesn't get much tastier, either!

- 6 boneless pork loin chops (1/2 inch thick and 4 ounces *each*)
- 2 jars (12 ounces *each*) pork gravy
- 1 can (10-3/4 ounces) condensed cream of mushroom soup, undiluted
- 2 tablespoons ketchup
- 1 tablespoon minced chives
- 1 teaspoon pepper
- 1 teaspoon soy sauce
- 1/2 teaspoon seasoned salt
- 3 medium potatoes, peeled and quartered
- 1 package (16 ounces) frozen mixed vegetables

1 Place pork chops in a greased 5-qt. slow cooker. In a large bowl, combine the gravy, soup, ketchup, chives, pepper, soy sauce and seasoned salt; pour over pork.

2 Stir in potatoes; cover and cook on low for 4 hours. Stir in vegetables; continue cooking 1 hour or until meat and potatoes are tender.

Yield: 6 servings.

> **Budget saver.** If you're trying to cut back your grocery bill, consider pork arm or blade chops when preparing Country Pork Chop Supper. Just trim the fat from the edge of the chops before cooking.

all-day red beans & rice

**PREP: 20 MIN. + SOAKING
COOK: 8-1/2 HOURS**

Celinda Dahlgren
Napa, California

My family loves New Orleans-style cooking, so I often make this authentic dish. Being a busy working woman, I appreciate how simple it is. Its smoky ham flavor is scrumptious.

- 1 cup dried red beans
- 7 cups water, *divided*
- 2 smoked ham hocks
- 1 medium onion, chopped
- 1-1/2 teaspoons minced garlic
- 1 teaspoon ground cumin
- 1 medium tomato, chopped
- 1 medium green pepper, chopped
- 1 teaspoon salt
- 4 cups hot cooked rice

1 Sort beans and rinse in cold water. Place beans in a 3-qt. slow cooker. Add 4 cups water; cover and let stand overnight.

2 Drain and rinse beans, discarding liquid. Return beans to slow cooker; add the ham hocks, onion, garlic, cumin and remaining water. Cover and cook on low for 8-10 hours or until beans are tender.

3 Remove ham hocks; cool slightly. Remove meat from bones. Finely chop meat and return to slow cooker; discard bones. Stir in the tomato, pepper and salt; cover and cook on high for 30 minutes or until pepper is tender. Serve with rice.

Yield: 6 servings.

tender spareribs

PREP: 10 MIN. • COOK: 5-1/2 HOURS

Julie Czmer
West Bloomfield, Michigan

Even my three little ones love this easy-to-make and delicious-to-eat meal. The succulent meat falls right off the bone!

> 4 pounds pork spareribs, cut into serving-size pieces
>
> 1/4 cup soy sauce

> 1/4 cup prepared mustard
>
> 1/4 cup molasses
>
> 3 tablespoons cider vinegar
>
> 2 tablespoons Worcestershire sauce
>
> 1 to 2 teaspoons hot pepper sauce

1 Place ribs in a 5-qt. slow cooker. Combine the remaining ingredients; pour over ribs. Cover and cook on low for 5-1/2 to 6 hours or until meat is tender.

Yield: 8 servings.

pork chops with fruit

PREP: 5 MIN. • COOK: 4 HOURS

Marian Platt
Sequim, Washington

This recipe came from a good friend, and it's been a big hit whenever I've served it. With rice pilaf and a green salad, a complete meal for two is on the table.

2 bone-in center-cut pork loin chops
(12 ounces *each*)

1 cup mixed dried fruit

1/3 cup unsweetened pineapple juice

1/4 cup dark corn syrup

1/4 teaspoon salt

1/4 teaspoon curry powder

1 teaspoon cornstarch

1 tablespoon cold water

1 Place pork chops in a 1-1/2-qt. oval or 3-qt. slow cooker. In a bowl, combine the fruit, pineapple juice, corn syrup, salt and curry powder; pour over chops. Cover and cook on low for 4 to 4-1/2 hours or until meat is tender.

2 With a slotted spoon, remove meat and fruit to a serving platter and keep warm. In a small saucepan, combine the cornstarch and cold water until smooth; stir in the cooking juices. Bring to a boil; cook and stir for 2 minutes or until thickened. Serve over chops and fruit.

Yield: 2 servings.

cider pork roast

PREP: 20 MIN. • COOK: 5 HOURS

Terry Danner
Rochelle, Illinois

Apple cider, dried cherries and fresh rosemary put the pizzazz in this pleasing pork roast. It's even more flavorful when the sweet pan juices are thickened and served on top.

- 1 boneless pork loin roast (2 pounds)
- 3/4 teaspoon salt
- 1/4 teaspoon pepper
- 2 cups apple cider *or* unsweetened apple juice, *divided*
- 3 sprigs fresh rosemary
- 1/2 cup dried cherries
- 5 teaspoons cornstarch

1 Sprinkle pork with salt and pepper. In a nonstick skillet coated with cooking spray, brown pork for about 4 minutes on each side. Pour 1 cup apple cider in a 3-qt. slow cooker. Place two sprigs rosemary in slow cooker; top with meat and remaining rosemary. Place cherries around roast. Cover and cook on low for 5-6 hours or until a meat thermometer reads 160°

2 Remove meat; keep warm. Strain cooking liquid; reserve liquid and transfer to a small saucepan. Stir in 3/4 cup cider; bring to a boil. Combine cornstarch and remaining cider until smooth. Gradually whisk into cider mixture. Bring to a boil; cook and stir for 1-2 minutes or until thickened. Serve with meat.

Yield: 6 servings.

christmas carol ham

PREP: 10 MIN. • COOK: 2 HOURS

Julie Williquette
Hartselle, Alabama

Made with healthy turkey ham, this slow-cooked entree is tender and delicious. My family loves it! Simmered in pineapple juice, the ham slices are so flavorful.

- 2 pounds fully cooked turkey ham, cut into eight slices
- 1/2 cup packed brown sugar
- 1/4 cup unsweetened pineapple juice
- 1-1/2 teaspoons white vinegar
- 1/4 teaspoon ground mustard

1 Place ham slices in a 3-qt. slow cooker. In a small bowl, combine the brown sugar, pineapple juice, vinegar and mustard; pour over ham. Cover and cook on low for 2-4 hours or until heated through.

Yield: 8 servings.

jambalaya

PREP: 20 MIN. • COOK: 6-1/4 HOURS

Sherry Huntwork
Gretna, Nebraska

Sausage, chicken and shrimp keep this dish hearty and satisfying. Made easy with canned items and other kitchen staples, it's perfect for casual get-togethers and serves a crowd.

1 pound smoked Polish sausage, cut into 1/2-inch slices

1/2 pound boneless skinless chicken breasts, cut into 1-inch cubes

1 can (14-1/2 ounces) beef broth

1 can (14-1/2 ounces) diced tomatoes, undrained

2 celery ribs, chopped

1/3 cup tomato paste

4 garlic cloves, minced

1 tablespoon dried parsley flakes

1-1/2 teaspoons dried basil

1 teaspoon cayenne pepper

1/2 teaspoon salt

1/2 teaspoon dried oregano

1 pound cooked medium shrimp, peeled and deveined

2 cups cooked rice

1 In a 5-qt. slow cooker, combine first 12 ingredients. Cover and cook on low for 6-7 hours or until chicken is no longer pink.

2 Stir in shrimp and rice. Cover and cook 15 minutes longer or until heated through.

Yield: 12 servings.

pork baby back ribs

PREP: 10 MIN. • COOK: 6 HOURS

LaVerne Parkin
Manitowoc, Wisconsin

These tender ribs get a touch of sweetness from brown sugar and apricot preserves. It's one slow-cooked recipe that you will enjoy time and again.

1 rack pork baby back ribs (2-1/2 pounds)

2 tablespoons canola oil

1 medium onion, thinly sliced

1/2 cup apricot preserves

1/3 cup beef broth

3 tablespoons white vinegar

2 tablespoons Worcestershire sauce

1 tablespoon brown sugar

1 Cut the ribs into five servings. In a Dutch oven, brown ribs in oil in batches. Place onion in a 5-qt. slow cooker; top with ribs. In a small bowl, combine the remaining ingredients. Pour over ribs. Cover and cook on low for 6-7 hours or until meat is tender.

Yield: 5 servings.

apricot pork roast

PREP: 15 MIN. • COOK: 6 HOURS

Patricia Defosse
Wilmington, Delaware

*Serve this lovely roast with rice or mashed potatoes.
We like leftovers with gravy, served on buns.*

> 1 boneless whole pork loin roast
> (2 to 3 pounds)
>
> 1 jar (12 ounces) apricot preserves
>
> 1 cup vegetable broth
>
> 2 tablespoons cornstarch
>
> 1/4 cup cold water

1 Place roast in a 3-qt. slow cooker. In a small bowl, combine preserves and broth; pour over roast. Cover and cook on low for 6-7 hours or until a meat thermometer reads 160°.

2 Remove meat to a serving platter; keep warm. Skim fat from cooking juices; transfer to a small saucepan. Bring liquid to a boil. Combine cornstarch and water until smooth. Gradually stir into pan. Bring to a boil; cook and stir for 2 minutes or until thickened. Serve with pork.

Yield: 6 servings.

slow-cooked ribs

PREP: 15 MIN. • COOK: 6 HOURS

Sharon Crider
Junction City, Kansas

Nothing says comfort like a plate full of mouth-watering ribs coated in barbecue sauce. These are delicious and tangy.

- 4 pounds boneless country-style pork ribs
- 1 cup barbecue sauce
- 1 cup Catalina salad dressing
- 1/2 teaspoon minced garlic
- 2 tablespoons all-purpose flour
- 1/4 cup cold water

1 Cut ribs into serving-size pieces. Place in a 5-qt. slow cooker. Combine barbecue sauce and salad dressing; pour over ribs. Sprinkle with garlic. Cover and cook on low for 6-7 hours or until meat is tender.

2 Remove meat to a serving platter; keep warm. Skim fat from cooking juices; transfer to a small saucepan. Bring liquid to a boil. Combine flour and water until smooth. Gradually stir into the pan. Bring to a boil; cook and stir for 2 minutes or until thickened. Serve with meat.

Yield: 8 servings.

melt-in-your-mouth sausages

PREP: 10 MIN. • COOK: 5 HOURS

Ilean Schultheiss
Cohocton, New York

This recipe is a good all-around dish, especially if you choose to eat the sausage with spaghetti.

- 8 Italian sausage links (2 pounds)
- 1 jar (26 ounces) meatless spaghetti sauce

- 1/2 cup water
- 1 can (6 ounces) tomato paste
- 1 large green pepper, thinly sliced
- 1 large onion, thinly sliced
- 1 tablespoon grated Parmesan cheese
- 1 teaspoon dried parsley flakes
- 8 brat buns, split
- Additional Parmesan cheese, optional

1 Place the sausages in a large skillet; cover with water. Bring to a boil. Reduce the heat; cover and simmer for 10 minutes; drain well.

2 Meanwhile, in a 3-qt. slow cooker, combine the spaghetti sauce, water, tomato paste, green pepper, onion, cheese and parsley. Add sausages. Cover and cook on low for 4 hours. Increase temperature to high; cook 1 hour longer.

3 Serve in buns. Sprinkle with additional cheese if desired.

Yield: 8 servings.

2 Remove roast; cover and let stand for 15 minutes. Meanwhile, strain cooking juices and return to slow cooker. Mix cornstarch and water until smooth; stir into juices. Cover and cook on high for 15 minutes or until thickened. Slice pork; serve with gravy.

Yield: 6-8 servings.

switch-and-go ribs

PREP: 10 MIN. • COOK: 6 HOURS

Lil Neuls
Caballo, New Mexico

A slightly sweet sauce gives these boneless ribs mild teriyaki flavor. Simmering them in the slow cooker adds to the ease of this recipe.

    1-1/2 pounds boneless country-style
    pork ribs

    1 tablespoon canola oil

    1/3 cup orange marmalade

    1/3 cup teriyaki sauce

    1 teaspoon minced garlic

1 In a large skillet, brown ribs in oil on both sides. In a small bowl, combine the marmalade, teriyaki sauce and garlic.

2 Pour half of the sauce into a 3-qt. slow cooker; top with the ribs. Drizzle with remaining sauce. Cover and cook on low for 6-8 hours or until meat is tender.

Yield: 4 servings.

teriyaki pork roast

PREP: 10 MIN.
COOK: 6-1/4 HOURS + STANDING

Debbie Dunaway
Kettering, Ohio

How good is this dish? Well, it's the only kind of meat my two young kids will eat and enjoy.

    1 boneless pork shoulder butt roast
    (3 to 4 pounds)

    1 cup packed brown sugar

    1/3 cup unsweetened apple juice

    1/3 cup soy sauce

    1/2 teaspoon salt

    1/4 teaspoon pepper

    2 tablespoons cornstarch

    3 tablespoons cold water

1 Cut roast in half; rub with brown sugar. Place in a 5-qt. slow cooker. Pour apple juice and soy sauce over roast. Sprinkle with salt and pepper. Cover and cook on low for 6 to 6-1/2 hours or until meat is tender.

Flavor punch. For additional sauce combinations for Switch-and-Go Ribs, try red plum jam, mango jam, apple jelly or apricot preserves instead of the orange marmalade called for in the recipe.

honey-glazed ham

PREP: 10 MIN. • COOK: 4-1/2 HOURS

Jacquie Stolz
Little Sioux, Iowa

Here's an easy solution for feeding a large group. The simple ham is perfect for family dinners where time in the kitchen is as valuable as space in the oven. Serve with mashed potatoes.

  1 boneless fully cooked ham (4 pounds)

  1-1/2 cups ginger ale

  1/4 cup honey

1/2 teaspoon ground mustard

1/2 teaspoon ground cloves

1/4 teaspoon ground cinnamon

Sour cream, optional

1 Cut ham in half; place in a 5-qt. slow cooker. Pour ginger ale over ham. Cover and cook on low for 4-5 hours or until heated through.

2 Combine the honey, mustard, cloves and cinnamon; stir until smooth. Spread over ham; cook 30 minutes longer. Garnish with sour cream if desired.

Yield: 14 servings.

secret's in the sauce bbq ribs

PREP: 10 MIN. • COOK: 6 HOURS

Tanya Reid
Winston-Salem, North Carolina

A sweet, rich sauce makes these ribs so tender that the meat literally falls off the bones. The aroma is wonderful. Yum!

2 racks pork baby back ribs
(about 4-1/2 pounds)

1-1/2 teaspoons pepper

2-1/2 cups barbecue sauce

3/4 cup cherry preserves

1 tablespoon Dijon mustard

1 garlic clove, minced

1 Cut ribs into serving-size pieces; sprinkle with pepper. Place in a 5– or 6-qt. slow cooker. Combine the remaining ingredients; pour over ribs. Cover and cook on low for 6-8 hours or until meat is tender. Serve with sauce.

Yield: 5 servings.

pork roast with mashed potatoes and gravy

PREP: 20 MIN. • COOK: 3 HOURS

Lee Bremson
Kansas City, Missouri

This home-style meal can be made ahead of time and reheated. Simply strain and skim the cooking juices and cover and store in the fridge. Finish the gravy in a pan before serving.

1 boneless whole pork loin roast
(3 to 4 pounds)

1 can (14-1/2 ounces) chicken broth

1 cup julienned sweet red pepper

1/2 cup chopped onion

1/4 cup cider vinegar

2 tablespoons Worcestershire sauce

1 tablespoon brown sugar

2 teaspoons Italian seasoning

1 teaspoon salt

1 teaspoon pepper

2 teaspoons cornstarch

2 teaspoons cold water

2 cups refrigerated mashed potatoes

1 Cut roast in half; transfer to a 5-qt. slow cooker. In a small bowl, combine the broth, red pepper, onion, vinegar, Worcestershire sauce, brown sugar and seasonings; pour over pork. Cover and cook on low for 3-4 hours or until meat is tender.

2 Remove pork; cut some into cubes measuring 2-1/2 cups and save for another use. (Keep remaining pork warm.)

3 For gravy, strain cooking juices and skim fat; pour 1 cup into a small saucepan. Combine cornstarch and water until smooth; stir into cooking juices. Bring to a boil; cook and stir for 2 minutes or until thickened.

4 Meanwhile, in a small microwave-safe bowl, cook potatoes on high for 2-3 minutes or until heated through. Slice remaining pork; serve with potatoes and gravy.

Yield: 4 servings + leftover pork.

EDITOR'S NOTE: This recipe was tested in a 1,100-watt microwave.

sweet onion & cherry pork chops

PREP: 15 MIN. • COOK: 3 HOURS

Stephanie Ray
Foley, Minnesota

When I want to jump-start supper for two of us, I opt for these tender pork chops. The sweet and savory cherry sauce makes this recipe a keeper. Try serving it with wild rice pilaf.

1/2 cup fresh *or* frozen pitted tart cherries, thawed

2 tablespoons chopped sweet onion

1 tablespoon honey

1/2 teaspoon seasoned salt

1/4 teaspoon pepper

2 boneless pork loin chops (5 ounces *each*)

1 teaspoon cornstarch

1 teaspoon cold water

1 In a 1-1/2-qt. slow cooker, combine the first five ingredients; top with pork chops. Cover and cook on low for 3-4 hours or until meat is tender.

2 Remove meat to a serving platter; keep warm. Skim fat from cooking juices; transfer to a small saucepan. Bring liquid

to a boil. Combine cornstarch and water until smooth. Gradually stir into the pan. Bring to a boil; cook and stir for 2 minutes or until thickened. Serve with meat.

Yield: 2 servings.

creamy cabbage-pork stew

PREP: 20 MIN. • COOK: 6 HOURS

Ruth Ann Stelfox
Raymond, Alberta

Savory flavors blend beautifully in this hearty meal-in-one dish. In a pinch, I use a ring of garlic bologna cut into chunks for the pork shoulder. Add a basket of bread and dinner is served!

1 boneless pork shoulder butt roast (1 pound), cut into 3/4-inch cubes

1 tablespoon canola oil

2 cans (10-3/4 ounces *each*) condensed cream of celery soup, undiluted

1-1/2 cups apple juice

2 medium red potatoes, cut into 1-inch chunks

3 medium carrots, sliced

1/4 teaspoon caraway seeds

1/4 teaspoon pepper

3 cups coarsely chopped cabbage

1/2 cup 2% milk

1 In a large skillet over medium-high heat, brown pork in oil on all sides; drain.

2 Transfer to a 3-qt. slow cooker; stir in the soup, apple juice, potatoes, carrots, caraway and pepper. Cover and cook on high for 3-1/2 hours.

3 Add the cabbage and milk. Cover and cook 2-1/2 hours longer or until meat and vegetables are tender.

Yield: 6 servings.

hash brown egg brunch

PREP: 20 MIN. • COOK: 4 HOURS

Barb Keith
Eau Claire, Wisconsin

Here's a recipe that combines slow cooking with brunch. It's a wonderful treat to take to a covered dish event or a morning get-together.

- 1 package (32 ounces) frozen shredded hash brown potatoes
- 1 pound bacon strips, cooked and crumbled
- 1 medium onion, chopped
- 1 medium green pepper, chopped
- 1-1/2 cups (6 ounces) shredded cheddar cheese
- 12 eggs
- 1 cup whole milk
- 1/2 teaspoon salt
- 1/2 teaspoon pepper

1 Layer a third of the potatoes, bacon, onion, green pepper and cheese in a 5-qt. slow cooker coated with cooking spray. Repeat layers twice. In a large bowl, whisk the eggs, milk, salt and pepper; pour over top.

2 Cover and cook on high for 30 minutes. Reduce heat to low; cook for 3-1/2 to 4 hours or until a thermometer reads 160°.

Yield: 10 servings.

tangy pork chops

PREP: 15 MIN. • COOK: 5-1/2 HOURS

Karol Hines
Kitty Hawk, North Carolina

Fancy enough for company, these mouth-watering pork chops also make a great family meal. I usually have all the ingredients on hand. Since my husband and I just had our first child, this recipe is very convenient.

4 bone-in pork loin chops (1/2 inch thick)

1/2 teaspoon salt, optional

1/8 teaspoon pepper

2 medium onions, chopped

2 celery ribs, chopped

1 large green pepper, sliced

1 can (14-1/2 ounces) stewed tomatoes

1/2 cup ketchup

2 tablespoons cider vinegar

2 tablespoons brown sugar

2 tablespoons Worcestershire sauce

1 tablespoon lemon juice

1 teaspoon beef bouillon granules

2 tablespoons cornstarch

2 tablespoons water

Hot cooked rice, optional

1 Place pork chops in a 3-qt. slow cooker; sprinkle with salt if desired and pepper. Add the onions, celery, green pepper and tomatoes. Combine the ketchup, vinegar, brown sugar, Worcestershire sauce, lemon juice and bouillon; pour over vegetables. Cover and cook on low for 5-6 hours or until meat is tender.

2 Mix cornstarch and water until smooth; stir into liquid in slow cooker. Cover and cook on high for 30 minutes or until thickened. Serve with rice if desired.

Yield: 4 servings.

asian pork roast

PREP: 25 MIN. • COOK: 4-1/2 HOURS

Sheree Shown
Junction City, Oregon

Slow-cooked dishes are a favorite in our home, and this one is just perfect for fall and winter evenings. A pork roast cooks all afternoon with sweet onions, honey, soy sauce and ginger for fabulous flavor. The aroma fills the house with a scent that cries out, "Welcome home!"

2 large onions, thinly sliced

3 garlic cloves, minced

1/2 teaspoon salt

1/2 teaspoon pepper

1 boneless whole pork loin roast (3 pounds)

1 tablespoon canola oil

3 bay leaves

1/4 cup hot water

1/4 cup honey

1/4 cup reduced-sodium soy sauce

2 tablespoons rice vinegar

1 teaspoon ground ginger

1/2 teaspoon ground cloves

3 tablespoons cornstarch

1/4 cup cold water

2 tablespoons sesame seeds, toasted

Hot cooked rice and sliced green onion tops, optional

1 Place the onions in a 5-qt. slow cooker. In a small bowl, combine the garlic, salt and pepper. Cut the roast in half; rub with garlic mixture. In a large nonstick skillet coated with cooking spray, brown the pork in oil on all sides. Transfer to slow cooker; add bay leaves.

2 In a small bowl, combine the hot water and honey; stir in the soy sauce, vinegar, ginger and cloves. Pour over pork. Cover and cook on low for 4-5 hours or until a meat thermometer reads 160°.

3 Remove meat and onions from slow cooker; keep warm. Discard bay leaves. In a small bowl, combine cornstarch and cold water until smooth. Gradually stir into slow cooker.

4 Cover and cook on high for 30 minutes or until thickened, stirring twice. Slice pork; top with onions, sauce and sesame seeds. Serve with rice and garnish with green onion tops if desired.

Yield: 12 servings.

Smart purchase. When selecting a pork roast, look for packages without any holes or tears. Be sure to purchase meat that is cold. Some grocery stores place their meat on sale the day of or the day before the "sell by" date. It is fine to take advantage of these great bargains as long as you cook or freeze the meat before the package date.

smoky bean stew

PREP: 10 MIN. • COOK: 4 HOURS

Glenda Holmes
Riley, Kansas

I get this satisfying sausage-and-bean stew started in the slow cooker, then spend the afternoon curled up with a good book. It's an effortless meal that tastes great.

1 package (16 ounces) miniature smoked sausage links

1 can (16 ounces) baked beans

2 cups frozen cut green beans

2 cups frozen lima beans

1/2 cup packed brown sugar

1/2 cup thinly sliced fresh carrots

1/2 cup chopped onion

1/2 cup ketchup

1 tablespoon cider vinegar

1 teaspoon prepared mustard

1 In a 3-qt. slow cooker, combine all ingredients. Cover and cook on high for 4-5 hours or until vegetables are tender.

Yield: 6-8 servings.

fruity pork roast

PREP: 25 MIN.
COOK: 8 HOURS + STANDING

Mary Jeppesen-Davis
St. Cloud, Minnesota

I like using the slow cooker because it gives me time for other preparations, frees the oven, and it usually doesn't matter if you serve your supper later than planned. This tender roast is jazzed up with dried cranberries, raisins and lemon slices.

1/2 medium lemon, sliced

1/2 cup dried cranberries

1/3 cup golden raisins

1/3 cup unsweetened apple juice

3 tablespoons sherry *or* additional unsweetened apple juice

1 teaspoon minced garlic

1/2 teaspoon ground mustard

1 boneless whole pork loin roast (about 3 pounds)

1/2 teaspoon salt

1/4 teaspoon pepper

1/8 to 1/4 teaspoon ground ginger

1 medium apple, peeled and sliced

1/2 cup packed fresh parsley sprigs

1 In a small bowl, combine the first seven ingredients; set aside. Sprinkle roast with salt, pepper and ginger.

2 Transfer to a 3-qt. slow cooker. Pour fruit mixture over roast. Place apple and parsley around roast. Cover and cook on low for 8-9 hours or until a meat thermometer reads 160°.

3 Transfer meat to a serving platter. Let stand for 10 minutes before slicing.

Yield: 8 servings.

slow cooker pork and apple curry

PREP: 5 MIN. • COOK: 5-1/2 HOURS

Nancy Reck
Mill Valley, California

Here's a gentle curry dish that's sure to please American palates. For fun, try varying the garnish.

2 pounds boneless pork loin roast, cut into 1-inch cubes

1 medium apple, peeled and chopped

1 small onion, chopped

1/2 cup orange juice

1 tablespoon curry powder

1 teaspoon chicken bouillon granules

1 garlic clove, minced

1/2 teaspoon salt

1/2 teaspoon ground ginger

1/4 teaspoon ground cinnamon

2 tablespoons cornstarch

2 tablespoons cold water

Hot cooked rice, optional

1/4 cup raisins

1/4 cup flaked coconut, toasted

1 In a 3-qt. slow cooker, combine the first 10 ingredients. Cover and cook on low for 5-6 hours or until meat is tender.

2 Increase heat to high. In a small bowl, combine cornstarch and water until smooth; stir into slow cooker. Cover and cook for 30 minutes or until thickened, stirring once.

3 Serve with rice if desired. Sprinkle with raisins and coconut.

Yield: 8 servings.

italian pork chops

PREP: 15 MIN. • COOK: 5-1/2 HOURS

Bonnie Marlow
Ottoville, Ohio

Not only is it easy to use my slow cooker, but the results are fabulous. Meat cooked this way is always so tender and juicy. These pork chops in a thick tomato sauce turn out great.

6 boneless pork loin chops (1/2 inch thick and 6 ounces *each*)

1 tablespoon canola oil

1 medium green pepper, diced

1 can (6 ounces) tomato paste

1 jar (4-1/2 ounces) sliced mushrooms, drained

1/2 cup water

1 envelope spaghetti sauce mix

1/2 to 1 teaspoon hot pepper sauce

1 In a large skillet, brown pork chops in oil over medium heat for 3-4 minutes on each side; drain. In a 5-qt. slow cooker, combine the remaining ingredients. Top with pork chops. Cover and cook on low for 5-1/2 to 6 hours or until meat is tender.

Yield: 6 servings.

slow-cooked pork loin

PREP: 20 MIN. • COOK: 5 HOURS

Kathleen Hendrick
Alexandria, Kentucky

Sweet apple undertones lend special flair to my low-calorie pork loin. I top it with gravy for down-home appeal, creating a slimmed-down dish that will keep them coming back for more!

1 boneless whole pork loin roast
(3-1/2 to 4 pounds)

1 tablespoon canola oil

1 medium onion, chopped

1 celery rib, cut into 1-inch pieces

1 envelope brown gravy mix

1 cup water

1 cup unsweetened apple juice

1/2 cup unsweetened applesauce

2 teaspoons Worcestershire sauce

1/2 teaspoon seasoned salt

1/2 teaspoon pepper

1 Cut roast in half. In a large skillet, brown roast in oil on all sides. Transfer halves to a 5-qt. slow cooker. In the same skillet, saute onion and celery until tender; add to slow cooker.

2 In a small bowl, combine gravy mix and water. Stir in the remaining ingredients; pour over pork. Cover and cook on low for 5-6 hours or until meat is tender. Skim fat from cooking juices; thicken if desired. Serve with roast.

Yield: 12 servings.

lazy man's ribs

PREP: 20 MIN. • COOK: 5-1/2 HOURS

Allan Stackhouse Jr.
Jennings, Louisiana

I'll have to admit these ribs are finger-lickin' good and fall-off-the-bone tender! I've made them for a lot of my buddies.

2-1/2 pounds pork baby back ribs, cut into eight pieces

2 teaspoons Cajun seasoning

1 medium onion, sliced

1 cup ketchup

1/2 cup packed brown sugar

1/3 cup orange juice

1/3 cup cider vinegar

1/4 cup molasses

2 tablespoons Worcestershire sauce

1 tablespoon barbecue sauce

1 teaspoon stone-ground mustard

1 teaspoon paprika

1/2 teaspoon garlic powder

1/2 teaspoon Liquid Smoke, optional

Dash salt

5 teaspoons cornstarch

1 tablespoon water

1 Rub meat with Cajun seasoning. Layer ribs and onion in a 5-qt. slow cooker. In a small bowl, combine the ketchup, brown sugar, orange juice, vinegar, molasses, Worcestershire sauce, barbecue sauce, mustard, paprika, garlic powder, Liquid Smoke if desired and salt. Pour over ribs. Cover and cook on low for 5-1/2 to 6-1/2 hours or until meat is tender.

2 Remove ribs and keep warm. Strain cooking juices and skim fat; transfer to a small saucepan. Combine cornstarch and water until smooth; stir into juices. Bring to a boil; cook and stir for 2 minutes or until thickened. Serve with ribs.

Yield: 4 servings.

southwestern pulled pork

PREP: 5 MIN. • COOK: 8-1/4 HOURS

Jill Hartung
Colorado Springs, Colorado

The best way to describe this easy pork recipe is "yummy!" Bottled barbecue sauce, canned green chilies and a few other kitchen staples make preparation fast and easy. We like to wrap the seasoned pork in flour tortillas.

2 cans (4 ounces *each*) chopped green chilies

1 can (8 ounces) tomato sauce

1 cup barbecue sauce

1 large sweet onion, thinly sliced

1/4 cup chili powder

1 teaspoon ground cumin

1 teaspoon dried oregano

1 boneless pork loin roast
(2 to 2-1/2 pounds)

Flour tortillas

TOPPINGS:
Sour cream, shredded lettuce and chopped tomatoes, optional

1 In a 3-qt. slow cooker, combine the chilies, tomato sauce, barbecue sauce, onion, chili powder, cumin and oregano. Cut pork in half; place on top of tomato sauce mixture. Cover and cook on low for 8-9 hours or until meat is tender.

2 Remove pork. When cool enough to handle, shred meat using two forks. Return to slow cooker and heat through. Spread on tortillas; top with sour cream, lettuce and tomatoes if desired; roll up.

Yield: 6-8 servings.

hearty pork stew

PREP: 10 MIN. • COOK: 8-1/2 HOURS

Rebecca Overy
Evanston, Wyoming

This spicy slow-cooked stew combines tasty chunks of pork with colorful tomatoes and green peppers. I garnish bowls of it with chopped hard-cooked eggs and green onions.

- 1-1/2 to 2 pounds boneless pork, cut into 1-inch cubes
- 4 cups water
- 1 can (14-1/2 ounces) stewed tomatoes
- 1 medium onion, chopped
- 1 medium green pepper, chopped
- 1/3 cup soy sauce
- 1 to 2 tablespoons chili powder
- 1 tablespoon dried celery flakes
- 1/2 teaspoon garlic powder
- 1/2 teaspoon pepper
- 1/3 cup cornstarch
- 1/3 cup cold water
- Hot cooked noodles

1 In a 3-qt. slow cooker, combine the first 10 ingredients. Cover and cook on low for 8 hours.

2 Combine cornstarch and water until smooth; gradually stir into slow cooker. Cover and cook on high for 30 minutes or until slightly thickened. Serve in bowls with noodles.

Yield: 8 servings.

mushroom pork ragout

PREP: 20 MIN. • COOK: 3 HOURS

Connie McDowell
Greenwood, Delaware

My savory pork tenderloin is luscious draped in a delightful tomato gravy and served over noodles. It's a nice change from regular pork roast.

1 pork tenderloin (3/4 pound)

1/8 teaspoon salt

1/8 teaspoon pepper

1 tablespoon cornstarch

3/4 cup canned crushed tomatoes, *divided*

1 tablespoon chopped sun-dried tomatoes (not packed in oil)

1-1/4 teaspoons dried savory

1-1/2 cups sliced fresh mushrooms

1/3 cup sliced onion

1-1/2 cups hot cooked egg noodles

1 Rub pork with salt and pepper; cut in half. In a 1-1/2-qt. slow cooker, combine the cornstarch, 1/2 cup crushed tomatoes, sun-dried tomatoes and savory. Top with mushrooms, onion and pork. Pour remaining tomatoes over pork. Cover and cook on low for 3-4 hours or until meat is tender.

2 Remove meat and cut into slices. Stir cooking juices until smooth; serve with pork and noodles.

Yield: 2 servings.

sweet 'n' sour sausage

PREP: 15 MIN. • COOK: 4-1/2 HOURS

Barbara Schutz
Pandora, Ohio

Bright carrots, green pepper and pineapple lend gorgeous color to this slow-simmered sausage supper. Serve this lovely dish over rice or chow mein noodles.

- 1 pound smoked kielbasa *or* Polish sausage, sliced
- 1 can (20 ounces) unsweetened pineapple chunks, undrained
- 1-1/2 cups fresh baby carrots, quartered lengthwise
- 1 large green pepper, cut into 1-inch pieces
- 1 medium onion, cut into chunks
- 1/3 cup packed brown sugar
- 1 tablespoon soy sauce
- 1/2 teaspoon chicken bouillon granules
- 1/4 teaspoon garlic powder
- 1/4 teaspoon ground ginger
- 2 tablespoons cornstarch
- 1/4 cup cold water
- Hot cooked rice *or* chow mein noodles

1 In a 3-qt. slow cooker, combine the first 10 ingredients. Cover and cook on low for 4-5 hours.

2 Mix cornstarch and water until smooth; stir into sausage mixture. Cover and cook on high for 30 minutes or until gravy is thickened. Serve with rice.

Yield: 6 servings.

pork chop supper

PREP: 20 MIN. • COOK: 3 HOURS

Pamela Shank
Parkersburg, West Virginia

You'll love the succulent taste of this easy meal-in-one that's ideal for a pair.

- 2 boneless pork loin chops (5 ounces *each*)
- 2 teaspoons canola oil
- 1 medium sweet potato, peeled and cut into 1/4-inch slices
- 1 small onion, sliced
- 1 small tart apple, peeled and sliced
- 1 tablespoon brown sugar
- 1/2 teaspoon ground cinnamon
- 1/4 teaspoon salt
- 1/4 teaspoon ground nutmeg
- 1/4 teaspoon pepper
- 1 can (8 ounces) sauerkraut, undrained

1 In a nonstick skillet, brown chops in oil. Place the sweet potato, onion and apple in a 1-1/2-qt. slow cooker. Combine brown sugar, cinnamon, salt, nutmeg and pepper; sprinkle over apple. Top with pork chops and sauerkraut. Cover and cook on low for 3 to 3-1/2 hours or until juices run clear.

Yield: 2 servings.

tender pork chops

PREP: 20 MIN. • COOK: 6 HOURS

Patricia Dick
Anderson, Indiana

My family has enjoyed these simple pork chops for years. They are so tender and juicy, the meat falls right off the bone!

1/2 cup all-purpose flour

1-1/2 teaspoons ground mustard

1 teaspoon seasoned salt

1/2 teaspoon garlic powder

6 bone-in pork loin chops (1 inch thick and 8 ounces *each*)

2 tablespoons canola oil

1 can (10-1/2 ounces) condensed chicken with rice soup, undiluted

1 In a large resealable plastic bag, combine the flour, mustard, seasoned salt and garlic powder. Add pork chops, one at a time, and shake to coat.

2 In a large skillet, brown chops in oil on both sides. Place in a 3-qt. slow cooker. Pour soup over pork. Cover and cook on low for 6-7 hours or until meat is tender.

Yield: 6 servings.

cranberry-apricot pork roast with potatoes

PREP: 15 MIN. • COOK: 5 HOURS

Pat Barnes
Panama City, Florida

Here's a tasty combination that makes weeknight dining a snap. The apricots blend well with the whole-berry cranberry sauce for a delightful sweet-and-tart taste. Cayenne pepper adds just the right touch of zing to this meat-and-potatoes meal.

1 boneless whole pork loin roast (3 pounds)

4 medium potatoes, peeled and quartered

1 can (14 ounces) whole-berry cranberry sauce

1 can (15 ounces) apricot halves, drained

1 medium onion, quartered

1/2 cup chopped dried apricots

1 tablespoon sugar

1/2 teaspoon ground mustard

1/4 teaspoon cayenne pepper

1 Cut roast in half. Place potatoes in a 5-qt. slow cooker. Add the pork.

2 In a blender, combine the cranberry sauce, apricots, onion, dried apricots, sugar, mustard, and cayenne. Cover and process for 30 seconds or until almost smooth. Pour over pork. Cover and cook on low for 5-6 hours or until a meat thermometer reads 160° and pork is tender.

3 Remove pork and potatoes to a serving platter and bowl. Pour cooking juices into a pitcher; serve with meat and potatoes.

Yield: 8 servings.

hawaiian pork roast

PREP: 30 MIN.
COOK: 3 HOURS + STANDING

Ruth Chiarenza
La Vale, Maryland

This is one of my favorite slow cooker recipes. It's wonderful with rice or potatoes and any vegetable. It also reheats well for lunch the next day.

1 boneless whole pork loin roast (3 pounds)

1/2 teaspoon salt

1/4 teaspoon pepper

3 tablespoons canola oil

2 cups unsweetened pineapple juice

1 can (8 ounces) unsweetened crushed pineapple, undrained

1/2 cup packed brown sugar

1/2 cup sliced celery

1/2 cup cider vinegar

1/2 cup soy sauce

1/4 cup cornstarch

1/3 cup cold water

1 Cut pork roast in half. Sprinkle with salt and pepper. In a large skillet, brown roast halves in oil on all sides; drain. Place in a 5-qt. slow cooker.

2 In a large bowl, combine the pineapple juice, pineapple, brown sugar, celery, vinegar and soy sauce. Pour over the roast. Cover and cook on low for 4-6 hours or until a meat thermometer reads 160°.

3 Remove roast and keep warm. Let stand for 10 minutes before slicing. Meanwhile, strain cooking juices; transfer to a large saucepan. Combine cornstarch and water until smooth; stir into cooking juices. Bring to a boil; cook and stir for 2 minutes or until thickened. Serve with pork.

Yield: 8 servings.

barbecue country ribs

PREP: 15 MIN. • COOK: 6 HOURS

Rebecca Knode
Mechanicsburg, Pennsylvania

Barbecue ribs are the perfect comfort food, and this recipe is sure to satisfy!

- 4 pounds boneless country-style pork ribs
- 1 bottle (12 ounces) chili sauce
- 1 cup ketchup
- 1/2 cup packed brown sugar
- 1/3 cup balsamic vinegar
- 2 tablespoons Worcestershire sauce
- 2 teaspoons onion powder
- 1 teaspoon salt
- 1 teaspoon garlic powder
- 1 teaspoon chili powder
- 1 teaspoon pepper
- 1/2 teaspoon hot pepper sauce, optional
- 1/4 teaspoon Liquid Smoke, optional

1 Place ribs in a 5-qt. slow cooker. Combine the chili sauce, ketchup, brown sugar, vinegar, Worcestershire sauce, seasonings and pepper sauce and Liquid Smoke if desired; pour over ribs.

2 Cover and cook on low for 6-7 hours or until meat is tender.

Yield: 10 servings.

creamy bratwurst stew

PREP: 20 MIN. • COOK: 6-1/2 HOURS

Susan Holmes
Germantown, Wisconsin

A rich sauce coats this hearty combo of potatoes and bratwurst chunks. It's great on cold nights.

- 4 medium potatoes, cubed
- 2 medium carrots, coarsely chopped
- 2 celery ribs, chopped
- 1 cup chopped onion
- 3/4 cup chopped green pepper
- 2 pounds fresh bratwurst links, cut into 1-inch slices
- 1/2 cup chicken broth
- 1 teaspoon salt
- 1 teaspoon dried basil
- 1/2 teaspoon pepper
- 2 cups half-and-half cream
- 3 tablespoons cornstarch
- 3 teaspoons cold water

1 In a 5-qt. slow cooker, combine the potatoes, carrots, celery, onion and green pepper. Top with bratwurst slices. Combine the broth, salt, basil and pepper; pour over top. Cover and cook on low for 6-7 hours or until vegetables are tender and sausage is no longer pink.

2 Stir in cream. Combine cornstarch and water until smooth; stir into stew. Cover and cook on high for 30 minutes or until gravy is thickened.

Yield: 8 servings.

1. Cut roast in half; place in a 5-qt. slow cooker. In a blender, combine the tomatoes, chili powder, garlic, lime juice, honey, jalapeno and salt; cover and process until smooth. Pour over pork. Cover and cook on low for 8-10 hours or until meat is tender.

2. Shred pork with two forks. Using a slotted spoon, place about 1/2 cup pork mixture down the center of each tortilla; top with avocado and sour cream if desired. Fold sides and ends over filling and roll up.

Yield: 10 burritos.

EDITOR'S NOTE: When cutting hot peppers, disposable gloves are recommended. Avoid touching your face.

maple pork ribs

PREP: 10 MIN. • COOK: 5 HOURS

Phyllis Eismann Schmalz
Kansas City, Kansas

These tender ribs are draped in a luscious maple-mustard sauce. This is one of our favorite recipes that serves two people.

  1 pound boneless country-style pork ribs, trimmed and cut into 3-inch pieces

  2 teaspoons canola oil

  1 medium onion, cut into 1/4-inch slices and separated into rings

  3 tablespoons maple syrup

  2 tablespoons spicy brown *or* Dijon mustard

1. In a large skillet, brown ribs in oil on all sides; drain. Place ribs and onion in a 1-1/2-qt. slow cooker. Combine syrup and mustard; pour over ribs. Cover and cook on low for 5-7 hours or until meat is tender.

Yield: 2 servings.

pork burritos

PREP: 25 MIN. • COOK: 8 HOURS

Kelly Gengler
Theresa, Wisconsin

These burritos are spicy but slightly sweet. I depend on the slow cooker to help feed my family.

  1 boneless pork shoulder butt roast (3 to 4 pounds)

  1 can (14-1/2 ounces) diced tomatoes with mild green chilies, undrained

  1/4 cup chili powder

  3 tablespoons minced garlic

  2 tablespoons lime juice

  2 tablespoons honey

  1 tablespoon chopped seeded jalapeno pepper

  1 teaspoon salt

  10 flour tortillas (8 inches), warmed

  Sliced avocado and sour cream, optional

creamy ham & potatoes

PREP: 20 MIN. • COOK: 5 HOURS

Wendy Rowley
Green River, Wyoming

If you love scalloped potatoes, this downsized version with hearty chunks of ham is just for you.

- 2 large red potatoes, cubed
- 1/3 cup cubed process cheese (Velveeta)
- 3/4 cup cubed fully cooked ham
- 1 tablespoon dried minced onion
- 2/3 cup condensed cream of celery soup, undiluted
- 2/3 cup 2% milk
- 1 tablespoon all-purpose flour
- 1/4 teaspoon pepper

1 In a 1-1/2-qt. slow cooker coated with cooking spray, layer the potatoes, cheese, ham and onion.

2 In a small bowl, combine soup and milk; whisk in flour and pepper. Pour over potatoes. Cover and cook on low for 5-6 hours or until potatoes are tender. Stir before serving.

Yield: 2 servings.

cranberry pork tenderloin

PREP: 10 MIN. • COOK: 5-1/4 HOURS

Betty Helton
Melbourne, Florida

I rely on a can of cranberry sauce to create the sweet sauce for this tender pork entree. I add orange juice and ground cloves to the mixture to season it nicely as it simmers.

> 1 pork tenderloin (1 pound)
>
> 1 can (14 ounces) whole-berry cranberry sauce
>
> 1/2 cup orange juice
>
> 1/4 cup sugar
>
> 1 tablespoon brown sugar
>
> 1 teaspoon ground mustard
>
> 1/4 to 1/2 teaspoon ground cloves
>
> 2 tablespoons cornstarch
>
> 3 tablespoons cold water

1 Place the tenderloin in a 3-qt. slow cooker. In a small bowl, combine the cranberry sauce, orange juice, sugars, mustard and cloves; pour over pork. Cover and cook on low for 5-6 hours or until a meat thermometer reads 160°.

2 Remove pork and keep warm. In a small bowl, combine cornstarch and cold water until smooth; gradually stir into cranberry mixture. Cover and cook on high for 15 minutes longer or until thickened. Serve with pork.

Yield: 4 servings.

sweet 'n' sour pork chops

PREP: 5 MIN. • COOK: 4-1/4 HOURS

Laurie Stafford
Waterville, New York

These tangy, tender pork chops are moist and simply delicious. They couldn't be much easier to make with only five ingredients! If you can't find honey barbecue sauce, substitute any barbecue sauce you like.

> 1 can (8 ounces) crushed pineapple, undrained
>
> 1 cup honey barbecue sauce
>
> 1/3 cup finely chopped onion
>
> 2 tablespoons chili sauce
>
> 4 bone-in pork loin chops (3/4 inch thick and 8 ounces *each*)

1 In a small bowl, combine the pineapple, barbecue sauce, onion and chili sauce. Pour half into a greased 3-qt. slow cooker. Top with pork chops and remaining sauce. Cover and cook on low for 4-1/4 to 5-1/4 hours or until meat is tender.

Yield: 4 servings.

mexican pork roast

PREP: 15 MIN. • COOK: 8 HOURS

Chuck Allen
Dana Point, California

A friend who lives in Mexico shared this recipe with me some years ago. They cooked the roast in a clay pot in a slow oven, but I found it works well in a slow cooker. The leftovers make great burritos and tacos.

- 2 medium onions, sliced
- 2 medium carrots, sliced
- 2 jalapeno peppers, seeded and chopped
- 2 tablespoons olive oil
- 3 garlic cloves, minced
- 1/2 cup water
- 1/2 cup chicken broth
- 1 teaspoon ground coriander
- 1/2 teaspoon salt
- 1/2 teaspoon ground cumin
- 1/2 teaspoon dried oregano
- 1/4 teaspoon pepper
- 1 boneless pork shoulder butt roast (3 pounds)

1 In a large skillet, saute the onions, carrots and jalapenos in oil for 3 minutes. Add garlic; cook 1 minute longer. Transfer to a 5-qt. slow cooker; add water and broth.

2 In a small bowl, combine the coriander, salt, cumin, oregano and pepper; rub over roast. Cut roast in half; place in the slow cooker. Cover and cook on low for 8-9 hours or until meat is tender.

3 Transfer roast and vegetables to a serving platter; keep warm. Strain cooking juices and skim fat. Pour into a small saucepan. Bring to a boil; cook until liquid is reduced to about 1 cup. Serve with roast and vegetables.

Yield: 8 servings.

EDITOR'S NOTE: When cutting hot peppers, disposable gloves are recommended. Avoid touching your face.

country-style pork loin

PREP: 20 MIN. • COOK: 5 HOURS

Corina Flansberg
Carson City, Nevada

This pork roast is so moist and tender, it melts in your mouth. It is my son's favorite dish!

- 1 boneless whole pork loin roast (3 pounds)
- 1/2 cup all-purpose flour
- 1 teaspoon onion powder
- 1 teaspoon ground mustard
- 2 tablespoons canola oil
- 2 cups chicken broth
- 1/4 cup cornstarch
- 1/4 cup cold water
- Hot mashed potatoes, optional

1 Cut pork roast in half. In a large resealable plastic bag, combine the flour, onion powder and mustard. Add pork, one portion at a time, and shake to coat.

2 In a large skillet, brown pork in oil over medium-high heat on all sides. Transfer to a 5-qt. slow cooker. Pour broth over pork. Cover and cook on low for 5-6 hours or until a meat thermometer reads 160°. Remove pork and keep warm.

3 For gravy, strain cooking juices and skim fat; pour 2-1/2 cups cooking juices into a large saucepan. Combine cornstarch and water until smooth; stir into juices. Bring to a boil; cook and stir for 2 minutes or until thickened. Slice pork; serve with gravy and mashed potatoes if desired.

Yield: 8 servings.

tasty pork ribs

PREP: 10 MIN. • COOK: 6 HOURS

Michelle Rominger
Albia, Iowa

I like to serve these tender, country-style ribs over rice. The tantalizing aroma and zippy Cajun barbecue sauce are sure to make these ribs a frequent request at your house, too.

8 bone-in country-style pork ribs (8 ounces *each*)

1 cup ketchup

1 cup barbecue sauce

1/4 cup packed brown sugar

1/4 cup Worcestershire sauce

1 tablespoon balsamic vinegar

1 tablespoon molasses

1 garlic clove, minced

2 tablespoons dried minced onion

1 teaspoon Cajun seasoning

1 teaspoon ground mustard

1/2 teaspoon salt

1/4 teaspoon pepper

1 Place ribs in a 5-qt. slow cooker. Combine the remaining ingredients; pour over ribs. Cover and cook on low for 6-7 hours or until meat is tender.

Yield: 8 servings.

chinese pork chops

PREP: 15 MIN. • COOK: 3 HOURS

Sharon Crider
Junction City, Kansas

These delicious pork chops are so saucy and tender. I got the recipe years ago and it's been a family favorite ever since.

6 boneless pork loin chops (4 ounces *each*)

1 small onion, finely chopped

1/3 cup ketchup

3 tablespoons brown sugar

3 tablespoons water

3 tablespoons reduced-sodium soy sauce

1 garlic clove, minced

1 teaspoon ground ginger

3 cups hot cooked rice

1 Place pork chops in a 3-qt. slow cooker coated with cooking spray. In a small bowl, combine the onion, ketchup, brown sugar, water, soy sauce, garlic and ginger. Pour over chops. Cover and cook on low for 3-4 hours or until meat is tender. Serve with rice and cooking juices.

Yield: 6 servings.

creole black beans 'n' sausage

PREP: 25 MIN. • COOK: 6 HOURS

Cheryl Landers
LaTour, Missouri

It's easy to add a Louisiana entree to my table with this recipe. I brown the meat, cut up veggies and measure spices the night before then assemble and start cooking it the next morning. When I get home, I make the rice...and dinner is served!

2 pounds smoked sausage, cut into 1-inch slices

3 cans (15 ounces *each*) black beans, rinsed and drained

1-1/2 cups *each* chopped onion, celery and green pepper

1 cup water

1 can (8 ounces) tomato sauce

4 garlic cloves, minced

2 teaspoons dried thyme

1 teaspoon chicken bouillon granules

1 teaspoon white pepper

1/4 teaspoon cayenne pepper

2 bay leaves

Hot cooked rice

1 In a large skillet, brown sausage over medium heat; drain. Transfer to a 5-qt. slow cooker.

2 In a large bowl, combine the beans, onion, celery, green pepper, water, tomato sauce, garlic, thyme, bouillon, white pepper, cayenne and bay leaves; pour over sausage. Cover and cook on low for 6 hours or until vegetables are tender. Discard bay leaves. Serve with rice.

Yield: 10 servings.

peachy pork chops

PREP: 15 MIN. • COOK: 5 HOURS

Bonnie Morrow
Spencerport, New York

I played around with many variations of this recipe until I came up with one that was just right. The warm peaches make an excellent side dish for the pork. Serve with noodles if you wish.

2 bone-in center-cut pork loin chops (7 ounces *each*)

2 teaspoons canola oil

1 can (8-1/4 ounces) sliced peaches

1 can (8 ounces) tomato sauce

1/2 cup water

1 teaspoon reduced-sodium soy sauce

1/8 teaspoon dried rosemary, crushed

1/8 teaspoon dried thyme

1/8 teaspoon dried basil

Dash to 1/8 teaspoon cayenne pepper

1 In a small skillet, brown pork chops in oil; drain. Transfer to a 1-1/2-qt. slow cooker.

2 Drain peaches, reserving juice. In a bowl, combine the tomato sauce, water, soy sauce, rosemary, thyme, basil, cayenne and reserved peach juice; pour over pork. Top with peaches. Cover and cook on low for 5 hours or until pork is tender.

Yield: 2 servings.

cheesy sausage gravy

PREP: 15 MIN. • COOK: 7 HOURS

P.J. Prusia
Raymore, Missouri

I appreciate the make-ahead convenience of this breakfast dish shared by a friend many years ago. I've served this to overnight guests, and they never fail to ask for the recipe.

1 pound bulk pork sausage

1/4 cup butter, cubed

1/4 cup all-purpose flour

1/4 teaspoon pepper

2-1/2 cups milk

2 cans (10-3/4 ounces *each*) condensed cheddar cheese soup, undiluted

6 hard-cooked eggs, chopped

1 jar (4-1/2 ounces) sliced mushrooms, drained

Warm biscuits

1 In a large skillet, cook sausage over medium heat until no longer pink; drain and remove sausage. In the same skillet, melt butter. Stir in flour and pepper until smooth. Gradually whisk in milk. Bring to a boil; cook and stir for 2 minutes or until thickened and bubbly.

2 Stir in soup until blended. Stir in eggs, mushrooms and sausage. Transfer to a 3-qt. slow cooker. Cover and cook on low for 7-8 hours. Stir; serve over biscuits.

Yield: 8 servings.

p. 204

p. 186

p. 199

poultry

p. 215

slow-cooked southwest chicken

PREP: 15 MIN. • COOK: 6 HOURS

Brandi Castillo
Santa Maria, California

With just 15 minutes of prep, you'll be out of the kitchen in no time. This deliciously low-fat dish gets even better served with reduced-fat sour cream and chopped cilantro.

2 cans (15 ounces *each*) black beans, rinsed and drained

1 can (14-1/2 ounces) reduced-sodium chicken broth

1 can (14-1/2 ounces) diced tomatoes with mild green chilies, undrained

1/2 pound boneless skinless chicken breast

1 jar (8 ounces) chunky salsa

1 cup frozen corn

1 tablespoon dried parsley flakes

1 teaspoon ground cumin

1/4 teaspoon pepper

3 cups hot cooked rice

1 In a 2- or 3-qt. slow cooker, combine the beans, broth, tomatoes, chicken, salsa, corn and seasonings. Cover and cook on low for 6-8 hours or until a meat thermometer reads 170°.

2 Shred chicken and return to the slow cooker; heat through. Serve with rice.

Yield: 6 servings.

lemon chicken

PREP: 20 MIN. • COOK: 4-1/4 HOURS

Elizabeth Hokanson
Arborg, Manitoba

This easy and attractive meal is bound to become a staple on your dinner menu. Made with everyday ingredients, there's nothing complicated or fancy about this great find.

1 teaspoon dried oregano

1/2 teaspoon seasoned salt

1/4 teaspoon pepper

6 boneless skinless chicken breast halves (6 ounces *each*)

2 teaspoons chicken bouillon granules

1/4 cup boiling water

3 tablespoons lemon juice

1-1/2 teaspoons minced garlic

1-1/2 cups (12 ounces) sour cream

2 teaspoons minced fresh parsley

Hot cooked brown rice, optional

1 Combine the oregano, seasoned salt and pepper; rub over the chicken. Place in a 3-qt. slow cooker.

2 In a small bowl, dissolve the bouillon in boiling water. Stir in the lemon juice and garlic. Pour over chicken. Cover and cook on low for 4 hours or until a meat thermometer reads 170°.

3 Remove chicken and keep warm. Stir in sour cream and parsley; cover and cook for 15 minutes or until heated through. Serve chicken with sauce and rice if desired.

Yield: 6 servings.

chicken, bean and rice nachos

PREP: 15 MIN. • COOK: 5 HOURS

Barbara Schweitzer
Chesapeake, Virginia

You can't go wrong with this sure-fire dinnertime hit. When you're craving nachos but need more than a snack, this makes one zesty meal.

- 1-1/2 pounds boneless skinless chicken breasts
- 1 jar (16 ounces) salsa
- 1 can (15 ounces) black beans, rinsed and drained
- 1 can (7 ounces) Mexicorn, drained
- 1 package (8 ounces) cream cheese, cubed
- 3 cups cooked rice
- 3/4 cup shredded Mexican cheese blend
- Tortilla chips

1 Place chicken in a 3-qt. slow cooker. In a small bowl, combine the salsa, beans and corn; pour over chicken. Cover and cook on low for 5-6 hours or until chicken is tender.

2 Shred chicken with two forks and return to cooker. Stir in cream cheese. To serve, place rice in serving bowls; top with chicken mixture and cheese blend. Serve with tortilla chips.

Yield: 6 servings.

moist drumsticks

PREP: 10 MIN. • COOK: 5 HOURS

Lianne Felton
Riverside, California

I found this in my mom's recipe box years ago. It's very quick to prepare and makes the house smell wonderful while it's cooking.

- 3 pounds chicken drumsticks, skin removed
- 1 can (8 ounces) tomato sauce
- 1/2 cup soy sauce
- 1/4 cup packed brown sugar
- 1 teaspoon minced garlic
- 3 tablespoons cornstarch
- 1/4 cup cold water

1 Place drumsticks in a 5-qt. slow cooker. In a small bowl, combine the tomato sauce, soy sauce, brown sugar and garlic; pour over chicken. Cover and cook on low for 5-6 hours or until a meat thermometer reads 180°.

2 Remove chicken to a serving platter; keep warm. Skim fat from cooking juices; transfer to a small saucepan. Bring liquid to a boil. Combine cornstarch and water until smooth. Gradually stir into the pan. Bring to a boil; cook and stir for 2 minutes or until thickened. Serve with chicken.

Yield: 6 servings.

> **Slow cooker know-how.** Unless the recipe has instructions to stir in or add ingredients, refrain from lifting the lid while the slow cooker is cooking. Every time you lift the lid, steam is lost and as much as 15 to 30 minutes may be added to the cooking time.

chicken with veggies 'n' gravy

PREP: 10 MIN. • COOK: 4 HOURS

Susan Dalrymple
Marathon, Florida

I couldn't bear the thought of going to the store one day and was determined to come up with something for dinner from what I had on hand. I created this comforting chicken mix for two, and my husband loved it!

3 medium carrots, chopped

2 celery ribs, chopped

1 medium onion, chopped

2 boneless skinless chicken breast halves (5 ounces *each*)

1/8 teaspoon pepper

1 can (10-3/4 ounces) condensed cream of chicken soup, undiluted

2/3 cup water

1/4 cup white wine *or* chicken broth

2 individually frozen biscuits

1 Place the carrots, celery and onion in a 1-1/2-qt. slow cooker; top with chicken. Sprinkle with pepper.

2 In a small bowl, combine the soup, water and wine; pour over chicken. Cover and cook on low for 4-5 hours or until a meat thermometer reads 170° and vegetables are tender.

3 If desired, thicken cooking juices. Meanwhile, bake biscuits according to package directions. Serve with chicken, vegetables and gravy.

Yield: 2 servings.

1. Place chicken in a 5-qt. slow cooker; sprinkle with salt and pepper. Drain peaches, reserving 1/2 cup juice; set peaches aside. In a small bowl, combine the broth, butter, onion, curry, garlic, ginger and reserved juice; pour over chicken. Cover and cook on low for 3-4 hours or until chicken juices run clear.

2. Remove chicken to a serving platter; keep warm. Mix cornstarch and water until smooth; stir into cooking juices. Add raisins. Cover and cook on high for 10-15 minutes or until gravy is thickened. Stir in peaches; heat through. Serve with chicken. Garnish with coconut if desired.

Yield: 4 servings.

curried chicken with peaches

PREP: 15 MIN. • COOK: 3-1/4 HOURS

Heidi Martinez
Colorado Springs, Colorado

I'm always looking for recipes I can prepare ahead of time. The chicken pieces bask for hours in snappy spices and seasonings, giving this recipe a lot of pizzazz.

- 1 broiler/fryer chicken (3 pounds), cut up
- 1/8 teaspoon salt
- 1/8 teaspoon pepper
- 1 can (29 ounces) sliced peaches
- 1/2 cup chicken broth
- 2 tablespoons butter, melted
- 1 tablespoon dried minced onion
- 2 teaspoons curry powder
- 2 garlic cloves, minced
- 1/4 teaspoon ground ginger
- 3 tablespoons cornstarch
- 3 tablespoons cold water
- 1/4 cup raisins
- Toasted flaked coconut, optional

moist & tender turkey breast

PREP: 10 MIN. • COOK: 4 HOURS

Heidi Vawdrey
Riverton, Utah

This easy dish will be very popular in your home, I promise! Your family will love the taste and you will love how quickly it comes together.

- 1 bone-in turkey breast (6 to 7 pounds)
- 4 fresh rosemary sprigs
- 4 garlic cloves, peeled
- 1 tablespoon brown sugar
- 1/2 teaspoon coarsely ground pepper
- 1/4 teaspoon salt

1. Place turkey breast in a 6-qt. slow cooker. Place rosemary and garlic around turkey. Combine the brown sugar, pepper and salt; sprinkle over turkey. Cover and cook on low for 4-6 hours or until turkey is tender.

Yield: 12 servings.

sweet 'n' sour curry chicken

PREP: 15 MIN. • COOK: 4 HOURS

Carol Conrad
Edmonton, Alberta

A little mango chutney goes a long way in adding a tangy twist to chicken. I add some curry powder to this dish for extra flair.

1 pound boneless skinless chicken breasts, cut into 1-inch pieces

1 can (14-1/2 ounces) stewed tomatoes, cut up

1 large green pepper, cut into 1-inch pieces

1 large onion, sliced

1/2 cup mango chutney

2 tablespoons cornstarch

1-1/2 teaspoons curry powder

1/4 cup water

1 In a 3-qt. slow cooker, combine the chicken, tomatoes, green pepper, onion and chutney. In a small bowl, combine the cornstarch, curry powder and water until smooth; stir into chicken mixture.

2 Cover and cook on low for 4 hours or until chicken is no longer pink and vegetables are tender.

Yield: 4 servings.

chicken and red potatoes

PREP: 20 MIN. • COOK: 3-1/2 HOURS

Michele Trantham
Waynesville, North Carolina

Try this moist and tender chicken-and-potato dish tonight! Just fix after lunch, then forget about it until dinnertime.

- 3 tablespoons all-purpose flour
- 4 boneless skinless chicken breast halves (6 ounces *each*)
- 2 tablespoons olive oil
- 4 medium red potatoes, cut into wedges
- 2 cups fresh baby carrots, halved lengthwise
- 1 can (4 ounces) mushroom stems and pieces, drained
- 4 canned whole green chilies, cut into 1/2-inch slices
- 1 can (10-3/4 ounces) condensed cream of onion soup, undiluted
- 1/4 cup 2% milk
- 1/2 teaspoon chicken seasoning
- 1/4 teaspoon salt
- 1/4 teaspoon dried rosemary, crushed
- 1/4 teaspoon pepper

1 Place flour in a large resealable plastic bag. Add chicken, one piece at a time; shake to coat. In a large skillet, brown chicken in oil on both sides.

2 Meanwhile, place the potatoes, carrots, mushrooms and chilies in a greased 5-qt. slow cooker. In a small bowl, combine the remaining ingredients. Pour half of soup mixture over vegetables.

3 Transfer chicken to slow cooker; top with remaining soup mixture. Cover and cook on low for 3-1/2 to 4 hours or until a meat thermometer reads 170°.

Yield: 4 servings.

maple mustard chicken

PREP: 5 MIN. • COOK: 3 HOURS

Jennifer Seidel
Midland, Michigan

This recipe is one of my husband's favorites. It only calls for a few ingredients, and we try to have them on hand regularly for a delicious and cozy meal anytime!

- 6 boneless skinless chicken breast halves (6 ounces *each*)
- 1/2 cup maple syrup
- 1/3 cup stone-ground mustard
- 2 tablespoons quick-cooking tapioca
- Hot cooked brown rice

1 Place chicken in a 3-qt. slow cooker. In a small bowl, combine the syrup, mustard and tapioca; pour over chicken. Cover and cook on low for 3-4 hours or until a meat thermometer reads 170°. Serve with rice.

Yield: 6 servings.

busy mom's chicken fajitas

PREP: 15 MIN. • COOK: 5 HOURS

Sarah Newman
Mahtomedi, Minnesota

Staying at home with a 9-month-old makes preparing dinner a challenge, but a slow cooker provides an easy way to make a low-fat meal. The tender meat in these fajitas is a hit, and the veggies and beans provide a dose of fiber!

1 pound boneless skinless chicken breast halves

1 can (16 ounces) kidney beans, rinsed and drained

1 can (14-1/2 ounces) diced tomatoes with mild green chilies, drained

1 *each* medium green, sweet red and yellow peppers, julienned

1 medium onion, halved and sliced

2 teaspoons ground cumin

2 teaspoons chili powder

1 garlic clove, minced

1/4 teaspoon salt

6 flour tortillas (8 inches), warmed

Shredded lettuce and chopped tomatoes, optional

1 In a 3-qt. slow cooker, combine the chicken, beans, tomatoes, peppers, onion and seasonings. Cover and cook on low for 5-6 hours or until chicken is tender.

2 Remove chicken; cool slightly. Shred chicken and return to the slow cooker; heat through.

3 Spoon about 3/4 cup chicken mixture down the center of each tortilla. Top with lettuce and tomatoes if desired.

Yield: 6 servings.

herbed turkey breasts

PREP: 15 MIN. + MARINATING
COOK: 3-1/2 HOURS

Laurie Mace
Los Ososo, California

Tender, moist turkey breasts are enhanced with an array of flavorful seasonings in this comforting slow cooker recipe.

2 cans (14-1/2 ounces *each*) chicken broth

1 cup lemon juice

1/2 cup packed brown sugar

1/2 cup fresh sage

1/2 cup minced fresh thyme

1/2 cup lime juice

1/2 cup cider vinegar

1/2 cup olive oil

2 envelopes onion soup mix

1/4 cup Dijon mustard

2 tablespoons minced fresh marjoram

3 teaspoons paprika

2 teaspoons garlic powder

2 teaspoons pepper

1 teaspoon salt

2 boneless turkey breasts (2 pounds *each*)

1 In a blender, process the first 15 ingredients in batches until blended. Pour 3-1/2 cups marinade into a large resealable plastic bag; add the turkey. Seal bag and turn to coat; refrigerate for 8 hours or overnight. Cover and refrigerate remaining marinade.

2 Drain and discard marinade. Place turkey in a 5-qt. slow cooker; add reserved marinade. Cover and cook on high for 3-1/2 to 4-1/2 hours or until a meat thermometer reads 170°.

Yield: 14-16 servings.

herbed chicken with wild rice

PREP: 20 MIN. • COOK: 4 HOURS

Becky Gifford
Conway, Arkansas

My family is always very busy. With three kids involved in many different after-school and evening activities, it's nice to come home to a meal that's already prepared and ready to eat!

1 package (6 ounces) long grain and wild rice mix

6 boneless skinless chicken breast halves (5 ounces *each*)

1 tablespoon canola oil

1 teaspoon butter

1/2 pound sliced fresh mushrooms

1 can (10-3/4 ounces) condensed cream of chicken soup, undiluted

1 cup water

3 bacon strips, cooked and crumbled

1 teaspoon dried parsley flakes

1/2 teaspoon dried thyme

1/4 teaspoon dried tarragon

1 Place rice in a 5-qt. slow cooker; set aside seasoning packet. In a large skillet, brown chicken in oil and butter. Add to slow cooker. In the same skillet, saute mushrooms until tender; place over chicken.

2 In a small bowl, combine the soup, water, bacon, herbs and contents of seasoning packet. Pour over top. Cover and cook on low for 4 hours or until a meat thermometer reads 170°.

Yield: 6 servings.

coconut curry chicken

PREP: 20 MIN. • COOK: 5 HOURS

Andi Kauffman
Beavercreek, Oregon

My husband and I love this yummy dish! It's a breeze to prepare in the slow cooker, and it tastes just like a meal you'd have at your favorite Indian or Thai restaurant.

2 medium potatoes, peeled and cubed

1 small onion, chopped

4 boneless skinless chicken breast halves (4 ounces *each*)

1 cup light coconut milk

4 teaspoons curry powder

1 garlic clove, minced

1 teaspoon reduced-sodium chicken bouillon granules

1/4 teaspoon salt

1/4 teaspoon pepper

2 cups hot cooked rice

1/4 cup thinly sliced green onions

Raisins, flaked coconut and chopped unsalted peanuts, optional

1 Place potatoes and onion in a 3- or 4-qt. slow cooker. In a large nonstick skillet coated with cooking spray, brown chicken on both sides.

2 Transfer to slow cooker. In a small bowl, combine the coconut milk, curry, garlic, bouillon, salt and pepper; pour over chicken. Cover and cook on low for 5 hours or until a meat thermometer reads 170°.

3 Serve chicken, vegetables and sauce with rice; sprinkle with green onions. Garnish with raisins, coconut and peanuts if desired.

Yield: 4 servings.

satisfying chicken and veggies

PREP: 20 MIN. • COOK: 4 HOURS

Kat Sadi
San Luis Obispo, California

I'm happy to share the recipe for this tasty meal-in-one supper. Chicken and vegetables are simmered in spaghetti with herbs. The nice thing about this delicious dish is that you have only one pot to clean.

2 medium potatoes, peeled and cut into 1-inch pieces (about 1-1/2 cups)

1 cup thickly sliced onion

1/2 cup sliced celery

1 medium carrot, cut into 1-inch pieces

1 medium sweet yellow pepper, cut into 1-inch pieces

1 broiler/fryer chicken (3 to 4 pounds), cut up and skin removed

1 jar (26 ounces) meatless spaghetti sauce

1 cup water

1-1/2 teaspoons minced garlic

1/4 teaspoon salt

1/4 teaspoon dried oregano

1/4 teaspoon dried basil

1/4 teaspoon pepper

1 Place the potatoes, onion, celery, carrot and yellow pepper in a 5-qt. slow cooker. Top with chicken. Combine the remaining ingredients; pour over chicken. Cover and cook on low for 4 to 4-1/2 hours or until chicken juices run clear and vegetables are tender.

Yield: 6 servings.

southwest turkey stew

PREP: 15 MIN. • COOK: 5 HOURS

Stephanie Hutchinson
Helix, Oregon

I prefer main dishes that enable me to stay on my diet but still eat what the rest of the family eats. This stew is a hit with my husband and our young children.

1-1/2 pounds turkey breast tenderloins, cubed

2 teaspoons canola oil

1 can (15 ounces) turkey chili with beans, undrained

1 can (14-1/2 ounces) diced tomatoes

1 medium sweet red pepper, cut into 3/4-inch pieces

1 medium green pepper, cut into 3/4-inch pieces

3/4 cup chopped onion

3/4 cup salsa

3 garlic cloves, minced

1-1/2 teaspoons chili powder

1/2 teaspoon salt

1/2 teaspoon ground cumin

1 tablespoon minced fresh cilantro, optional

1 In a nonstick skillet, brown turkey in oil; transfer to a 3-qt. slow cooker. Stir in the chili, tomatoes, peppers, onion, salsa, garlic, chili powder, salt and cumin. Cover and cook on low for 5-6 hours or until turkey is no longer pink. Garnish with cilantro if desired.

Yield: 6 servings.

herbed slow cooker chicken

PREP: 5 MIN. • COOK: 4 HOURS

Sundra Hauck
Bogalusa, Louisiana

I use my slow cooker to prepare these well-seasoned chicken breasts that cook up moist and tender. My daughter, who has two young sons to keep up with, gave this great recipe to me several years ago. I've made it repeatedly.

1 tablespoon olive oil

1 teaspoon paprika

1/2 teaspoon garlic powder

1/2 teaspoon seasoned salt

1/2 teaspoon dried thyme

1/2 teaspoon dried basil

1/2 teaspoon pepper

1/2 teaspoon browning sauce, optional

4 bone-in chicken breast halves
(6 ounces *each*)

1/2 cup chicken broth

1 In a small bowl, combine the first eight ingredients; rub over chicken. Place in a 5-qt. slow cooker; add broth. Cover and cook on low for 4-5 hours or until a meat thermometer reads 170°.

Yield: 4 servings.

southern barbecue spaghetti sauce

PREP: 10 MIN. • COOK: 4 HOURS

Rhonda Melanson
Sarnia, Ontario

I revamped our favorite sloppy joe recipe into this thick spaghetti sauce that simmers in the slow cooker. The flavor is jazzy enough to be interesting to adults, yet mild enough to be enjoyed by children.

1 pound lean ground turkey

2 medium onions, chopped

1-1/2 cups sliced fresh mushrooms

1 medium green pepper, chopped

2 garlic cloves, minced

1 can (14-1/2 ounces) diced tomatoes, undrained

1 can (12 ounces) tomato paste

1 can (8 ounces) tomato sauce

1 cup ketchup

1/2 cup beef broth

2 tablespoons Worcestershire sauce

2 tablespoons brown sugar

1 tablespoon ground cumin

2 teaspoons chili powder

12 cups hot cooked spaghetti

1 In a large nonstick skillet, cook the turkey, onions, mushrooms and green pepper over medium heat until meat is no longer pink. Add garlic; cook 1 minute longer. Drain.

2 Transfer to a 3-qt. slow cooker. Stir in the tomatoes, tomato paste, tomato sauce, ketchup, broth, Worcestershire sauce, brown sugar, cumin and chili powder. Cover and cook on low for 4-5 hours or until vegetables are tender. Serve with spaghetti.

Yield: 12 servings.

italian chicken and peppers

PREP: 20 MIN. • COOK: 4 HOURS

Brenda Nolen
Simpsonville, South Carolina

I put this recipe together one day when I had leftover peppers and wanted to make something easy with spagetti sauce. To my delight, the taste reminds me of pizza.

- 6 boneless skinless chicken breast halves (4 ounces *each*)
- 1 jar (26 ounces) garden-style spaghetti sauce
- 1 medium onion, sliced
- 1/2 *each* small green, sweet yellow and red peppers, julienned
- 1/4 cup grated Parmesan cheese
- 2 garlic cloves, minced
- 1 teaspoon dried oregano
- 1 teaspoon dried basil
- 1/2 teaspoon salt
- 1/4 teaspoon pepper
- 4-1/2 cups uncooked spiral pasta
- Shaved Parmesan cheese, optional

1 Place chicken in a 3-qt. slow cooker. In a large bowl, combine the spaghetti sauce, onion, peppers, cheese, garlic, oregano, basil, salt and pepper. Pour over chicken. Cover and cook on low for 4-5 hours or until a meat thermometer reads 170°.

2 Meanwhile, cook pasta according to package directions; drain. Serve chicken with pasta and sauce. Top with shaved Parmesan cheese if desired.

Yield: 6 servings.

soy-garlic chicken

PREP: 10 MIN. • COOK: 4 HOURS

Colleen Faber
Buffalo, Montana

Being a full-time mother as well as helping my husband on our ranch, I'm always looking for simple meals for the slow cooker. My family really likes this hearty main dish.

- 6 chicken leg quarters, skin removed
- 1 can (8 ounces) tomato sauce
- 1/2 cup soy sauce
- 1/4 cup packed brown sugar
- 2 teaspoons minced garlic

1 With a sharp knife, cut leg quarters at the joints if desired. Place in a 4-qt. slow cooker. In a small bowl, combine the tomato sauce, soy sauce, brown sugar and garlic; pour over chicken. Cover and cook on low for 4-5 hours or until a meat thermometer reads 180°.

Yield: 6 servings.

cornish hens with potatoes

PREP: 20 MIN. • COOK: 6 HOURS

Deborah Randall
Abbeville, Louisiana

For a wonderful holiday meal with only a fraction of the work, consider this savory dish. This special slow-cooked dinner is delicious. I serve it with green beans and French bread.

4 Cornish game hens (20 to 24 ounces *each*)

2 tablespoons canola oil

4 large red potatoes, cut into 1/8-inch slices

4 bacon strips, cut into 1-inch pieces

Lemon-pepper seasoning and garlic powder to taste

Minced fresh parsley

1 In a large skillet, brown hens in oil. Place the potatoes in a 5-qt. slow cooker. Top with the hens and bacon. Sprinkle with lemon-pepper and garlic powder.

2 Cover and cook on low for 6-8 hours or until a meat thermometer reads 180° and potatoes are tender. Thicken the cooking juices if desired. Sprinkle the hens with parsley. Serve with the potatoes.

Yield: 4 servings.

slow-cooked italian chicken

PREP: 10 MIN • COOK: 4-1/4 HOURS

Deanna D'Auria
Banning, California

With its nicely seasoned tomato sauce, this enticing chicken entree is especially good over pasta or rice. My father loved this dish.

4 boneless skinless chicken breast halves (4 ounces *each*)

1 can (14-1/2 ounces) chicken broth

1 can (14-1/2 ounces) stewed tomatoes, cut up

1 can (8 ounces) tomato sauce

1 medium green pepper, chopped

1 green onion, chopped

1 garlic clove, minced

3 teaspoons chili powder

1 teaspoon ground mustard

1/2 teaspoon garlic salt *or* garlic powder

1/2 teaspoon onion salt *or* onion powder

1/2 teaspoon pepper

1/3 cup all-purpose flour

1/2 cup cold water

Hot cooked pasta

1 Place chicken in a 3-qt. slow cooker. In a bowl, combine the broth, tomatoes, tomato sauce, green pepper, onion, garlic and seasonings; pour over chicken. Cover and cook on low for 4-5 hours or until a meat thermometer reads 170°.

2 Remove chicken and keep warm. Pour cooking juices into a large saucepan; skim fat. Combine flour and cold water until smooth; stir into juices. Bring to a boil; cook and stir for 2 minutes or until thickened. Serve with chicken and pasta.

Yield: 4 servings.

teriyaki chicken

PREP: 15 MIN. • COOK: 4 HOURS

Gigi Miller
Stoughton, Wisconsin

Chicken, rice and a sweet and salty sauce create an entree that's packed with Asian flavor. Your family will love this moist and tender meal.

12 boneless skinless chicken thighs
(about 3 pounds)

3/4 cup sugar

3/4 cup soy sauce

6 tablespoons cider vinegar

3/4 teaspoon ground ginger

3/4 teaspoon minced garlic

1/4 teaspoon pepper

4-1/2 teaspoons cornstarch

4-1/2 teaspoons cold water

Hot cooked rice, optional

1 Place chicken in a 4-qt. slow cooker. In a large bowl, combine the sugar, soy sauce, vinegar, ginger, garlic and pepper. Pour over chicken. Cover and cook on low for 4-5 hours or until chicken is tender.

2 Remove chicken to a serving platter; keep warm. Skim fat from cooking juices; transfer to a small saucepan. Bring liquid to a boil. Combine cornstarch and water until smooth. Gradually stir into the pan. Bring to a boil; cook and stir for 2 minutes or until thickened. Serve with chicken and rice if desired.

Yield: 6 servings.

creamy chicken and carrots

PREP: 5 MIN. • **COOK: 4 HOURS**

Valma O'Neill
Utica, Michigan

Mushroom soup makes a creamy gravy for this tender chicken. Use other vegetables or thick sliced potatoes for a change.

2 boneless skinless chicken breast halves (6 ounces *each*)

1/2 pound fresh baby carrots, cut in half lengthwise

1 can (10-3/4 ounces) condensed cream of mushroom soup, undiluted

1 can (4 ounces) mushroom stems and pieces, drained

Hot cooked rice, optional

1 Place the chicken in a 1-1/2-qt. slow cooker. Top with carrots, soup and mushrooms. Cover and cook on high for 4-5 hours or until chicken juices run clear. Serve over rice if desired.

Yield: 2 servings.

chicken stew with gnocchi

PREP: 25 MIN. • **COOK: 6-1/2 HOURS**

Marge Drake
Juniata, Nebraska

My hearty chicken stew makes the house smell wonderful as it gently bubbles in the slow cooker.

3 medium parsnips, peeled and cut into 1/2-inch pieces

2 large carrots, cut into 1/2-inch slices

2 celery ribs, chopped

1 large sweet potato, peeled and cut into 1-inch cubes

4 green onions, chopped

3 pounds bone-in chicken thighs, skin removed

1/2 teaspoon dried sage leaves

1/4 teaspoon salt

1/4 teaspoon pepper

4 cups chicken broth

1 cup water

3 tablespoons cornstarch

1/4 cup cold water

1 package (16 ounces) potato gnocchi

Hot pepper sauce, optional

1 Place the parsnips, carrots, celery, sweet potato and onions in a 5-qt. slow cooker. Top with chicken; sprinkle with the sage, salt and pepper. Add broth and water. Cover and cook on low for 6 hours or until a meat thermometer reads 180°.

2 Remove chicken; when cool enough to handle, remove meat from bones and discard bones. Cut meat into bite-size pieces and return to the slow cooker.

3 Mix cornstarch and cold water until smooth; stir into stew. Add gnocchi. Cover and cook on high for 30 minutes or until thickened. Season with hot pepper sauce if desired.

Yield: 8 servings (3 quarts).

spicy beans with turkey sausage

PREP: 25 MIN. • COOK: 5 HOURS

Dorothy Jordan
College Station, Texas

Here's a jambalaya-type dish that comes together in the slow cooker. It's a wonderful way to warm up cold winter nights.

1 pound smoked turkey sausage, halved lengthwise and cut into 1/2-inch slices

1 can (16 ounces) kidney beans, rinsed and drained

1 can (15-1/2 ounces) great northern beans, rinsed and drained

1 can (15 ounces) black beans, rinsed and drained

1-1/2 cups frozen corn

1-1/2 cups salsa

1 large green pepper, chopped

1 large onion, chopped

1/2 to 1 cup water

3 garlic cloves, minced

1 teaspoon ground cumin

1 In a 5-qt. slow cooker, combine all ingredients. Cover and cook on low for 5-6 hours or until meat is tender. Stir before serving.

Yield: 6 servings.

mushroom chicken cacciatore

PREP: 20 MIN. • COOK: 4 HOURS

Jane Bone
Cape Coral, Florida

I give an Italian treatment to chicken by slow-cooking it in a zesty tomato sauce and serving it over spaghetti.

4 boneless skinless chicken breast halves (about 1-1/2 pounds)

2 tablespoons canola oil

1 can (15 ounces) tomato sauce

2 cans (4 ounces *each*) sliced mushrooms, drained

1 medium onion, chopped

1/4 cup red wine *or* chicken broth

2 garlic cloves, minced

1-1/4 teaspoons dried oregano

1/2 teaspoon dried thyme

1/8 to 1/4 teaspoon salt

1/8 teaspoon pepper

Hot cooked spaghetti

1 In a large skillet, brown chicken in oil on both sides. Transfer to a 3-qt. slow cooker. In a bowl, combine the tomato sauce, mushrooms, onion, wine, garlic, oregano, thyme, salt and pepper; pour over chicken.

2 Cover and cook on low for 4-5 hours or until a meat thermometer reads 170°. Serve with spaghetti.

Yield: 4 servings.

stuffed chicken rolls

PREP: 25 MIN. + CHILLING
COOK: 4 HOURS

Jean Sherwood
Kenneth City, Florida

The wonderful aroma of these moist, delicious chicken roll-ups sparks our appetites. The ham and cheese tucked inside is a tasty surprise. They're especially nice served over rice or pasta.

6 boneless skinless chicken breast halves
(8 ounces *each*)

6 slices fully cooked ham

6 slices Swiss cheese

1/4 cup all-purpose flour

1/4 cup grated Parmesan cheese

1/2 teaspoon rubbed sage

1/4 teaspoon paprika

1/4 teaspoon pepper

1/4 cup canola oil

1 can (10-3/4 ounces) condensed cream of chicken soup, undiluted

1/2 cup chicken broth

Chopped fresh parsley, optional

1 Flatten chicken to 1/8-in. thickness. Place ham and cheese on each breast. Roll up and tuck in ends; secure with a toothpick.

2 In a large shallow bowl, combine the flour, cheese, sage, paprika and pepper; coat chicken on all sides. Cover and refrigerate for 1 hour.

3 In a large skillet, brown chicken in oil over medium-high heat. Transfer to a 5-qt. slow cooker. Combine soup and broth; pour over chicken. Cover and cook on low for 4-5 hours or until chicken is no longer pink. Remove toothpicks. Garnish with parsley if desired.

Yield: 6 servings.

soft chicken tacos

PREP: 30 MIN. • COOK: 5 HOURS

Cheryl Newendorp
Pella, Iowa

My family loves these tacos. The chicken filling cooks in the slow cooker, so it's convenient to throw it together before I leave for work. At the end of the day, I just have to roll it up in a tortilla with the remaining ingredients and dinner's ready in minutes. The chicken also makes a great topping for a main-dish salad.

1 broiler/fryer chicken (3-1/2 pounds), cut up and skin removed

1 can (8 ounces) tomato sauce

1 can (4 ounces) chopped green chilies

1/3 cup chopped onion

2 tablespoons chili powder

2 tablespoons Worcestershire sauce

1/4 teaspoon garlic powder

10 flour tortillas (8 inches), warmed

1-1/4 cups shredded cheddar cheese

1-1/4 cups salsa

1-1/4 cups shredded lettuce

1 large tomato, chopped

3/4 cup sour cream, optional

1 Place the chicken in a 3-qt. slow cooker. In a small bowl, combine the tomato sauce, chilies, onion, chili powder, Worcestershire sauce and garlic powder; pour over chicken. Cover and cook on low for 5-6 hours or until chicken is tender and juices run clear.

2 Remove the chicken. Shred meat with two forks and return to the slow cooker; heat through. Spoon 1/2 cup chicken mixture down the center of each tortilla. Top with cheese, salsa, lettuce, tomato and sour cream if desired; roll up.

Yield: 5 servings.

slow 'n' easy barbecued chicken

PREP: 20 MIN. • COOK: 3 HOURS

Dreama Hughes
London, Kentucky

I rely on this yummy recipe often during the summer and fall when I know I'm going to be out working in the yard all day. I just pair it with a side vegetable and salad...and supper is served! It's also delicious with pork or beef and easy to double for a crowd.

1/4 cup water

3 tablespoons brown sugar

3 tablespoons white vinegar

3 tablespoons ketchup

2 tablespoons butter

2 tablespoons Worcestershire sauce

1 tablespoon lemon juice

1 teaspoon salt

1 teaspoon paprika

1 teaspoon ground mustard

1/2 teaspoon cayenne pepper

1 broiler/fryer chicken (2-1/2 to 3 pounds), cut up and skin removed

4 teaspoons cornstarch

1 tablespoon cold water

1 In a small saucepan, combine the first 11 ingredients. Bring to a boil. Reduce heat; simmer, uncovered, for 5 minutes. Remove from the heat.

2 Place the chicken in a 3-qt. slow cooker. Top with sauce. Cover and cook on low for 3-4 hours or until chicken juices run clear.

3 Remove chicken to a serving platter; keep warm. Skim fat from cooking juices; transfer to a small saucepan. Bring liquid to a boil. Combine cornstarch and water until smooth. Gradually stir into the pan. Bring to a boil; cook and stir for 2 minutes or until thickened. Spoon some of the sauce over chicken and serve the remaining sauce on the side.

Yield: 4 servings.

turkey leg pot roast

PREP: 15 MIN. • COOK: 5 HOURS

Rick and Vegas Pearson
Cadillac, Michigan

Well-seasoned turkey legs and tender potatoes, carrots and celery make this meal ideal for a crisp fall day. Moist and satisfying, the recipe couldn't be more comforting!

3 medium potatoes, peeled and quartered

2 cups fresh baby carrots

2 celery ribs, cut into 2-1/2-inch pieces

1 medium onion, peeled and quartered

3 garlic cloves, peeled and quartered

1/2 cup chicken broth

3 turkey drumsticks (8 ounces *each*), skin removed

2 teaspoons seasoned salt

1 teaspoon dried thyme

1 teaspoon dried parsley flakes

1/4 teaspoon pepper

1 In a greased 5-qt. slow cooker, combine the first six ingredients. Place drumsticks over vegetables. Sprinkle with the seasoned salt, thyme, parsley and pepper. Cover; cook on low for 5 to 5-1/2 hours or until a meat thermometer reads 180°.

Yield: 3 servings.

chicken athena

PREP: 15 MIN. • COOK: 4 HOURS

Radelle Knappenberger
Oviedo, Florida

Greek flavors abound in this tasty chicken dish that's cooked in the slow cooker. Olives, sun-dried tomatoes, lemon juice and balsamic vinegar combine with chicken for a special treat.

6 boneless skinless chicken breast halves (6 ounces *each*)

2 medium onions, chopped

1/3 cup sun-dried tomatoes (not packed in oil), chopped

1/3 cup pitted Greek olives, chopped

2 tablespoons lemon juice

1 tablespoon balsamic vinegar

3 garlic cloves, minced

1/2 teaspoon salt

1 Place chicken in a 3-qt. slow cooker. Add the remaining ingredients. Cover and cook on low for 4 hours or until a meat thermometer reads 170°.

Yield: 6 servings.

saucy chicken thighs

PREP: 20 MIN. • COOK: 4 HOURS

Kim Puckett
Reagan, Tennessee

Everyone raves about how sweet the sauce is for these slow-cooked chicken thighs. They're such a breeze because they simmer away while you do other things. Simply add oven-fresh rolls and your favorite side for a nice meal.

9 bone-in chicken thighs (about 3-1/4 pounds)

1/2 teaspoon salt

1/4 teaspoon pepper

1-1/2 cups barbecue sauce

1/2 cup honey

2 teaspoons prepared mustard

2 teaspoons Worcestershire sauce

1/8 to 1/2 teaspoon hot pepper sauce

1 Sprinkle chicken with salt and pepper. Place on a broiler pan. Broil 4-5 in. from the heat for 3-4 minutes on each side or until lightly browned. Transfer to a 5-qt. slow cooker.

2 In a small bowl, combine the barbecue sauce, honey, mustard, Worcestershire sauce and pepper sauce. Pour over chicken; stir to coat. Cover and cook on low for 4-5 hours or until meat is tender.

Yield: 9 servings.

> **Crystallized honey.** Heating honey is the only way to dissolve the crystals that form when honey remains untouched for too long. Place the jar in warm water and stir until the crystals dissolve. Or set honey in a microwave-safe container and microwave on high, stirring every 30 seconds. Store honey in a tightly sealed container and in a cool dry place.

greek chicken dinner

PREP: 20 MIN. • **COOK: 5 HOURS**

Terri Christensen
Montague, Michigan

I got this recipe from my sister and my family really likes it a lot. It makes the house smell so good! The amount of garlic might seem high, but it's just right. You get every bit of the flavor but it doesn't overpower the other ingredients.

6 medium Yukon Gold potatoes, quartered

1 broiler/fryer chicken (3-1/2 pounds), cut up and skin removed

2 large onions, quartered

1 whole garlic bulb, separated and peeled

3 teaspoons dried oregano

1 teaspoon salt

3/4 teaspoon pepper

1/2 cup plus 1 tablespoon water, *divided*

1 tablespoon olive oil

4 teaspoons cornstarch

1 Place potatoes in a 5-qt. slow cooker. Add the chicken, onions and garlic. Combine the oregano, salt, pepper and 1/2 cup water; pour over chicken and vegetables. Drizzle with oil. Cover and cook on low for 5-6 hours or until chicken juices run clear and vegetables are tender.

2 Remove the chicken and the vegetables to a serving platter; keep warm. Strain cooking juices and skim fat; transfer to a small saucepan. Bring liquid to a boil. Combine cornstarch and remaining water until smooth. Gradually stir into the pan. Bring to a boil; cook and stir for 2 minutes or until thickened. Serve gravy with the chicken and vegetables.

Yield: 6 servings.

squash 'n' chicken stew

PREP: 15 MIN. • **COOK: 6 HOURS**

Taste of Home Test Kitchen

We created this satisfying stew that's colorful, full-flavored and family-friendly. Chicken thighs are slowly simmered with vegetables for tasty meal-in-one convenience.

2 pounds boneless skinless chicken thighs, cut into 1/2-inch pieces

1 can (28 ounces) stewed tomatoes, cut up

3 cups cubed butternut squash

2 medium green peppers, cut into 1/2-inch pieces

1 small onion, sliced and separated into rings

1 cup water

1 teaspoon salt

1 teaspoon ground cumin

1/2 teaspoon ground coriander

1/2 teaspoon pepper

2 tablespoons minced fresh parsley

Hot cooked couscous, optional

1 In a 5-qt. slow cooker, combine first 10 ingredients. Cover and cook on low for 6-7 hours or until no longer pink. Sprinkle with minced parsley. Serve with the couscous if desired.

Yield: 5 servings.

stuffed sweet peppers

PREP: 15 MIN. • COOK: 4 HOURS

Judy Earl
Sarasota, Florida

Italian sausage gives zest to the rice filling in these tender peppers I've often prepared over the years. When I was married in 1970, slow cookers were the rage. In our home, it's one appliance that's never gone out of style.

  3 medium sweet red peppers

  2 medium sweet yellow peppers

  1 jar (14 ounces) spaghetti sauce, *divided*

  3/4 pound Italian turkey sausage links

  3/4 cup uncooked instant rice

  1/2 cup crumbled feta cheese

  1/2 cup chopped onion

  1/4 cup chopped tomato

  1/4 cup minced fresh parsley

  2 tablespoons sliced ripe olives

  1/4 to 1/2 teaspoon garlic powder

  1/2 teaspoon salt

  1/2 teaspoon Italian seasoning

  1/2 teaspoon crushed red pepper flakes

1 Cut tops off peppers and remove seeds; set aside. Reserve 3/4 cup spaghetti sauce; pour the remaining sauce into a 5-qt. slow cooker.

2 In a large bowl, combine the sausage, rice, cheese, onion, tomato, parsley, olives, garlic powder, salt, Italian seasoning, red pepper flakes and reserved chopped peppers and spaghetti sauce. Spoon into peppers.

3 Transfer peppers to a 3-qt. slow cooker. Cover and cook on low for 4-5 hours or until peppers are tender.

Yield: 5 servings.

simple chicken stew

PREP: 20 MIN. • COOK: 6 HOURS

Amy Dulling
Rockwood, Tennessee

This comforting stew for two was one of my husband's experiments that turned out to be one of our favorite Sunday dinners.

  1 can (10-3/4 ounces) condensed cream of chicken soup, undiluted

  1 cup water

  1/2 pound boneless skinless chicken breasts, cut into cubes

  1 large potato, peeled and cut into 3/4-inch cubes

  2 medium carrots, cut into 1/4-inch slices

  1/2 cup sliced fresh mushrooms

  1/4 cup chopped onion

  1 teaspoon chicken bouillon granules

  1/4 teaspoon poultry seasoning

1 In a 3-qt. slow cooker, combine all ingredients. Cover and cook on low for 6-7 hours or until chicken is no longer pink and vegetables are tender.

Yield: 2 servings.

lemon chicken with gravy

PREP: 25 MIN. • COOK: 3 HOURS

Shona Germino
Casa Grande, Arizona

Chicken tenders are nicely seasoned with lovely lemon and thyme flavors in this recipe. They're especially tasty served alongside brown rice.

1 pound chicken tenderloins

1/4 cup chicken broth

3 tablespoons lemon juice

3 tablespoons butter, cubed

1 tablespoon grated lemon peel

2 large garlic cloves, peeled and sliced

1/2 teaspoon salt

1/2 teaspoon white pepper

2 tablespoons minced fresh parsley *or* 2 teaspoons dried parsley flakes

2 tablespoons minced fresh thyme *or* 2 teaspoons dried thyme

2 teaspoons cornstarch

2 teaspoons cold water

Hot cooked rice, optional

1 In a 1-1/2-qt. slow cooker, combine the first eight ingredients. Cover and cook on low for 2-1/2 hours. Add parsley and thyme; cover and cook 30 minutes longer or until chicken is no longer pink.

2 Remove chicken to a serving plate and keep warm. Transfer juices to a small saucepan. Combine cornstarch and water until smooth; add to juices. Bring to a boil; cook and stir for 2 minutes or until thickened. Serve with chicken and rice if desired.

Yield: 4 servings.

spicy meatballs with sauce

PREP: 30 MIN. • COOK: 5 HOURS

Rosanne Bergman
Alta Loma, California

I rely on ground turkey and Italian sausage to make my meatballs. Not only do they taste great, but they also cook to perfection in the slow cooker along with a homemade sauce.

1 egg, lightly beaten

3/4 cup crushed seasoned salad croutons

1/2 cup finely chopped onion

1/4 cup finely chopped green pepper

1 teaspoon garlic powder

1 teaspoon ground cumin

1 teaspoon dried oregano

1 teaspoon pepper

1 pound ground turkey

1 pound bulk Italian sausage

SAUCE:

3 tablespoons cornstarch

1 tablespoon sugar

3/4 cup beef broth

2 cans (28 ounces *each*) crushed tomatoes

3 medium carrots, diced

1 can (6 ounces) tomato paste

1 envelope onion soup mix

3 garlic cloves, minced

1 teaspoon dried basil

1/2 teaspoon crushed red pepper flakes

Hot cooked pasta

1 In a large bowl, combine the egg, croutons, onion, green pepper, garlic powder, cumin, oregano and pepper. Crumble turkey and sausage over mixture and mix well. Shape into 1-in. balls. Place in a 5-qt. slow cooker.

2 In a large bowl, combine the cornstarch, sugar and broth until smooth; stir in the tomatoes, carrots, tomato paste, soup mix, garlic, basil and pepper flakes. Pour over meatballs. Cover and cook on low for 5-6 hours or until meat is no longer pink. Serve with pasta.

Yield: 8 servings (1 cup sauce with 5 meatballs each).

Meaty Method. For meatballs to cook evenly, they need to be the same size. The easiest way to do this is by using a 1- or 1-1/2-inch cookie scoop. Scoop the meat mixture, level off the top, then gently roll into a ball. If you don't have a cookie scoop, then lightly pat meat mixture into a 1-in.-thick rectangle, cut into an equal number of squares as meatballs in the recipe, then gently roll each square.

pepper jack chicken

PREP: 20 MIN. • COOK: 5 HOURS

Linda Foreman
Locust Grove, Oklahoma

Simmer up a low-fat, delicious meal with just a few basic ingredients. Your family is sure to love this colorful medley with tender chicken and a zippy cheese sauce.

6 boneless skinless chicken breast halves
(5 ounces *each*), cut into chunks

1 *each* small green, sweet red and orange
pepper, cut into thin strips

1 can (10-3/4 ounces) condensed nacho
cheese soup, undiluted

1/2 cup chunky salsa

1/8 teaspoon chili powder

4-1/2 cups hot cooked rice

1 In a 3-qt. slow cooker, combine the chicken, peppers, soup, salsa and chili powder. Cover and cook on low for 5-6 hours or until chicken is no longer pink. Serve with rice.

Yield: 6 servings.

orange chicken with sweet potatoes

PREP: 25 MIN. • COOK: 3-1/2 HOURS

Vicki Smith
Okeechobee, Florida

Orange peel and pineapple juice lend a fruity flavor to this super chicken and sweet potato combo. Serve it over rice.

3 medium sweet potatoes, peeled and sliced

2/3 cup plus 3 tablespoons all-purpose flour,
divided

1 teaspoon *each*, salt, onion powder, ground
nutmeg, ground cinnamon and pepper

4 boneless skinless chicken breast halves
(5 ounces *each*)

2 tablespoons butter

1 can (10-3/4 ounces) condensed cream of
chicken soup, undiluted

3/4 cup unsweetened pineapple juice

2 teaspoons brown sugar

1 teaspoon grated orange peel

1/2 pound sliced fresh mushrooms

Hot cooked rice

1 Layer sweet potatoes in a 3-qt. slow cooker. In a large resealable plastic bag, combine 2/3 cup flour and seasonings; add chicken, one piece at a time, and shake to coat.

2 In a large skillet over medium heat, cook chicken in butter for 3 minutes on each side or until lightly browned. Arrange chicken over sweet potatoes.

3 Place remaining flour in a small bowl. Stir in the soup, pineapple juice, brown sugar and orange peel until blended. Add mushrooms; pour over chicken. Cover and cook on low for 3-1/2 to 4 hours or until a meat thermometer reads 170° and potatoes are tender. Serve with rice.

Yield: 4 servings.

italian shrimp 'n' pasta

PREP: 10 MIN. • COOK: 7-1/4 HOURS

Karen Scaglione
Nanuet, New York

This dish is always a hit! The shrimp, orzo, tomatoes and cayenne pepper remind me of a Creole favorite, but the Italian seasoning adds a different twist. The strips of chicken thighs stay nice and moist while cooking.

1 pound boneless skinless chicken thighs, cut into 2-inch x 1-inch strips

2 tablespoons canola oil

1 can (28 ounces) crushed tomatoes

2 celery ribs, chopped

1 medium green pepper, cut into 1-inch pieces

1 medium onion, coarsely chopped

2 garlic cloves, minced

1 tablespoon sugar

1/2 teaspoon salt

1/2 teaspoon Italian seasoning

1/8 to 1/4 teaspoon cayenne pepper

1 bay leaf

1/2 cup uncooked orzo pasta *or* other small pasta

1 pound cooked medium shrimp, peeled and deveined

1 In a large skillet, brown chicken in oil; transfer to a 3-qt. slow cooker. Stir in the next 10 ingredients. Cover and cook on low for 7-8 hours or until the chicken is no longer pink.

2 Discard bay leaf. Stir in pasta; cover and cook on high for 10-15 minutes or until pasta is tender. Stir in shrimp; cover and cook for 5 minutes longer or until it is heated through.

Yield: 6-8 servings.

harvest chicken with walnut gremolata

PREP: 25 MIN. • COOK: 5-1/4 HOURS

Patricia Harmon
Baden, Pennsylvania

This original recipe is based on a classic veal or lamb dish but made more simply in the slow cooker. To lighten up the recipe, I use fat-free chicken broth and remove the skin and excess fat from the chicken legs. It's an elegant dinner that always gets compliments.

1 medium butternut squash (about 3 pounds), peeled and cubed

1 can (14-1/2 ounces) diced tomatoes, drained

1 medium onion, chopped

1 celery rib, chopped

1/2 cup reduced-sodium chicken broth

1/4 cup white wine *or* additional reduced-sodium chicken broth

1 garlic clove, minced

1 teaspoon Italian seasoning

1/4 teaspoon coarsely ground pepper, *divided*

1/4 cup all-purpose flour

1 teaspoon seasoned salt

6 chicken drumsticks, skin removed

1 cup uncooked orzo pasta

GREMOLATA:

2 tablespoons finely chopped walnuts

2 tablespoons minced fresh parsley

1 garlic clove, minced

1 teaspoon grated lemon peel

1 In a 5-qt. slow cooker, combine butternut squash, tomatoes, onion, celery, broth, white wine, garlic, Italian seasoning and 1/8 teaspoon pepper.

2 In a large resealable plastic bag, combine the flour, seasoned salt and remaining pepper. Add chicken, a few pieces at a time, and shake to coat. Place chicken on top of vegetables. Cover and cook on low for 5 hours or until a meat thermometer reads 180°. Remove the chicken and keep it warm.

3 Stir orzo into vegetable mixture; cover and cook 15-20 minutes longer or until orzo is tender. Meanwhile, combine the gremolata ingredients.

4 Transfer vegetable mixture to a serving platter; top with chicken. Sprinkle chicken with gremolata.

Yield: 6 servings.

nostalgic chicken and dumplings

PREP: 20 MIN. • COOK: 5 HOURS

Brenda Edwards
Herford, Arizona

Enjoy old-fashioned goodness without all the fuss when you fix this supper in your slow cooker. It features tender chicken, wonderfully light dumplings and a full-flavored sauce.

6 bone-in chicken breast halves (10 ounces *each*), skin removed

2 whole cloves

1/2 cup frozen pearl onions, thawed

1 bay leaf

1 garlic clove, minced

1/2 teaspoon salt

1/2 teaspoon dried thyme

1/2 teaspoon dried marjoram

1/4 teaspoon pepper

1/2 cup reduced-sodium chicken broth

1/2 cup white wine *or* additional chicken broth

3 tablespoons cornstarch

1/4 cup cold water

1/2 teaspoon browning sauce, optional

1 cup reduced-fat biscuit/baking mix

6 tablespoons fat-free milk

1 tablespoon minced fresh parsley

1 Place the chicken in a 5-qt. slow cooker. Insert cloves into one onion; add to slow cooker. Add bay leaf and remaining onions. Sprinkle mixture with the garlic, salt, thyme, marjoram and pepper. Add the broth and wine. Cover and cook on low for 4-1/2 to 5 hours or until a meat thermometer reads 170°.

2 Remove chicken to a serving platter and keep warm. Discard cloves and bay leaf. In a small bowl, combine cornstarch, water and browning sauce if desired until smooth. Stir into slow cooker. Cover and cook on high until mixture reaches a simmer.

3 Meanwhile, combine the biscuit mix, milk and parsley. Drop by tablespoonfuls onto simmering liquid. Reduce heat to low; cover and cook for 20-25 minutes or until a toothpick inserted into dumplings comes out clean (do not lift cover while simmering). Serve dumplings and sauce with chicken.

Yield: 6 servings.

sweet pepper chicken

PREP: 10 MIN. • COOK: 4 HOURS

Ann Johnson
Dunn, North Carolina

Sweet red and green pepper strips add attractive color to this delicious chicken. Prepare it after lunch and it's ready by dinnertime.

6 bone-in chicken breast halves, skin removed

1 tablespoon canola oil

2 cups sliced fresh mushrooms

1 medium onion, halved and sliced

1 each medium green pepper and sweet red pepper, julienned

1 can (10-3/4 ounces) condensed cream of chicken soup, undiluted

1 can (10-3/4 ounces) condensed cream of mushroom soup, undiluted

Hot cooked rice

1 In a large skillet, brown chicken in oil on both sides. Transfer to a 5-qt. slow cooker. Top with mushrooms, onion and peppers. Combine the soups; pour over vegetables. Cover and cook on low for 4-5 hours or until a meat thermometer reads 170°. Serve with rice.

Yield: 6 servings.

citrus turkey roast

PREP: 15 MIN. • COOK: 5-1/4 HOURS

Kathy Kittell
Lenexa, Kansas

I was skeptical at first about fixing turkey in a slow cooker, but once I tasted this dish, I was hooked. With a little cornstarch to thicken the juices, the gravy is easily made.

1 frozen boneless turkey roast, thawed (3 pounds)

1 tablespoon garlic powder

1 tablespoon paprika

1 tablespoon olive oil

2 teaspoons Worcestershire sauce

1/2 teaspoon salt

1/2 teaspoon pepper

8 garlic cloves, peeled

1 cup chicken broth, *divided*

1/4 cup water

1/4 cup white wine *or* additional chicken broth

1/4 cup orange juice

1 tablespoon lemon juice

2 tablespoons cornstarch

1 Cut roast in half. Combine the garlic powder, paprika, oil, Worcestershire sauce, salt and pepper; rub over turkey. Place in a 5-qt. slow cooker. Add the garlic, 1/2 cup broth, water, wine or additional broth, orange juice and lemon juice. Cover and cook on low for 5-6 hours or until a meat thermometer reads 170°.

2 Remove turkey and keep warm. Discard garlic cloves. For gravy, combine cornstarch and remaining broth until smooth; stir into cooking juices. Cover and cook on high for 15 minutes or until thickened. Slice turkey; serve with gravy.

Yield: 12 servings.

chicken in sour cream sauce

PREP: 15 MIN. • COOK: 6 HOURS

Jane Carlovsky
Sebring, Florida

Tender chicken is deliciously dressed up in a flavorful cream sauce with fresh mushrooms. This is an excellent entree for your family or guests.

 1-1/2 teaspoons salt

 1/4 teaspoon pepper

 1/4 teaspoon paprika

 1/4 teaspoon lemon-pepper seasoning

 6 bone-in chicken breast halves, skin removed (7 ounces *each*)

 1 can (10-3/4 ounces) condensed cream of mushroom soup, undiluted

 1 cup (8 ounces) sour cream

 1/2 cup dry white wine *or* chicken broth

 1/2 pound fresh mushrooms, sliced

1 In a small bowl, combine the first four ingredients; rub over chicken. Place in a 3-qt. slow cooker. In a large bowl, combine the soup, sour cream, and wine; stir in mushrooms. Pour over chicken.

2 Cover and cook on low for 6-8 hours or until a meat thermometer reads 170°. Thicken the sauce if desired.

Yield: 6 servings.

sunday chicken supper

PREP: 15 MIN. • COOK: 6 HOURS

Ruthann Martin
Louisville, Ohio

This convenient slow cooker dish makes a hearty supper that's special any day of the week.

 2 small carrots, cut into 2-inch pieces

 1/2 medium onion, chopped

 1/2 celery rib, cut into 2-inch pieces

 1 cup cut fresh green beans (2-inch pieces)

 2 small red potatoes, halved

 2 bone-in chicken breast halves (7 ounces *each*), skin removed

 2 bacon strips, cooked and crumbled

 3/4 cup hot water

 1 teaspoon chicken bouillon granules

 1/4 teaspoon salt

 1/4 teaspoon dried thyme

 1/4 teaspoon dried basil

 Pinch pepper

1 In a 3-qt. slow cooker, layer the first seven ingredients in the order listed. Combine the water, bouillon, salt, thyme, basil and pepper; pour over the top. Do not stir. Cover and cook on low for 6-8 hours or until vegetables are tender and a meat thermometer reads 170°. Remove chicken and vegetables. Thicken cooking juices for gravy if desired.

Yield: 2 servings.

forgotten jambalaya

PREP: 35 MIN. • COOK: 4-1/4 HOURS

Cindi Coss
Coppell, Texas

During chilly months, I fix this jambalaya at least once a month. It's so easy...just chop the vegetables, dump everything in the slow cooker and forget it! Even my sons, who are picky about spicy things, like this dish.

- 1 can (14-1/2 ounces) diced tomatoes, undrained
- 1 can (14-1/2 ounces) beef *or* chicken broth
- 1 can (6 ounces) tomato paste
- 2 medium green peppers, chopped
- 1 medium onion, chopped
- 3 celery ribs, chopped
- 5 garlic cloves, minced
- 3 teaspoons dried parsley flakes
- 2 teaspoons dried basil
- 1-1/2 teaspoons dried oregano
- 1-1/4 teaspoons salt
- 1/2 teaspoon cayenne pepper
- 1/2 teaspoon hot pepper sauce
- 1 pound boneless skinless chicken breasts, cut into 1-inch cubes
- 1 pound smoked sausage, halved and cut into 1/4-inch slices
- 1/2 pound uncooked medium shrimp, peeled and deveined
- Hot cooked rice

1 In a 5-qt. slow cooker, combine the tomatoes, broth and tomato paste. Stir in the green peppers, onion, celery, garlic and seasonings. Stir in chicken and sausage.

2 Cover and cook on low for 4 hours or until chicken is tender. Stir in shrimp. Cover and cook 15-30 minutes longer or until shrimp turn pink. Serve with rice.

Yield: 11 servings.

1 Place the celery, carrots, onion and chicken in a 5-qt. slow cooker. In a small bowl, combine the soup, soup mix, thyme, pepper and tarragon; pour over chicken. Cover and cook on low for 4-5 hours or until a meat thermometer reads 170°.

2 Mix cornstarch and wine until smooth; stir into slow cooker. Cover on high for 30 minutes or until gravy is thickened. Serve with rice.

Yield: 6 servings.

citrus chicken

PREP: 15 MIN. • COOK: 4 HOURS

Barbara Easton
North Vancouver, British Columbia

Bold-flavored ingredients are tempered by the taste of oranges, creating a mouthwatering dish that's guaranteed to impress.

2 medium oranges, cut into wedges

1 medium green pepper, chopped

1 broiler/fryer chicken (3 to 4 pounds), cut up and skin removed

1 cup orange juice

1/2 cup chili sauce

2 tablespoons soy sauce

1 tablespoon molasses

1 teaspoon ground mustard

1 teaspoon minced garlic

1/4 teaspoon pepper

Hot cooked rice

1 Place oranges and green pepper in a 5-qt. slow cooker coated with cooking spray. Top with chicken. Combine the remaining ingredients; pour over chicken. Cover and cook on low for 4-5 hours or until chicken juices run clear. Serve with rice.

Yield: 4 servings.

saucy chicken with veggies and rice

PREP: 15 MIN. • COOK: 4-1/2 HOURS

Teri Lindquist
Gurnee, Illinois

I'm proud to share this recipe. I created it many years ago for a slow cooker contest and won first place! It's rich and flavorful, yet so easy.

3 cups sliced celery

3 cups sliced fresh carrots

2 cups sliced onion

6 boneless skinless chicken breast halves (5 ounces *each*)

1 can (10-3/4 ounces) condensed cream of mushroom soup, undiluted

1 envelope onion soup mix

1 teaspoon dried thyme

1 teaspoon pepper

1/2 teaspoon dried tarragon

2 tablespoons cornstarch

1/3 cup white wine *or* chicken broth

Hot cooked rice

chicken cacciatore

PREP: 20 MIN. • COOK: 4 HOURS

Denise Hollebeke
Penhold, Alberta

Here's an all-time favorite Italian dish made easy in the slow cooker! Dried herbs and fresh garlic give it an aromatic flavor, and green pepper, sliced mushrooms and diced tomatoes round out the juicy chicken entree.

   1/3 cup all-purpose flour

   1 broiler/fryer chicken (3 to 4 pounds), cut up

   2 tablespoons canola oil

   2 medium onions, cut into wedges

   1 medium green pepper, cut into strips

   1 jar (6 ounces) sliced mushrooms, drained

   1 can (14-1/2 ounces) diced tomatoes, undrained

   2 garlic cloves, minced

   1/2 teaspoon salt

   1/2 teaspoon dried oregano

   1/4 teaspoon dried basil

   1/2 cup shredded Parmesan cheese

1 Place flour in a large resealable plastic bag. Add chicken, a few pieces at a time, and shake to coat. In a large skillet, brown chicken in oil on all sides.

2 Transfer to a 5-qt. slow cooker. Top with onions, green pepper and mushrooms. In a small bowl, combine the tomatoes, garlic, salt, oregano and basil; pour over the vegetables. Cover and cook on low for 4-5 hours or until chicken juices run clear and the vegetables are tender. Serve with Parmesan cheese.

Yield: 6 servings.

fruited chicken

PREP: 10 MIN. • COOK: 4 HOURS

Mirien Church
Aurora, Colorado

*I've worked full-time for more than 30 years, and
this super slow cooker recipe has been a lifesaver. It
cooks while I'm away and smells heavenly when I
walk in the door in the evening.*

  1 large onion, sliced

  6 boneless skinless chicken breast halves
  (6 ounces *each*)

  1/3 cup orange juice

  2 tablespoons soy sauce

  2 tablespoons Worcestershire sauce

  2 tablespoons Dijon mustard

  1 tablespoon grated orange peel

  2 garlic cloves, minced

  1/2 cup chopped dried apricots

  1/2 cup dried cranberries

  Hot cooked rice

1 Place onion and chicken in a 5-qt. slow
  cooker. In a small bowl, combine the
  orange juice, soy sauce, Worcestershire
  sauce, mustard, orange peel and garlic;
  pour over chicken. Sprinkle with apricots
  and cranberries. Cover and cook on low for
  4-5 hours or until a meat thermometer
  reads 170°. Serve with rice.

Yield: 6 servings.

tender chicken dinner

PREP: 10 MIN. • COOK: 5-1/4 HOURS

Wanda Sanner
Amarillo, Texas

This all-in-one poultry dinner is quick to assemble and provides lots of family appeal.

4 boneless skinless chicken breast halves
(4 ounces *each*)

1 can (14-1/2 ounces) chicken broth

1 can (14-1/2 ounces) chicken gravy

2 cups sliced peeled potatoes

1 package (16 ounces) frozen sliced
carrots, thawed

1 package (16 ounces) frozen cut green
beans, thawed

1 teaspoon pepper

2 tablespoons cornstarch

1/3 cup cold water

1 cup french-fried onions

1 Place chicken in a 5-qt. slow cooker.
Add broth, gravy, vegetables and
pepper. Cover and cook on low for
5 to 5-1/2 hours or until chicken juices
run clear.

2 Mix cornstarch and water until smooth;
stir into cooking juices. Sprinkle with
onions. Cover and cook on high for
15 minutes or until thickened.

Yield: 4 servings.

lemon chicken breasts

PREP: 20 MIN. • COOK: 4 HOURS

Kathy Evans
Lacey, Washington

*Dijon mustard, rosemary and lemon juice season
chicken breasts wonderfully well in this dish.*

6 boneless skinless chicken breast halves
(5 ounces *each*)

1 cup chicken broth, *divided*

1/4 cup lemon juice

3 tablespoons Dijon mustard

3 garlic cloves, minced

2 tablespoons butter, melted

1/4 teaspoon dried rosemary, crushed

3 tablespoons cornstarch

Hot cooked rice

1/2 cup slivered almonds, toasted

3 tablespoons minced fresh parsley

1 Place chicken in a 3-qt. slow cooker. In
a small bowl, combine 3/4 cup broth,
lemon juice, mustard, garlic, butter and
rosemary; pour over chicken. Cover and
cook on low for 4-5 hours or until a meat
thermometer reads 170°. Remove chicken;
keep warm.

2 Skim fat from cooking juices; transfer to
a small saucepan. Bring liquid to a boil.
Combine cornstarch and remaining broth
until smooth. Gradually stir into the pan.
Bring to a boil; cook and stir for 2 minutes
or until thickened. Serve chicken with rice
and sauce. Sprinkle with almonds and
minced parsley.

Yield: 6 servings.

honey pineapple chicken

PREP: 15 MIN. • COOK: 3 HOURS

Carol Gillespie
Chambersburg, Pennsylvania

Sweet pineapple and salty soy sauce season this flavorful chicken dish that serves a crowd. I adapted the recipe for my slow cooker because it's so easy to do the preparation hours in advance and let it simmer all day.

  3 pounds boneless skinless chicken breast halves

  2 tablespoons canola oil

  1 can (8 ounces) unsweetened crushed pineapple, undrained

  1 cup packed brown sugar

  1/2 cup honey

  1/3 cup lemon juice

  1/4 cup butter, melted

  2 tablespoons prepared mustard

  2 teaspoons soy sauce

1 In a large skillet, brown chicken in oil in batches on both sides; transfer to a 5-qt. slow cooker. Combine the remaining ingredients; pour over chicken. Cover and cook on low for 3-4 hours or until a meat thermometer reads 170°.

2 Strain pan juices, reserving pineapple. Serve pineapple with the chicken.

Yield: 12 servings.

apricot-orange salsa chicken

PREP: 10 MIN. • COOK: 2-1/2 HOURS

LaDonna Reed
Ponca City, Oklahoma

This easy entree is just five ingredients away! Sweet orange juice and apricot preserves blend perfectly with zippy salsa in this dish. Keep the heat to your liking with mild, medium or hot salsa.

  3/4 cup salsa

  1/3 cup apricot preserves

  1/4 cup orange juice

  2 boneless skinless chicken breast halves (5 ounces *each*)

  1 cup hot cooked rice

1 In a small bowl, combine the salsa, apricot preserves and orange juice. In a 1-1/2-qt. slow cooker coated with cooking spray, layer 1/3 cup salsa mixture and a chicken breast. Repeat layers. Top with remaining salsa.

2 Cover and cook on low for 2-1/2 to 3 hours or until tender and a meat thermometer reads 170°. If desired, thicken pan juices. Serve with rice.

Yield: 2 servings.

fiesta chicken burritos

PREP: 30 MIN. • COOK: 4-1/4 HOURS

Margaret Latta
Paducah, Kentucky

Looking for some heat with supper but still want a cool kitchen? Try these slow-cooked burritos with a spicy touch the whole family will love! This is a simple recipe to double if you're catering to a crowd. And for those who prefer a spicier dish, add a teaspoon of cayenne pepper.

1-1/2 pounds boneless skinless chicken breasts

1 can (15-1/4 ounces) whole kernel corn, drained

1 can (15 ounces) black beans, rinsed and drained

1 can (10 ounces) diced tomatoes and green chilies, undrained

1 jalapeno pepper, seeded and finely chopped

3 tablespoons ground cumin

1 teaspoon salt

1 teaspoon paprika

1/2 teaspoon pepper

Dash cayenne pepper

Dash crushed red pepper flakes

1 package (8 ounces) reduced-fat cream cheese

8 flour tortillas (8 inches), warmed

Optional toppings: sour cream, shredded cheddar cheese, shredded lettuce and chopped tomatoes

1 Place chicken in a greased 4-qt. slow cooker. In a large bowl, combine the corn, beans, tomatoes, jalapeno and seasonings; pour over chicken. Cover and cook on low for 4-5 hours or until chicken is tender.

2 Remove chicken; cool slightly. Shred meat with two forks and return to the slow cooker. Stir in cream cheese. Cover and cook 15 minutes longer or until heated through.

3 Spoon 3/4 cup chicken mixture down the center of each tortilla; add toppings of your choice. Fold sides and ends over filling and roll up.

Yield: 8 servings.

EDITOR'S NOTE: When cutting hot peppers, disposable gloves are recommended. Avoid touching your face.

Chicken breast basics. Buying skinned and boned chicken breasts can cut up to 15 minutes off your cooking time. Save money by buying larger size packages, then rewrap individually or in family-size portions and freeze. Use an instant-read thermometer to check if the chicken breasts are thoroughly cooked. Chicken breasts should register 170°.

tropical bbq chicken

PREP: 15 MIN. • **COOK: 5 HOURS**

Yvonne McKim
Vancouver, Washington

*This is my favorite slow cooker recipe. The delicious,
slightly spicy sauce will win you over, too!*

  6 chicken leg quarters
  3/4 cup ketchup
  1/2 cup orange juice
  1/4 cup packed brown sugar
  1/4 cup red wine vinegar
  1/4 cup olive oil
  4 teaspoons minced fresh parsley
  2 teaspoons Worcestershire sauce
  1 teaspoon garlic salt
  1/2 teaspoon pepper

  2 tablespoons plus 2 teaspoons cornstarch
  1/4 cup water

1 With a sharp knife, cut leg quarters at the joints. Place chicken in a 4-qt. slow cooker. In a small bowl, combine the ketchup, orange juice, brown sugar, vinegar, oil, parsley, Worcestershire sauce, garlic salt and pepper; pour over chicken.

2 Cover and cook on low for 5-6 hours or until a meat thermometer reads 180°.

3 Remove chicken to a serving platter; keep warm. Skim fat from cooking juices; transfer 2 cups to a small saucepan. Bring liquid to a boil. Combine cornstarch and water until smooth. Gradually stir into the pan. Bring to a boil; cook and stir for 2 minutes or until thickened. Serve with chicken.

Yield: 12 servings.

sweet-and-sour chicken

PREP: 15 MIN. • COOK: 3-1/4 HOURS

Dorothy Hess
Hartwell, Georgia

No one will believe this dish is cooked in the slow cooker. Adding the onions, pineapple and snow peas later keeps them from becoming over-cooked.

1-1/4 pounds boneless skinless chicken breasts, cut into 1-inch strips

1 tablespoon canola oil

Salt and pepper to taste

1 can (8 ounces) pineapple chunks

1 can (8 ounces) sliced water chestnuts, drained

2 medium carrots, sliced

2 tablespoons soy sauce

4 teaspoons cornstarch

1 cup sweet-and-sour sauce

1/4 cup water

1-1/2 teaspoons ground ginger

3 green onions, cut into 1-inch pieces

1-1/2 cups fresh *or* frozen snow peas

Hot cooked rice

1 In a large skillet, saute chicken in oil for 4-5 minutes; drain. Sprinkle with salt and pepper. Drain pineapple, reserving juice; set pineapple aside. In a 5-qt. slow cooker, combine the chicken, water chestnuts, carrots, soy sauce and pineapple juice. Cover and cook on low for 3 hours or until chicken juices run clear.

2 Combine cornstarch, sweet-and-sour sauce, water and ginger until smooth. Stir into slow cooker. Add onions and reserved pineapple; cover and cook on high for 10- 15 minutes or until thickened. Add peas; cook 5 minutes longer. Serve with hot cooked rice.

Yield: 5 servings.

italian chicken

PREP: 20 MIN. • COOK: 3 HOURS

Judi Guizado
Rancho Cucamonga, California

*A friend gave me this easy, low-fat recipe years ago,
and I've tweaked the spices to my family's tastes.
I'm asked to make it at least twice a month.*

6 boneless skinless chicken breast halves
(about 8 ounces *each*)

1 can (14-1/2 ounces) Italian stewed
tomatoes

3/4 cup plus 3 tablespoons water, *divided*

2 tablespoons dried minced onion

2 teaspoons chicken bouillon granules

2 teaspoons chili powder

1/2 teaspoon dried tarragon

1/2 teaspoon Italian seasoning

1/4 teaspoon garlic powder

3 tablespoons cornstarch

Hot cooked rice

1 Place chicken in a 5-qt. slow cooker. In
a small bowl, combine the tomatoes,
3/4 cup water, onion, bouillon and
seasonings; pour over chicken. Cover and
cook on low for 3-4 hours or until a meat
thermometer reads 170°.

2 Transfer the chicken to a serving platter;
keep warm. Skim fat from cooking juices;
transfer to a small saucepan. Bring liquid
to a boil. Combine the cornstarch and
remaining water until smooth. Gradually
stir into the pan. Bring to a boil; cook and
stir for 2 minutes or until thickened. Serve
with the chicken and rice.

Yield: 6 servings.

zesty mexican chicken

PREP: 15 MIN. • COOK: 3-1/2 HOURS

Michelle Sheldon
Middletown, Delaware

A hint of lime juice helps tame the heat in this zesty, tender chicken with crunchy vegetables. Because it's all prepared in the slow cooker, you and your kitchen will stay cool, too! Serve it with a green salad for a quick meal.

> 6 boneless skinless chicken breast halves (4 ounces *each*)
>
> 1 can (14-1/2 ounces) diced tomatoes
>
> 1 large onion, chopped
>
> 1 medium green pepper, chopped
>
> 3 garlic cloves, minced
>
> 2 tablespoons lime juice
>
> 1 tablespoon hot pepper sauce
>
> 1/4 teaspoon salt
>
> 1/4 teaspoon pepper
>
> 3 cups hot cooked rice

1 Place chicken in a 3- or 4-qt. slow cooker coated with cooking spray. In a large bowl, combine the tomatoes, onion, green pepper, garlic, lime juice, pepper sauce, salt and pepper. Pour over chicken.

2 Cover and cook on low for 3-1/2 to 4 hours or until a meat thermometer reads 170°. Serve with rice.

Yield: 6 servings.

chicken mushroom stew

PREP: 20 MIN. • COOK: 4 HOURS

Kim Marie Van Rheenen
Mendota, Illinois

The flavors blend beautifully in this pot of chicken, vegetables and herbs as it simmers in a slow cooker. Folks with busy schedules will love this convenient recipe.

> 6 boneless skinless chicken breast halves (4 ounces *each*)
>
> 2 tablespoons canola oil, *divided*
>
> 8 ounces fresh mushrooms, sliced
>
> 1 medium onion, diced
>
> 3 cups diced zucchini
>
> 1 cup chopped green pepper
>
> 4 garlic cloves, minced
>
> 3 medium tomatoes, chopped
>
> 1 can (6 ounces) tomato paste
>
> 3/4 cup water
>
> 2 teaspoons *each* dried thyme, oregano, marjoram, and basil

1 Cut chicken into 1-in. cubes; brown in 1 tablespoon oil. Transfer to a 3-qt. slow cooker. Saute mushrooms, onion, zucchini and green pepper in remaining oil until crisp-tender; add minced garlic; cook 1 minute longer.

2 Place in slow cooker. Add the tomatoes, tomato paste, water and seasonings. Cover and cook on low for 4-5 hours or until the meat is no longer pink and vegetables are tender.

Yield: 6 servings.

prosciutto chicken cacciatore

PREP: 30 MIN. • COOK: 4 HOURS

Sandra Putnam
Corvallis, Montana

I tailored my mother's recipe for this hearty entree to take advantage of the slow cooker's convenience.

2 pounds boneless skinless chicken thighs

1-1/2 pounds boneless skinless chicken breast halves

1/2 cup all-purpose flour

1 teaspoon salt

1/4 teaspoon pepper

3 tablespoons olive oil

1 can (14-1/2 ounces) chicken broth

1 can (14-1/2 ounces) diced tomatoes, undrained

1 cup sliced fresh mushrooms

1 medium onion, chopped

1 package (3 ounces) thinly sliced prosciutto *or* deli ham, coarsely chopped

1 tablespoon diced pimientos

2 garlic cloves, minced

1/2 teaspoon Italian seasoning

Hot cooked linguine

Grated Parmesan cheese

1 Cut chicken into serving-size pieces. In a large resealable plastic bag, combine the flour, salt and pepper. Add chicken, a few pieces at a time, and shake to coat.

2 In a large skillet, brown chicken in oil in batches. Transfer to a 5-qt. slow cooker.

3 Stir in the broth, tomatoes, mushrooms, onion, prosciutto, pimientos, garlic and Italian seasoning. Cover and cook on low for 4 to 4-1/2 hours or until chicken juices run clear. Serve with a slotted spoon over linguine; sprinkle with cheese.

Yield: 6-8 servings.

p. 249

seafood & more

p. 242

p. 247

p. 248

egg and broccoli casserole

PREP: 10 MIN. • COOK: 3-1/2 HOURS

Janet Sliter
Kennewick, Washington

For years, I've prepared this egg casserole that's filled with the taste of broccoli and cheese.

3 cups (24 ounces) 4% cottage cheese

3 cups frozen chopped broccoli, thawed and drained

2 cups (8 ounces) shredded cheddar cheese

6 eggs, lightly beaten

1/3 cup all-purpose flour

1/4 cup butter, melted

3 tablespoons finely chopped onion

1/2 teaspoon salt

Additional shredded cheddar cheese, optional

1 In a large bowl, combine the first eight ingredients. Pour into a greased 3-qt. slow cooker. Cover and cook on high for 1 hour. Stir.

2 Reduce heat to low; cover and cook 2-1/2 to 3 hours longer or until a thermometer reads 160°. Sprinkle with cheese if desired.

Yield: 6 servings.

vegetarian tortilla lasagna

PREP: 20 MIN. • COOK: 3 HOURS

Connie McDowell
Greenwood, Delaware

You won't miss the meat in this savory delight. The layered main course is as tasty as it is impressive. Serve warm wedges alongside tortilla chips or a green salad.

1 can (14-1/2 ounces) diced tomatoes with basil, oregano and garlic

1 cup chunky salsa

1 can (6 ounces) tomato paste

1/2 teaspoon ground cumin

2 cans (15-1/2 ounces *each*) hominy, rinsed and drained

1 can (15 ounces) black beans, rinsed and drained

3 flour tortillas (10 inches)

2 cups (8 ounces) shredded Monterey Jack cheese

1/4 cup sliced ripe olives

1 Cut three 25-in. x 3-in. strips of heavy-duty foil; crisscross so they resemble spokes of a wheel. Place strips on the bottom and up the sides of a round 5-qt. slow cooker. Coat strips with cooking spray.

2 In a large bowl, combine the tomatoes, salsa, tomato paste and cumin. Stir in hominy and beans. Place one tortilla on the bottom of slow cooker. Top with a third of the hominy mixture and cheese. Repeat layers twice. Sprinkle with olives. Cover and cook on low for 3 to 3-1/2 hours or until heated through.

3 Using foil strips as handles, remove the lasagna to a platter. Let stand for 5 minutes before cutting into wedges.

Yield: 8 servings.

spicy seafood stew

PREP: 30 MIN. • COOK: 4-3/4 HOURS

Bonnie Marlow
Ottoville, Ohio

This zippy stew is very easy and quick to prepare. The hardest part is peeling and dicing the potatoes, and even that can be done the night before. Place the potatoes in water and store them in the refrigerator overnight to speed up assembly the next day.

2 pounds potatoes, peeled and diced

1 pound carrots, sliced

1 jar (26 ounces) spaghetti sauce

2 jars (6 ounces *each*) sliced mushrooms, drained

1-1/2 teaspoons ground turmeric

1-1/2 teaspoons minced garlic

1 teaspoon cayenne pepper

3/4 teaspoon salt

1-1/2 cups water

1 pound sea scallops

1 pound uncooked medium shrimp, peeled and deveined

1 In a 5-qt. slow cooker, combine the first eight ingredients. Cover and cook on low for 4-1/2 to 5 hours or until potatoes are tender.

2 Stir in the water, scallops and shrimp. Cover and cook for 15-20 minutes or until scallops are opaque and shrimp turn pink.

Yield: 9 servings.

red clam sauce

PREP: 25 MIN. • COOK: 3 HOURS

JoAnn Brown
LaTrobe, Pennsylvania

This recipe tastes like it's been slaved over all day. Instead, it cooks while you do other things. What a great way to jazz up pasta sauce.

    1 medium onion, chopped

    1 tablespoon canola oil

    2 garlic cloves, minced

    2 cans (6-1/2 ounces *each*) chopped clams, undrained

    1 can (14-1/2 ounces) diced tomatoes, undrained

    1 can (6 ounces) tomato paste

    1/4 cup minced fresh parsley

    1 bay leaf

    1 teaspoon sugar

    1 teaspoon dried basil

    1/2 teaspoon dried thyme

    6 ounces linguine, cooked and drained

1 In a small skillet, saute onion in oil until tender. Add garlic; cook 1 minute longer.

2 Transfer to a 1-1/2 – or 2-qt. slow cooker. Stir in the clams, tomatoes, tomato paste, parsley, bay leaf, sugar, basil and thyme. Cover and cook on low for 3-4 hours or until heated through. Discard bay leaf. Serve with linguine.

Yield: 4 servings.

sweet potato lentil stew

PREP: 5 MIN. • COOK: 5 HOURS

Heather Gray
Little Rock, Arkansas

Years ago, I fell in love with the spicy flavor and wonderful aroma of this hearty slow cooker recipe. You can serve the stew alone or as a topper for meat or poultry. It's great either way!

    4 cups vegetable broth

    3 cups sweet potatoes, peeled and cubed (about 1-1/4 pounds)

    1-1/2 cups dried lentils, rinsed

    3 medium carrots, cut into chunks

    1 medium onion, chopped

    4 garlic cloves, minced

    1/2 teaspoon ground cumin

    1/4 teaspoon ground ginger

    1/4 teaspoon cayenne pepper

    1/4 cup minced fresh cilantro

    1/4 teaspoon salt

1 In a 3-qt. slow cooker, combine the first nine ingredients. Cover and cook on low for 5-6 hours or until vegetables are tender. Stir in cilantro and salt.

Yield: 6 servings.

lamb with orzo

PREP: 30 MIN. • COOK: 8 – 10 HOURS

Dan Kelmenson
West Bloomfield, Michigan

Served over fresh spinach and sprinkled with feta cheese, this will leave everyone wanting seconds.

1 boneless lamb shoulder roast (3 pounds)

3 tablespoons lemon juice

3 garlic cloves, minced

2 teaspoons dried oregano

2 teaspoons grated lemon peel

1/4 teaspoon salt

1 package (16 ounces) orzo pasta

2 packages (9 ounces *each*) fresh spinach, torn, *divided*

1 cup (4 ounces) crumbled feta cheese, *divided*

1 Cut roast in half. Place in a 5-qt. slow cooker. Drizzle with lemon juice. Sprinkle with the garlic, oregano, lemon peel and salt. Cover and cook on low for 8-10 hours or until meat is tender.

2 Cook orzo according to package directions. Remove lamb from slow cooker. Shred meat with two forks; set aside and keep warm.

3 Skim fat from cooking juices if necessary; return 1 cup cooking juices to slow cooker. Add one package of spinach. Cook on high for 5-10 minutes or until spinach is wilted. Drain orzo; add to spinach mixture. Stir in reserved meat and 1/2 cup feta cheese.

4 To serve, arrange remaining fresh spinach on nine individual plates. Top with lamb mixture. Sprinkle each with remaining feta cheese.

Yield: 9 servings.

hunter's delight

PREP: 15 MIN. • COOK: 6 HOURS

Terry Paull
Eagle River, Wisconsin

This is a recipe our mom made often, and it's one of our all-time favorites.

1/2 pound sliced bacon, diced

2-1/2 pounds red potatoes, thinly sliced

2 medium onions, sliced

1-1/2 pounds boneless venison steak, cubed

2 cans (14-3/4 ounces *each*) cream-style corn

3 tablespoons Worcestershire sauce

1 teaspoon sugar

1/2 to 1 teaspoon seasoned salt

1 In a large skillet, cook bacon over medium heat until crisp; drain. Place potatoes and onions in a 5-qt. slow cooker. Top with venison and bacon.

2 In a large bowl, combine the corn, Worcestershire sauce, sugar and seasoned salt; pour over the top. Cover and cook on low for 6-8 hours or until meat and potatoes are tender.

Yield: 8 servings.

Temper the flavor of venison. If you have picky eaters in your family and want to cut the wild flavor of venison, simply sprinkle a tad of apple pie spice and black pepper to the meat. Venison cooked this way in a slow cooker will yield a taste very similar to that of beef.

venison meatballs

PREP: 30 MIN. • COOK: 4 HOURS

Geraldine Mennear
Mastic, New York

These meatballs are a savory blend of ground venison and pork sausage, with water chestnuts for crunch. This is my husband's favorite venison recipe. Even my co-workers, who normally don't like game meat, enjoy it.

1 egg, lightly beaten

1 cup soft bread crumbs

1 can (8 ounces) water chestnuts, drained and finely chopped

1/4 cup soy sauce

2 teaspoons ground ginger

1 garlic clove, minced

1 pound ground venison

1 pound bulk pork sausage

3 to 4 teaspoons canola oil, *divided*

1/2 pound fresh mushrooms, sliced

1 can (14-1/2 ounces) chicken broth

1-1/4 cups cold water, *divided*

3 tablespoons cornstarch

Hot cooked noodles

1 In a large bowl, combine the egg, bread crumbs, water chestnuts, soy sauce, ginger and garlic. Crumble the venison and sausage over the mixture and mix well. Shape into 1-in. balls. In a skillet over medium heat, brown meatballs in batches in 2 teaspoons oil, adding 1 teaspoon oil if needed. Transfer meatballs to a 3-qt. slow cooker.

2 In the same skillet, saute mushrooms in 1 teaspoon oil until tender. Stir in the broth and 1 cup cold water. Pour over the meatballs. Cover and cook on low for 4-5 hours or until a meat thermometer, inserted into a meatball, reads 160°.

3 Remove meatballs and mushrooms with a slotted spoon; keep warm. Strain cooking juices into a saucepan. Combine cornstarch and remaining water until smooth; add to saucepan. Bring to a boil; cook and stir for 2 minutes or until thickened. Serve over the meatballs, mushrooms and noodles.

Yield: 8-10 servings.

thai shrimp and rice

PREP: 30 MIN. • COOK: 3 HOURS 20 MIN.

Paula Marchesi
Lenhartsville, Pennsylvania

Raisins and coconut milk add a lovely hint of sweetness to this Thai dish. Your kitchen will be filled with the wonderful aroma of freshly grated lime peel and minced gingerroot as this cooks.

2 cans (14-1/2 ounces *each*) chicken broth

2 cups uncooked converted rice

1 large carrot, shredded

1 medium onion, chopped

1/2 cup *each* chopped sweet red and green pepper

1/2 cup water

1/2 cup coconut milk

1/3 cup lime juice

1/4 cup flaked coconut

1/4 cup *each* raisins and golden raisins

8 garlic cloves, minced

1 tablespoon grated lime peel

1 tablespoon minced fresh gingerroot

1 teaspoon salt

1 teaspoon *each* ground coriander and cumin

1/2 teaspoon cayenne pepper

1 pound cooked medium shrimp, peeled and deveined

1/2 cup fresh snow peas, cut into thin strips

1 In a 5-qt. slow cooker, combine the broth, rice, vegetables, water, milk, lime juice, coconut, raisins, garlic, lime peel and seasonings. Cover and cook on low for 3 hours or until rice is tender.

2 Stir in shrimp and peas. Cover and cook 20 minutes longer or until heated through.

Yield: 8 servings.

slow-cooked lamb chops

PREP: 10 MIN. • COOK: 4 HOURS

Sandra McKenzie
Braham, Minnesota

Chops are without a doubt the cut of lamb we like best. I simmer them on low for hours in a slow cooker. The aroma is irresistible, and they come out so tender they practically melt in your mouth!

1 medium onion, sliced

1 teaspoon dried oregano

1/2 teaspoon dried thyme

1/2 teaspoon garlic powder

1/4 teaspoon salt

1/8 teaspoon pepper

8 lamb loin chops (about 1-3/4 pounds)

2 garlic cloves, minced

1 Place onion in a 3-qt. slow cooker. Combine the oregano, thyme, garlic powder, salt and pepper; rub over the lamb chops. Place chops over onion. Top with garlic. Cover and cook on low for 4-6 hours or until the meat is tender.

Yield: 4 servings.

corn bread-topped frijoles

PREP: 20 MIN. • COOK: 3 HOURS

Suzanne Caldwell
Artesia, New Mexico

My family often requests this economical, slow-cooker favorite. It's loaded with fresh Southwestern flavors and is even good for comapny!

1 medium onion, chopped

1 medium green pepper, chopped

1 tablespoon canola oil

2 garlic cloves, minced

1 can (16 ounces) kidney beans, rinsed and drained

1 can (15 ounces) pinto beans, rinsed and drained

1 can (14-1/2 ounces) diced tomatoes, undrained

1 can (8 ounces) tomato sauce

1 teaspoon chili powder

1/2 teaspoon pepper

1/8 teaspoon hot pepper sauce

CORN BREAD TOPPING:

1 cup all-purpose flour

1 cup yellow cornmeal

1 tablespoon sugar

1-1/2 teaspoons baking powder

1/2 teaspoon salt

2 eggs, lightly beaten

1-1/4 cups fat-free milk

1 can (8-3/4 ounces) cream-style corn

3 tablespoons canola oil

1 In a large skillet, saute the onion and green pepper in oil until tender. Add garlic; cook 1 minute longer. Transfer to a greased 5-qt. slow cooker.

2 Stir in the beans, tomatoes, tomato sauce, chili powder, pepper and hot pepper sauce. Cover and cook on high for 1 hour.

3 In a large bowl, combine the flour, cornmeal, sugar, baking powder and salt. Combine the eggs, milk, corn and oil; add to dry ingredients and mix well. Spoon evenly over bean mixture.

4 Cover and cook on high 2 hours longer or until a toothpick inserted near the center of corn bread comes out clean.

Yield: 8 servings.

PREP: 25 MIN. • COOK: 3-1/2 HOURS

Laura Davister
Little Suamico, Wisconsin

This "veggie-licious" alternative to traditional lasagna makes use of slow-cooker convenience. I suggest using chunky spaghetti sauce.

3/4 cup meatless spaghetti sauce

1/2 cup sliced zucchini

1/2 cup shredded part-skim mozzarella cheese

3 tablespoons 1% cottage cheese

2 tablespoons grated Parmesan cheese

2 tablespoons beaten egg

1/2 teaspoon Italian seasoning

1/8 teaspoon garlic powder

2 no-cook lasagna noodles

4 cups fresh baby spinach

1/2 cup sliced fresh mushrooms

1 Spread 1 tablespoon spaghetti sauce in a 1-1/2-qt. slow cooker coated with cooking spray. Top with half of the zucchini. Combine the cheeses, egg, Italian seasoning and garlic powder; spoon a third over zucchini.

2 Break noodles into 1-in. pieces; sprinkle half over cheese mixture. Spread 1 tablespoon sauce over noodles. Top with half of the spinach and mushrooms. Repeat layers. Top with remaining cheese mixture and spaghetti sauce. Cover and cook on low for 3-1/2 to 4 hours or until noodles are tender.

Yield: 2 servings.

shrimp marinara

PREP: 30 MIN. • COOK: 3 HOURS 20 MIN.

Sue Mackey
Jackson, Wisconsin

This flavorful marinara sauce simmers for most of the day. Shortly before mealtime, I add cooked shrimp, which doesn't take too long to warm. Served over spaghetti, it makes a delicious dressed-up main dish.

1 can (14-1/2 ounces) Italian diced tomatoes, undrained

1 can (6 ounces) tomato paste

1/2 to 1 cup water

2 garlic cloves, minced

2 tablespoons minced fresh parsley

1 teaspoon salt

1 teaspoon dried oregano

1/2 teaspoon dried basil

1/4 teaspoon pepper

1 pound uncooked medium shrimp, peeled and deveined

1 pound spaghetti, cooked and drained

Shredded Parmesan cheese, optional

1 In a 3-qt. slow cooker, combine the first nine ingredients. Cover and cook on low for 3-4 hours.

2 Stir in shrimp. Cover and cook 20 minutes longer or just until shrimp turn pink. Serve with spaghetti. Sprinkle with cheese if desired.

Yield: 6 servings.

beef and lamb stew

PREP: 50 MIN. + MARINATING
COOK: 8-1/2 HOURS

Dennis Kuyper
Creston, Iowa

This stew includes lots of fresh garden vegetables and meat. I've made it for friends on several occasions, and they thought it was great and enjoyed the interesting combination of flavors. It's best served with brown rice or pumpkin fritters.

1/2 cup dry red wine *or* beef broth

1/2 cup olive oil

4 garlic cloves, minced, *divided*

1-1/2 teaspoons salt, *divided*

1-1/2 teaspoons dried thyme, *divided*

1-1/4 teaspoons dried marjoram, *divided*

3/4 teaspoon dried rosemary, crushed, *divided*

3/4 teaspoon pepper, *divided*

1 pound beef stew meat, cut into 1–inch cubes

1 pound lamb stew meat, cut into 1-inch cubes

10 small red potatoes, halved

1/2 pound medium fresh mushrooms, halved

2 medium onions, thinly sliced

2 cups fresh cauliflowerets

1 can (16 ounces) kidney beans, rinsed and drained

1-1/2 cups fresh green beans, trimmed and cut in half

3 medium carrots, cut into 1/2-inch slices

1 celery rib, thinly sliced

1 cup beef broth

2 tablespoons minced fresh parsley

2 teaspoons sugar

3 tablespoons cornstarch

1/4 cup cold water

6 cups cooked brown rice

1 In a large resealable plastic bag, combine the wine, oil, 2 minced garlic cloves, 1/2 teaspoon salt, 1 teaspoon thyme, 3/4 teaspoon marjoram, 1/2 teaspoon rosemary and 1/4 teaspoon pepper; add beef and lamb. Seal bag and turn to coat; refrigerate for 8 hours.

2 In a 5– or 6-qt. slow cooker, layer the potatoes, mushrooms, onions, cauliflower, kidney beans, green beans, carrots, and celery.

3 Drain and discard marinade. Place meats over vegetables. Combine the broth, parsley, sugar and remaining garlic, salt, thyme, marjoram, rosemary and pepper; pour over meats.

4 Cover and cook on low for 8-10 hours or until meat and vegetables are tender. Combine cornstarch and water until smooth; stir into stew. Cover and cook for 30 minutes longer or until thickened. Serve with rice.

Yield: 12 servings (3 quarts).

p. 259

p. 256

p. 263

p. 261

nacho hash brown casserole

PREP: 15 MIN. • COOK: 3-1/4 HOURS

Pat Habiger
Spearville, Kansas

This tasty slow cooker recipe will free up your oven and produce the best hash browns ever. Soft and super cheesy, they make a comforting side dish for meat or poultry.

  1 package (32 ounces) frozen cubed hash brown potatoes, thawed

  1 can (10-3/4 ounces) condensed cream of celery soup, undiluted

1 can (10-3/4 ounces) condensed nacho cheese soup, undiluted

1 large onion, finely chopped

1/3 cup butter, melted

1 cup (8 ounces) reduced-fat sour cream

1 In a 3-qt. slow cooker coated with cooking spray, combine the first five ingredients. Cover and cook on low for 3-4 hours or until potatoes are tender. Stir in sour cream. Cover and cook 15-30 minutes longer or until heated through.

Yield: 8 servings.

green beans and new potatoes

PREP: 15 MIN. • COOK: 6 HOURS

Ann Baker
Texarkana, Texas

This colorful side dish comes together in a pinch. The vegetables come out tender, and the onion soup mix and onion add lots of flavor to the broth.

- 1 pound fresh green beans, trimmed
- 1 pound small red potatoes, quartered
- 1/2 pound medium fresh mushrooms, halved
- 1/2 cup thinly sliced sweet onion
- 2 cans (14-1/2 ounces *each)* beef broth
- 2 tablespoons beefy onion soup mix
- 2 teaspoons Worcestershire sauce
- 1 teaspoon grated lemon peel
- 1/2 teaspoon salt
- 1/2 teaspoon pepper
- 1/4 teaspoon garlic powder

1 In a 5-qt. slow cooker, layer the green beans, potatoes, mushrooms and onion. In a small bowl, combine the remaining ingredients; pour over vegetables. Cover and cook on low for 6-7 hours or until vegetables are tender. Serve with a slotted spoon.

Yield: 10 servings.

Easy Entree. It's a snap to clean out your refrigerator and cut kitchen time! Simply turn Green Beans and New Potatoes into an entree. After the dish has simmered for 5 hours, stir in any cooked meats you have on hand. Chop up last night's chicken or pork and mix the pieces into the veggies for a fast dinner fix.

everything stuffing

PREP: 30 MIN. • COOK: 3 HOURS

Bette Votral
Bethlehem, Pennsylvania

My husband and father go crazy for this stuffing! It also freezes well so we can enjoy it even after Thanksgiving.

- 1/2 pound bulk Italian sausage
- 4 cups seasoned stuffing cubes
- 1-1/2 cups crushed corn bread stuffing
- 1/2 cup chopped toasted chestnuts *or* pecans
- 1/2 cup minced fresh parsley
- 1 tablespoon minced fresh sage *or* 1 teaspoon rubbed sage
- 1/8 teaspoon salt
- 1/8 teaspoon pepper
- 1-3/4 cups sliced baby portobello mushrooms
- 1 package (5 ounces) sliced fresh shiitake mushrooms
- 1 large onion, chopped
- 1 medium apple, peeled and chopped
- 1 celery rib, chopped
- 3 tablespoons butter
- 1 can (14-1/2 ounces) chicken broth

1 In a large skillet, cook sausage over medium heat until no longer pink; drain. Place in a large bowl. Stir in the stuffing cubes, corn bread stuffing, chestnuts, parsley, sage, salt and pepper.

2 In the same skillet, saute the mushrooms, onion, apple and celery in butter until tender. Stir into stuffing mixture. Add enough broth to reach desired moistness. Transfer to a 5-qt. slow cooker. Cover and cook on low for 3 hours, stirring once.

Yield: 9 servings.

creamed corn

PREP: 10 MIN. • COOK: 3 HOURS

Barbara Brizendine
Harrisonville, Missouri

Five ingredients are all you'll need for my popular dinner accompaniment. It's wonderful no matter what the occasion is. Try it on a barbecue buffet or holiday menu.

- 2 packages (one 16 ounces, one 10 ounces) frozen corn
- 1 package (8 ounces) cream cheese, softened and cubed
- 1/4 cup butter, cubed
- 1 tablespoon sugar
- 1/2 teaspoon salt

1 In a 3-qt. slow cooker coated with cooking spray, combine all ingredients. Cover and cook on low for 3 to 3-1/2 hours or until cheese is melted and corn is tender. Stir just before serving.

Yield: 5 servings.

corn and broccoli in cheese sauce

PREP: 10 MIN. • COOK: 3 HOURS

Joyce Johnson
Uniontown, Ohio

This dish is a standby. My daughter likes to add leftover ham to it. Save room in the oven by making this savory side in your slow cooker.

- 1 package (16 ounces) frozen corn, thawed
- 1 package (16 ounces) frozen broccoli florets, thawed
- 4 ounces reduced-fat process cheese (Velveeta), cubed
- 1/2 cup shredded cheddar cheese
- 1 can (10-1/4 ounces) reduced-fat reduced-sodium condensed cream of chicken soup, undiluted
- 1/4 cup fat-free milk

1 In a 4-qt. slow cooker, combine the corn, broccoli and cheeses. In a small bowl, combine soup and milk; pour over vegetable mixture. Cover and cook on low for 3-4 hours or until heated through. Stir before serving.

Yield: 8 servings.

italian spaghetti squash

PREP: 15 MIN. • COOK: 6-1/4 HOURS

Melissa Brooks
Sparta, Wisconsin

This is a unique and easy way to cook spaghetti squash. Be sure the squash is on the small or medium side so that it fits into the slow cooker after being cut in half.

- 1 medium spaghetti squash
- 1 cup sliced fresh mushrooms
- 1 can (14-1/2 ounces) diced tomatoes, undrained
- 1 teaspoon dried oregano
- 1 teaspoon salt
- 1/4 teaspoon pepper
- 3/4 cup shredded part-skim mozzarella cheese

1 Cut squash in half lengthwise; discard seeds. Place squash, cut side up, in a 6– or 7-qt. slow cooker. Layer with mushrooms, tomatoes, oregano, salt and pepper. Cover and cook on low for 6-8 hours or until squash is tender.

2 Sprinkle with cheese. Cover and cook for 15 minutes or until cheese is melted. When squash is cool enough to handle, use a fork to separate spaghetti squash strands.

Yield: 4 servings.

> **Oven Alternative.** You can also bake the squash. Cut it in half, and lay the pieces cut side down in a greased baking dish; bake at 350° for 45-60 minutes or until the shell is pierced easily with a fork. Top with the remaining ingredients and heat through.

ratatouille

PREP: 20 MIN. + STANDING
COOK: 3 HOURS

Jolene Walters
North Miami, Florida

Not only does this French-style recipe make a phenomenal side dish, but you can also serve it with sliced French bread for a warm appetizer. It's especially good in the summer with your garden-fresh vegetables.

1 large eggplant, peeled and cut into 1-inch cubes

2 teaspoons salt, *divided*

3 medium tomatoes, chopped

3 medium zucchini, halved lengthwise and sliced

2 medium onions, chopped

1 large green pepper, chopped

1 large sweet yellow pepper, chopped

1 can (6 ounces) pitted ripe olives, drained and chopped

1 can (6 ounces) tomato paste

1/2 cup minced fresh basil

2 garlic cloves, minced

1/2 teaspoon pepper

2 tablespoons olive oil

1 Place eggplant in a colander over a plate; sprinkle with 1 teaspoon salt and toss. Let stand for 30 minutes. Rinse and drain well. Transfer to a 5-qt. slow cooker coated with cooking spray.

2 Stir in the tomatoes, zucchini, onions, green and yellow peppers, olives, tomato paste, basil, garlic, pepper and remaining salt. Drizzle with oil. Cover and cook on high for 3-4 hours or until vegetables are tender.

Yield: 10 servings.

slow-cooked pork & beans

PREP: 25 MIN. • COOK: 6 HOURS

Sue Livermore
Detroit Lakes, Minnesota

Bacon adds subtle smokiness to this hearty side that's loaded with flavor. Serve it over rice for a tasty main dish.

1 package (1 pound) sliced bacon, chopped

1 cup chopped onion

2 cans (15 ounces *each*) pork and beans, undrained

1 can (16 ounces) kidney beans, rinsed and drained

1 can (15-1/4 ounces) lima beans, rinsed and drained

1 can (16 ounces) butter beans, rinsed and drained

1 can (15 ounces) black beans, rinsed and drained

1 cup packed brown sugar

1/2 cup cider vinegar

1 tablespoon molasses

2 teaspoons garlic powder

1/2 teaspoon ground mustard

1 In a large skillet, cook bacon and onion over medium heat until bacon is crisp. Remove to paper towels to drain.

2 In a 4-qt. slow cooker, combine remaining ingredients; stir in the bacon mixture. Cover and cook on low for 6-7 hours or until heated through.

Yield: 12 servings.

winter fruit compote

PREP: 10 MIN.
COOK: 1-1/4 HOURS + COOLING

Esther Chesney
Carthage, Missouri

Orange juice and raspberry vinegar add a wonderful touch to this no-fuss change-of-pace dish that features apricots and raisins. Walnuts add an earthy flavor.

1 package (12 ounces) fresh *or* frozen cranberries, thawed

2/3 cup packed brown sugar

1/4 cup orange juice concentrate

2 tablespoons raspberry vinegar

1/2 cup chopped dried apricots

1/2 cup golden raisins

1/2 cup chopped walnuts, toasted

1 In a 1-1/2-qt. slow cooker, combine the cranberries, brown sugar, orange juice concentrate and vinegar. Cover and cook on low for 1-1/4 to 1-3/4 hours or until cranberries pop and mixture is thickened.

2 Turn off heat; stir in the apricots, raisins and walnuts. Cool to room temperature. Serve or refrigerate.

Yield: 2-1/2 cups.

Company's coming. Save time when hosting guests by preparing this lovely compote up to a week in advance. Simply store it, covered, in the refrigerator until your gathering. It makes a great addition to turkey, chicken or pork—particularly during the busy holiday season.

---

hot fruit salad

PREP: 10 MIN. • COOK: 2 HOURS

Debbie Kimbrough
Lexington, Mississippi

This comforting side dish is convenient to make in the slow cooker when your oven and stovetop are occupied with other dishes. The warm medley can also be served over sliced pound cake for dessert.

3/4 cup sugar

1/2 cup butter, melted

1/4 teaspoon ground cinnamon

1/4 teaspoon ground nutmeg

1/8 teaspoon salt

2 cans (15-1/4 ounces *each*) sliced peaches, drained

2 cans (15-1/4 ounces *each*) sliced pears, undrained

1 jar (23 ounces) chunky applesauce

1/2 cup dried apricots, chopped

1/4 cup dried cranberries

1 In a 3-qt. slow cooker, combine the sugar, butter, cinnamon, nutmeg and salt. Stir in the remaining ingredients. Cover and cook on high for 2 hours or until heated through.

Yield: 10 servings.

ranch beans

PREP: 10 MIN. • COOK: 3 HOURS

Barbara Gordon
Roswell, Georgia

This sweet and tangy side dish uses lots of convenient canned goods, so it's a snap to throw together. Best of all, you can use whatever beans you have on hand or whichever variety your family enjoys most. The recipe was sent to me by a friend, and I like to share it at group picnics.

1 can (16 ounces) kidney beans, rinsed and drained

1 can (15-3/4 ounces) pork and beans, undrained

1 can (15 ounces) lima beans, rinsed and drained

1 can (14-1/2 ounces) cut green beans, drained

1 bottle (12 ounces) chili sauce

3/4 cup packed brown sugar

1 small onion, chopped

1 In a 3-qt. slow cooker, combine all ingredients. Cover and cook on high for 3-4 hours or until heated through.

Yield: 8-10 servings.

Easy Adjustment. Ranch Beans can also be prepared in the oven. Simply assemble the dish as directed. Cover and bake the beans at 350° for 40 minutes. Remover the cover, and continue cooking for an additional 10 minutes or until beans are heated through and bubbly.

coconut-pecan sweet potatoes

PREP: 20 MIN. • COOK: 5 HOURS

Rebecca Clark
Warrior, Alabama

It's great to be able to make a tempting sweet potato dish well ahead by putting it in the slow cooker. This tasty recipe includes sweet coconut and crunchy pecans. It's yummy!

2 pounds sweet potatoes, peeled and cut into 3/4-inch cubes

1/4 cup packed brown sugar

2 tablespoons flaked coconut

2 tablespoons chopped pecans, toasted

1 teaspoon vanilla extract

1/2 teaspoon salt

1/4 teaspoon ground cinnamon

1 tablespoon butter, melted

1/2 cup miniature marshmallows

1 Place sweet potatoes in a 3-qt. slow cooker coated with cooking spray. In a small bowl combine the brown sugar, coconut, pecans, vanilla, salt and cinnamon; sprinkle over sweet potatoes. Drizzle with butter.

2 Cover and cook on low for 5-6 hours or until potatoes are tender, sprinkling with marshmallows during last 5 minutes of cooking time.

Yield: 6 servings.

comforting slow-cooked mac 'n' cheese

PREP: 25 MIN. • COOK: 2-3/4 HOURS

Shelby Molina
Whitewater, Wisconsin

Mac 'n' Cheese...the words alone are enough to make most mouths water. This recipe is a clear example of comfort food at its finest: it's rich, hearty and extra-cheesy. And because it's made in the slow cooker, it's also extremely easy.

> 2 cups uncooked elbow macaroni
>
> 1 can (12 ounces) reduced-fat evaporated milk
>
> 1-1/2 cups fat-free milk
>
> 1/3 cup egg substitute
>
> 1 tablespoon butter, melted
>
> 8 ounces reduced-fat process cheese (Velveeta), cubed
>
> 2 cups (8 ounces) shredded sharp cheddar cheese, *divided*

1 Cook macaroni according to package directions; drain and rinse in cold water. In a large bowl, combine the evaporated milk, milk, egg substitute and butter. Stir in the process cheese, 1-1/2 cups sharp cheddar cheese and macaroni.

2 Transfer to a 3-qt. slow cooker coated with cooking spray. Cover and cook on low for 2-3/4 to 3 hours or until center is set, stirring once. Sprinkle with remaining sharp cheddar cheese.

slow-cooked creamy rice

PREP: 25 MIN. • COOK: 2-1/2 HOURS

Laura Crane
Leetonia, Ohio

This wonderful side dish goes well with any meat stew. I use fresh herbs I have on hand along with the chopped parsley to add even more flavor.

- 3 cups cooked rice
- 2 eggs, lightly beaten
- 1 can (12 ounces) evaporated milk
- 1 cup (4 ounces) shredded Swiss cheese
- 1 cup (4 ounces) shredded cheddar cheese
- 1 medium onion, chopped
- 1/2 cup minced fresh parsley
- 6 tablespoons water
- 2 tablespoons canola oil
- 1 garlic clove, minced
- 1-1/2 teaspoons salt
- 1/4 teaspoon pepper

1 In a 3-qt. slow cooker, combine all ingredients. Cover and cook on low for 2-1/2 to 3 hours or until a thermometer reads 160°.

Yield: 8 servings.

creamy red potatoes

PREP: 5 MIN. • COOK: 5 HOURS

Elaine Ryan
Holley, New York

I put my slow cooker to work to fix these saucy spuds. The side dish features cubed red potatoes that are cooked in a creamy coating until tender. Be sure to stir the mixture before serving to help the sauce thicken.

- 7 cups cubed uncooked red potatoes
- 1 cup (8 ounces) 4% cottage cheese
- 1/2 cup sour cream
- 1/2 cup cubed process cheese (Velveeta)
- 1 tablespoon dried minced onion
- 2 garlic cloves, minced
- 1/2 teaspoon salt
- Paprika and minced chives, optional

1 Place the potatoes in a 3-qt. slow cooker. In a blender, puree cottage cheese and sour cream until smooth. Transfer to a large bowl; stir in the process cheese, onion, garlic and salt. Pour over potatoes and mix well.

2 Cover and cook on low for 5-6 hours or until potatoes are tender. Stir well before serving. Garnish with paprika and chives if desired.

Yield: 8 servings.

p. 295

snacks & sweets

p. 269

p. 275

p. 289

reuben spread

PREP: 5 MIN. • COOK: 3 HOURS

Pam Rohr
Troy, Ohio

You'll need only five ingredients to stir up this hearty dip that tastes like a Reuben sandwich. It's requested at all the gatherings we attend.

2-1/2 cups cubed cooked corned beef

1 jar (16 ounces) sauerkraut, rinsed and well drained

2 cups (8 ounces) shredded Swiss cheese

2 cups (8 ounces) shredded cheddar cheese

1 cup mayonnaise

Snack rye bread

1 In a 3-qt. slow cooker, combine the first five ingredients. Cover and cook on low for 3 hours, stirring occasionally. Serve warm with rye bread.

Yield: about 5 cups.

caramel hot chocolate

PREP: 5 MIN. • COOK: 4 HOURS

Maureen Mitchell
Calgary, Alberta

Perfect on a chilly day, this recipe makes homemade hot chocolate even more luscious thanks to the addition of a caramel candy bar.

4 cups nonfat dry milk powder

3/4 cup baking cocoa

1/2 cup sugar

8 cups water

1 Caramello candy bar (2.7 ounces), chopped

Whipped cream and grated chocolate, optional

1 In a 3-qt. slow cooker, combine the milk powder, cocoa and sugar; gradually whisk in water until smooth. Cover and cook on low for 4 hours or until hot.

2 Add candy bar; stir until melted. Garnish with whipped cream and grated chocolate if desired.

Yield: about 2 quarts.

party meatballs

PREP: 10 MIN. • **COOK: 3 HOURS**

Debbie Paulsen
Apollo Beach, Florida

Meatballs are always great to serve at parties. This is an easy twist on the usual recipe, and it's very fast to make.

1 package (32 ounces) frozen fully cooked homestyle meatballs, thawed

1 bottle (14 ounces) ketchup

1/4 cup A.1. steak sauce

1 tablespoon minced garlic

1 teaspoon Dijon mustard

1 Place the meatballs in a 3-qt. slow cooker. In a small bowl, combine the ketchup, steak sauce, garlic and mustard. Pour over the meatballs. Cover and cook on low for 3-4 hours or until the meatballs are heated through.

Yield: about 6 dozen.

hot chili cheese dip

PREP: 20 MIN. • COOK: 4 HOURS

Jeanie Carrigan
Madera, California

I simplify party preparation by using my slow cooker to create this thick cheesy dip. Your guests won't believe how good it is.

1 medium onion, finely chopped

2 teaspoons canola oil

2 garlic cloves, minced

2 cans (15 ounces *each*) chili without beans

2 cups salsa

2 packages (3 ounces *each*) cream cheese, cubed

2 cans (2-1/4 ounces *each*) sliced ripe olives, drained

Tortilla chips

1 In a small skillet, saute onion in oil until tender. Add garlic; cook 1 minute longer.

2 Transfer to a 3-qt. slow cooker. Stir in the chili, salsa, cream cheese and olives. Cover and cook on low for 4 hours or until heated through, stirring occasionally. Stir before serving with tortilla chips.

Yield: 6 cups.

wassail bowl punch

PREP: 10 MIN. • COOK: 1 HOUR

Margaret Harms
Jenkins, Kentucky

All ages will enjoy this warming punch. The blend of spice, fruit and citrus flavors is scrumptious. You can assemble it before heading out for a winter activity and sip away the chill when you return. It's ready whenever you are.

4 cups hot brewed tea

4 cups cranberry juice

4 cups unsweetened apple juice

2 cups orange juice

1 cup sugar

3/4 cup lemon juice

3 cinnamon sticks (3 inches)

12 whole cloves

1 In a 5-qt. slow cooker, combine the first six ingredients. Place the cinnamon sticks and cloves on a double thickness of cheesecloth; bring up corners of cloth and tie with string to form a bag. Add to slow cooker. Cover and cook on high for 1 hour or until punch begins to boil. Discard spice bag. Serve warm.

Yield: 3-1/2 quarts.

chipotle ham 'n' cheese dip

PREP: 15 MIN. • COOK: 1 HOUR

Lisa Renshaw
Kansas City, Missouri

During the busy holiday season, you just can't beat convenient slow cooker recipes like this tasty snack that let you visit with guests instead of working away in the kitchen.

2 packages (8 ounces *each*) cream cheese, cubed

1 can (12 ounces) evaporated milk

8 ounces Gouda cheese, shredded

1 cup (4 ounces) shredded cheddar cheese

2 tablespoons chopped chipotle pepper in adobo sauce

1 teaspoon ground cumin

2 cups diced fully cooked ham

Fresh vegetables *or* tortilla chips

1 In a 3-qt. slow cooker, combine the first six ingredients. Cover and cook on low for 40 minutes.

2 Stir in ham; cook 20 minutes longer or until heated through. Serve warm with vegetables or tortilla chips.

Yield: 7 cups.

gingered pears

PREP: 35 MIN. • **COOK: 4 HOURS**

Catherine Mueller
St. Paul, Minnesota

My slow cooker allows me to serve this heart-warming dessert without much effort. Topped with caramel sauce, these tender pears feature a surprise filling of nuts and brown sugar.

- 1/2 cup finely chopped crystallized ginger
- 1/4 cup packed brown sugar
- 1/4 cup chopped pecans
- 1-1/2 teaspoons grated lemon peel
- 6 medium Bartlett *or* D'Anjou pears
- 2 tablespoons butter, cubed
- Vanilla ice cream and caramel ice cream topping, optional

1 In a small bowl, combine the ginger, brown sugar, pecans and lemon peel. Using a melon baller or long-handled spoon, core pears to within 1/4-in. of bottom. Spoon ginger mixture into the center of each.

2 Place pears upright in a 5-qt. slow cooker. Top each with butter. Cover and cook on low for 4-5 hours or until pears are tender. Serve with ice cream and caramel topping if desired.

Yield: 6 servings.

> **Core values.** To core a fresh pear, insert an apple corer into the bottom of the pear to within 1 inch of its top. Twist the corer to cut around the core, then slowly pull the corer out of the pear to remove the core. If you don't have an apple corer, use a melon baller, long-handled spoon, sharp knife or vegetable peeler to cut the core from the bottom of the pear.

cheesy pizza fondue

PREP/TOTAL TIME: 30 MIN.

Julie Barwick
Mansfield, Ohio

While I was growing up, I would sit for hours reading cookbooks from cover to cover. I've carried that love of cooking with me through the years. I found this recipe when we lived in Wisconsin.

- 1/2 pound ground beef
- 1 medium onion, chopped
- 2 cans (15 ounces *each*) pizza sauce
- 1-1/2 teaspoons dried basil *or* dried oregano
- 1/4 teaspoon garlic powder
- 2-1/2 cups (10 ounces) shredded sharp cheddar cheese
- 1 cup (4 ounces) shredded part-skim mozzarella cheese
- Breadsticks

1 In a large saucepan, cook beef and onion over medium heat until meat is no longer pink; drain. Stir in the pizza sauce, basil and garlic powder. Reduce heat to low. Add cheeses; stir until melted.

2 Transfer to a small fondue pot or 1-1/2-qt. slow cooker; keep warm. Serve with breadsticks.

Yield: about 5 cups.

hot crab spread

PREP: 15 MIN. • COOK: 1-1/2 HOURS

Christine Woody
Cottage Grove, Oregon

After my mother and sister described the hot crab sandwiches they had eaten at a San Francisco restaurant, I developed this recipe. It's become a family favorite, especially during vacations to the Oregon coast, where we can catch fresh crabs.

1-1/2 cups chopped green onions

1 tablespoon butter

6 garlic cloves, minced

1 tablespoon mayonnaise

8 cups (32 ounces) shredded Monterey Jack cheese

4 cans (6 ounces *each*) crabmeat, drained, flaked and cartilage removed

Assorted crackers

1 In a large skillet, saute onions in butter until tender. Add garlic, cook 1 minute longer. Transfer to a 3-qt. slow cooker; add mayonnaise. Stir in cheese. Cover and cook on low for 30 minutes or until cheese is melted, stirring occasionally.

2 Stir in crab; cover and cook 1 hour longer or until heated through. Serve spread warm with crackers.

Yield: 6 cups.

warm broccoli cheese dip

PREP: 15 MIN. • COOK: 2-1/2 HOURS

Barbara Maiol
Conyers, Georgia

When my family gathers for a party, this flavorful, creamy dip is served. Everyone loves its zip from the jalapeno pepper and the crunch of the broccoli.

2 jars (8 ounces *each*) process cheese sauce

1 can (10-3/4 ounces) condensed cream of chicken soup, undiluted

3 cups frozen chopped broccoli, thawed and drained

1/2 pound fresh mushrooms, chopped

2 tablespoons chopped seeded jalapeno pepper

Assorted fresh vegetables

1 In a 1-1/2-qt. slow cooker, combine the cheese sauce and soup. Cover and cook on low for 30 minutes or until cheese is melted, stirring occasionally. Stir in the broccoli, mushrooms and jalapeno. Cover and cook on low for 2 hours or until heated through. Serve with vegetables.

Yield: 5-1/2 cups.

EDITOR'S NOTE: When cutting hot peppers, disposable gloves are recommended. Avoid touching your face.

> **Jazz it up.** Want to bring a little extra kick to Warm Broccoli Cheese Dip? Simply stir in a few drops of hot pepper sauce or even a tablespoon or two of your favorite salsa. When you add the veggies, you can also consider stirring in a dash of dried red pepper flakes.

hot fudge cake

PREP: 20 MIN. • COOK: 4 HOURS

Marleen Adkins
Placentia, California

A cake baked in a slow cooker may seem unusual, but chocolaty smiles around the table prove how tasty it is. Sometimes, for a change of pace, I like to substitute butterscotch chips for chocolate.

- 1-3/4 cups packed brown sugar, *divided*
- 1 cup all-purpose flour
- 6 tablespoons baking cocoa, *divided*
- 2 teaspoons baking powder
- 1/2 teaspoon salt
- 1/2 cup 2% milk
- 2 tablespoons butter, melted
- 1/2 teaspoon vanilla extract
- 1-1/2 cups semisweet chocolate chips
- 1-3/4 cups boiling water
- Vanilla ice cream

1 In a small bowl, combine 1 cup brown sugar, flour, 3 tablespoons cocoa, baking powder and salt. In another bowl, combine the milk, butter and vanilla; stir into dry ingredients just until combined. Spread evenly into a 3-qt. slow cooker coated with cooking spray. Sprinkle with chocolate chips.

2 In another small bowl, combine the remaining brown sugar and cocoa; stir in boiling water. Pour over batter (do not stir). Cover and cook on high for 4 to 4-1/2 hours or until a toothpick inserted near the center of the cake comes out clean. Serve warm with ice cream.

Yield: 6-8 servings.

EDITOR'S NOTE: This recipe does not use eggs.

nacho salsa dip

PREP: 15 MIN. • COOK: 3 HOURS

Sally Hull
Homestead, Florida

This zesty dip is great for any get-together and allows me to spend more time with my guests. I always have requests to bring it when my husband and I attend parties.

1 pound ground beef

1/3 cup chopped onion

2 pounds process cheese (Velveeta), cubed

1 jar (16 ounces) chunky salsa

1/4 teaspoon garlic powder

Tortilla chips *or* cubed French bread

1 In a large skillet, cook beef and onion over medium heat until meat is no longer pink; drain well.

2 Transfer to a greased 3-qt. slow cooker; stir in the cheese, salsa and garlic powder. Cover and cook on low for 3 hours. Stir; serve with tortilla chips or cubed bread.

Yield: 7 cups.

sweet-and-sour chicken wings

PREP: 15 MIN. • COOK: 3 HOURS

June Eberhardt
Marysville, California

These wings are perfect for holiday gatherings. Because they come with plenty of sauce, I sometimes serve them over rice as a main dish. Any way you do it, this sweet and tangy combo will be a hit!

1 cup sugar

1 cup cider vinegar

1/2 cup ketchup

2 tablespoons reduced-sodium soy sauce

1 teaspoon chicken bouillon granules

16 chicken wings

6 tablespoons cornstarch

1/2 cup cold water

1 In a small saucepan, combine the first five ingredients. Bring to a boil; cook and stir until sugar is dissolved. Place chicken wings in a 3-qt. slow cooker; add vinegar mixture. Cover and cook on low for 3 to 3-1/2 hours or until chicken juices run clear.

2 Transfer wings to a serving dish and keep warm. Skim fat from cooking juices; transfer to a small saucepan. Bring liquid to a boil. Combine cornstarch and water until smooth. Gradually stir into the pan. Bring to a boil; cook and stir for 2 minutes or until thickened. Spoon over chicken. Serve with a slotted spoon.

Yield: 4 servings.

zesty smoked links

PREP: 5 MIN. • COOK: 30 MIN.

Jackie Boothman
LaGrande, Oregon

These flavorful sausages prepared in a slow cooker are great when entertaining. Men in the family can't resist these satisfying snacks.

1 bottle (12 ounces) chili sauce

1 cup grape jelly

2 tablespoons lemon juice

2 packages (1 pound *each*) miniature smoked sausage links *and/or* hot dogs

1 In a large skillet, combine the chili sauce, jelly and lemon juice; cook over medium-low heat until jelly is melted. Stir in sausages. Reduce heat; cover and cook for 30 minutes or until heated through, stirring occasionally. Serve immediately or keep warm in a 1-1/2-qt. slow cooker.

Yield: about 32 servings.

strawberry rhubarb sauce

PREP: 15 MIN. • COOK: 4-1/4 HOURS

Nancy Cowlishaw
Boise, Idaho

The perfect addition to vanilla ice cream, my colorful fruit sauce features a delightful combination of rhubarb, apple and strawberry flavors. The warm compote is so comforting any time of year.

6 cups sliced fresh *or* frozen rhubarb, thawed

1 cup sugar

1/2 cup unsweetened apple juice

3 cinnamon sticks (3 inches)

1/2 teaspoon grated orange peel

1/4 teaspoon ground ginger

1 pint fresh strawberries, halved

Vanilla ice cream

1 Place the rhubarb, sugar, juice, cinnamon sticks, orange peel and ginger in a 3-qt. slow cooker. Cover and cook on low for 4-5 hours or until rhubarb is tender. Stir in strawberries; cover and cook 15 minutes longer or until heated through. Discard cinnamon sticks. Serve with ice cream.

Yield: 4-1/2 cups.

Smart Sauce. You can use Strawberry Rhubarb Sauce as more than just an ice cream topping. Spoon it over pound cake or angel food cake for a special treat. It's also a wonderful addition to brunch. Use it instead of syrup on pancakes, waffles and French toast!

hot crab dip

PREP: 10 MIN. • COOK: 2 HOURS

Terri Perrier
Simonton, Texas

One batch of this slow-cooked appetizer isn't enough for my family so I often double the recipe. Bits of sweet onion give the creamy dip a bit of crunch.

1 package (8 ounces) cream cheese, softened

1/2 cup finely chopped sweet onion

1/4 cup grated Parmesan cheese

1/4 cup mayonnaise

2 garlic cloves, minced

2 teaspoons sugar

1 can (6 ounces) crabmeat, drained, flaked and cartilage removed

Assorted crackers

1 In a 1-1/2-qt. slow cooker, combine the first six ingredients; stir in crab. Cover and cook on low for 2-3 hours or until heated through. Serve with crackers.

Yield: 2 cups.

italian appetizer meatballs

PREP: 40 MIN. • COOK: 2 HOURS

Rene McCrory
Indianapolis, Indiana

Store-bought spaghetti sauce speeds up the prep for these homemade meatball appetizers. Leftovers make terrific sub sandwiches.

2 eggs, lightly beaten

1/2 cup dry bread crumbs

1/4 cup whole milk

2 teaspoons grated Parmesan cheese

1 teaspoon salt

1/4 teaspoon pepper

1/8 teaspoon garlic powder

1 pound ground beef

1 pound bulk Italian sausage

2 jars (26 ounces *each*) spaghetti sauce

1 In a large bowl, combine the first seven ingredients. Crumble beef and sausage over mixture and mix well. Shape into 1-in. balls.

2 Place the meatballs on a greased rack in a shallow baking pan. Bake, uncovered, at 400° for 15-20 minutes or until they are no longer pink.

3 Transfer meatballs to a 4-qt. slow cooker; add the spaghetti sauce. Cover and cook on high for 2-3 hours or until meatballs are heated through.

Yield: 4 dozen.

ginger tea drink

PREP: 15 MIN. • COOK: 2 HOURS

Alexandra Marcotty
Cleveland Heights, Ohio

Looking for something new and special to serve to guests? Let this soothing green tea simmer while you concentrate on preparing other dishes for your gathering. Everyone is sure to ask for this heartwarming recipe.

4 cups boiling water

15 individual green tea bags

4 cups white grape juice

1 to 2 tablespoons honey

1 tablespoon minced fresh gingerroot

Crystallized ginger, optional

1 In a 3-qt. slow cooker, combine boiling water and tea bags. Cover and let stand for 10 minutes. Discard tea bags. Stir in the remaining ingredients. Cover and cook on low for 2-3 hours or until heated through.

2 Strain if desired before serving warm. Garnish with candied ginger if desired.

Yield: 2 quarts.

sunshine chicken wings

PREP: 25 MIN. • BAKE: 45 MIN.

Ami Miller
Plain City, Ohio

Casual get-togethers get a flavorful boost when these finger-licking-good wings are served from the slow cooker. Add as much hot pepper sauce as you like, or omit altogether if you'd prefer a milder appetizer.

> 2 jars (12 ounces *each*) orange marmalade
>
> 3 cups ketchup
>
> 1 cup packed brown sugar
>
> 1 large onion, finely chopped
>
> 1/2 cup butter, cubed
>
> 3 tablespoons chili powder
>
> 3 tablespoons white vinegar
>
> 1 tablespoon Worcestershire sauce
>
> Hot pepper sauce to taste
>
> 8 pounds whole chicken wings (about 40)

1 In a large saucepan, combine the first nine ingredients. Bring to a boil. Reduce heat; simmer, uncovered, for 15 minutes.

2 Meanwhile, cut chicken wings into three sections; discard wing tips. Dip wings into sauce and place on two foil-lined 15-in. x 10-in. x 1-in. baking pans.

3 Bake at 350° for 45 minutes, reversing the pans once during baking time. Serve immediately or cover and refrigerate for up to 2 days before serving. Keep warm in 6-qt. slow cooker.

Yield: 15-20 servings.

EDITOR'S NOTE: Uncooked chicken wing sections (wingettes) may be substituted for whole chicken wings.

peachy spiced cider

PREP: 5 MIN. • COOK: 4 HOURS

Rose Harman
Hays, Kansas

I served this spiced cider at a party and received so many compliments. Everyone enjoys the subtle peach flavor.

> 4 cans (5-1/2 ounces *each*) peach nectar *or* apricot nectar
>
> 2 cups apple juice
>
> 1/4 to 1/2 teaspoon ground ginger
>
> 1/4 teaspoon ground cinnamon
>
> 1/4 teaspoon ground nutmeg
>
> 4 fresh orange slices (1/4-inch thick), halved

1 In a 1-1/2-qt. slow cooker, combine the first five ingredients. Top with the orange slices. Cover and cook on low for 4-6 hours or until heated through. Stir before serving.

Yield: about 1 quart.

raspberry fondue dip

PREP/TOTAL TIME: 25 MIN.

Edna Hoffman
Hebron, Indiana

I delight guests with this fun non-traditional fruit fondue. Creamy apple butter and cinnamon red-hot candies add tangy flair!

1 package (10 ounces) frozen sweetened raspberries
1 cup apple butter
1 tablespoon red-hot candies
2 teaspoons cornstarch
Assorted fresh fruit

1 Place raspberries in a small bowl; set aside to thaw. Strain raspberries, reserving 1 tablespoon juice; discard seeds.

2 In a small saucepan, combine the strained berries, apple butter and red-hots; cook over medium heat until candies are dissolved, stirring occasionally.

3 In a small bowl, combine the cornstarch and reserved juice until smooth; stir into the berry mixture. Bring to a boil; cook and stir over medium heat for 1-2 minutes or until thickened.

4 Transfer to a small fondue pot or 1-1/2-qt. slow cooker. Serve the dip warm or cold with fresh fruit.

Yield: 1 cup.

cider cheese fondue

PREP/TOTAL TIME: 15 MIN.

Kim Marie Van Rheenen
Mendota, Illinois

Cheese lovers are sure to enjoy dipping into this creamy, quick-to-fix fondue that has just a hint of apple. You can also serve this appetizer with apple or pear wedges.

　3/4 cup apple cider *or* apple juice

　2 cups (8 ounces) shredded cheddar cheese

　1 cup (4 ounces) shredded Swiss cheese

　1 tablespoon cornstarch

　1/8 teaspoon pepper

　Cubed French bread

1 In a large saucepan, bring cider to a boil. Reduce heat to medium-low. Toss the cheeses with cornstarch and pepper; stir into cider. Cook and stir for 3-4 minutes or until cheese is melted.

2 Transfer to a small fondue pot or 1-1/2-qt. slow cooker; keep warm. Serve with bread cubes.

Yield: 2-2/3 cups.

cranberry-stuffed apples

PREP: 10 MIN. • COOK: 4 HOURS

Graciela Sandvigen
Rochester, New York

Cinnamon, nutmeg and walnuts add a homey autumn flavor to these stuffed apples, but the slow cooker does most of the work for me.

　5 medium apples

　1/3 cup fresh *or* frozen cranberries, thawed and chopped

　1/4 cup packed brown sugar

　2 tablespoons chopped walnuts

　1/4 teaspoon ground cinnamon

　1/8 teaspoon ground nutmeg

　Whipped cream *or* vanilla ice cream, optional

1 Core apples, leaving bottoms intact. Peel top third of each apple; place in a 5-qt. slow cooker. Combine the cranberries, brown sugar, walnuts, cinnamon and nutmeg; spoon into apples.

2 Cover and cook on low for 4-5 hours or until apples are tender. Serve with whipped cream or ice cream if desired.

Yield: 5 servings.

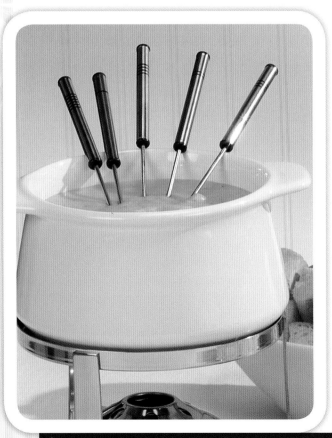

viennese coffee

PREP: 10 MIN. • COOK: 3 HOURS

Sharon Delaney-Chronis
South Milwaukee, Wisconsin

This isn't your regular cup of coffee! I dress it up with chocolate, whipped cream and more, making it a drink to savor!

3 cups strong brewed coffee

3 tablespoons chocolate syrup

1 teaspoon sugar

1/3 cup heavy whipping cream

1/4 cup creme de cacao *or* Irish cream liqueur

Whipped cream and chocolate curls, optional

1 In a 1-1/2-qt. slow cooker, combine the coffee, chocolate syrup and sugar. Cover and cook on low for 2-1/2 hours.

2 Stir in heavy cream and creme de cacao. Cover and cook 30 minutes longer or until heated through.

3 Ladle coffee into mugs. Garnish with whipped cream and chocolate curls if desired.

Yield: 4 servings.

> **Chocolate shavings.** Adding a pretty chocolate garnish to coffee beverages is a cinch. Use a vegetable peeler to "peel" curls from a solid block of chocolate. To keep the strips intact, allow them to fall gently onto the top of the beverage or a single layer of waxed paper. If you get only shavings, the chocolate may be too hard, so warm it slightly.

caramel apple fondue

PREP/TOTAL TIME: 25 MIN.

Katie Koziolek
Hartland, Minnesota

I like to serve this warm caramel dip with sliced apples while we're watching football games on Sunday afternoons. It really warms us up.

1/2 cup butter, cubed

2 cups packed brown sugar

1 can (14 ounces) sweetened condensed milk

1 cup light corn syrup

2 tablespoons water

1 teaspoon vanilla extract

Apple slices

1 In a heavy 3-qt. saucepan, combine the butter, brown sugar, milk, corn syrup and water; bring to a boil over medium heat. Cook and stir until a candy thermometer reads 230° (thread stage), about 8-10 minutes. Remove from the heat; stir in the vanilla extract.

2 Transfer to a small fondue pot or 1-1/2-qt. slow cooker; keep warm. Serve with the apple slices.

Yield: 3-1/2 cups.

EDITOR'S NOTE: We recommend that you test your candy thermometer before each use by bringing water to a boil; the thermometer should read 212°. Adjust your recipe temperature up or down based on your test.

barbecue chicken wings

PREP: 20 MIN. • COOK: 1 HOUR, 35 MIN.

Jean Ann Herritt
Canton, Ohio

I got this spicy recipe from a friend but altered the ingredient amounts to adjust the hotness of the sauce. Make sure everyone has extra napkins...these wings are messy to eat but oh, so good!

- 3 pounds whole chicken wings
- 2 cups ketchup
- 1/2 cup honey
- 2 tablespoons lemon juice
- 2 tablespoons canola oil
- 2 tablespoons soy sauce
- 2 tablespoons Worcestershire sauce
- 1 tablespoon paprika
- 4 garlic cloves, minced
- 1-1/2 teaspoons curry powder
- 1/2 teaspoon pepper
- 1/8 teaspoon hot pepper sauce

1 Cut the chicken wings into three sections; discard wing tips. Place the wings in a greased 15-in. x 10-in. x 1-in. baking pan. Bake at 350° for 35-40 minutes or until juices run clear.

2 In a large bowl, combine the remaining ingredients. Pour 1/2 cup into a 3-qt. slow cooker. Drain the chicken wings; add to slow cooker. Drizzle with the remaining sauce. Cover and cook on low for 1 hour, basting occasionally.

Yield: 10 servings.

EDITOR'S NOTE: Uncooked chicken wing sections (wingettes) may be substituted for whole chicken wings.

slow cooker mexican dip

PREP: 15 MIN. • COOK: 1-1/2 HOURS

Heather Courtney
Ames, Iowa

My husband, Jamie, and I love to entertain and this hearty, seven-ingredient dip is always a hit... as well as a request. It couldn't be much easier to put together, and using our slow cooker leaves us free to share some quality time with our guests. After all, isn't that the purpose of a holiday party?

1-1/2 pounds ground beef

1 pound bulk hot Italian sausage

1 cup chopped onion

1 package (8.8 ounces) ready-to-serve Spanish rice

1 can (16 ounces) refried beans

1 can (10 ounces) enchilada sauce

1 pound process cheese (Velveeta), cubed

1 package tortilla chip scoops

1 In a Dutch oven, cook the beef, sausage and onion over medium heat until meat is no longer pink; drain. Heat rice according to package directions.

2 In a 3-qt. slow cooker, combine the meat mixture, rice, beans, enchilada sauce and cheese. Cover and cook on low for 1-1/2 to 2 hours or until cheese is melted. Serve with tortilla scoops.

Yield: 8 cups.

saucy cocktail meatballs

PREP: 10 MIN. • COOK: 3 HOURS

Susie Snyder
Bowling Green, Ohio

I received this recipe from my grandmother many years ago. She would serve it at Christmas while I was growing up. Now I serve it every year.

1 package (32 ounces) frozen fully cooked homestyle meatballs, thawed

1 can (10-3/4 ounces) condensed tomato soup, undiluted

1/3 cup chopped onion

1/3 cup chopped green pepper

2 tablespoons brown sugar

4 teaspoons Worcestershire sauce

1 tablespoon white vinegar

1 tablespoon prepared mustard

1 Place meatballs in a 3-qt. slow cooker. In a small bowl, combine the remaining ingredients. Pour over meatballs.

2 Cover and cook on low for 3-4 hours or until heated through.

Yield: about 6 dozen.

warm spiced cider punch

PREP: 5 MIN. • COOK: 4 HOURS

Susan Smith
Forest, Virginia

Orange juice concentrate and spices perk up apple cider to make this nice warm-up punch.

4 cups apple cider *or* unsweetened apple juice

2-1/4 cups water

3/4 cup orange juice concentrate

3/4 teaspoon ground nutmeg

3/4 teaspoon ground ginger

3 whole cloves

2 cinnamon sticks

Orange slices and additional cinnamon sticks, optional

1 In a 3-qt. slow cooker, combine the apple cider, water, orange juice concentrate, nutmeg and ginger. Place cloves and cinnamon sticks on a double thickness of cheesecloth; bring up corners of cloth and tie with string to form a bag. Place bag in slow cooker.

2 Cover and cook on low for 4-5 hours or until heated through. Remove and discard spice bag. Garnish with orange slices and additional cinnamon sticks if desired.

Yield: 8 servings.

beer cheese fondue

PREP/TOTAL TIME: 15 MIN.

Chrystie Wear
Oak Ridge, North Carolina

This thick fondue originated in my kitchen when I didn't have all of the ingredients I needed to make the recipe I initially planned to prepare. Served with bread cubes, it has since become a staple, particularly while we watch football games on television.

1 loaf (1 pound, about 20 inches) French bread, cubed

1/4 cup chopped onion

1 tablespoon butter

1 teaspoon minced garlic

1 cup beer *or* nonalcoholic beer

4 cups (16 ounces) shredded cheddar cheese

1 tablespoon all-purpose flour

2 to 4 tablespoons half-and-half cream

1 Place bread cubes in a single layer in an ungreased 15-in. x 10-in. x 1-in. baking pan. Bake at 450° for 5-7 minutes or until lightly crisp, stirring twice.

2 Meanwhile, in a small saucepan, saute onion in butter until tender. Add garlic; cook 1 minute longer. Stir in beer. Bring to a boil; reduce heat to medium-low. Toss cheese and flour; stir into saucepan until melted. Stir in 2 tablespoons cream.

3 Transfer to a small fondue pot or 1-1/2-qt. slow cooker. Keep warm; add additional cream if fondue thickens. Serve with toasted bread cubes.

Yield: about 3 cups.

slow cooker cider

PREP: 5 MIN. • COOK: 2 HOURS

Alpha Wilson
Roswell, New Mexico

There's no last-minute rush when you simmer this sweet, spiced punch.

2 cinnamon sticks (3 inches)

1 teaspoon whole cloves

1 teaspoon whole allspice

2 quarts apple cider

1/2 cup packed brown sugar

1 orange, sliced

1 Place cinnamon, cloves and allspice in a double thickness of cheesecloth; bring up corners of cloth and tie with a string to form a bag.

2 Place cider and brown sugar in a 3-qt. slow cooker; stir until sugar dissolves. Add spice bag. Place orange slices on top. Cover and cook on low for 2-3 hours or until heated through. Discard spice bag.

Yield: 2 quarts.

nutty apple streusel dessert

PREP: 20 MIN. • BAKE: 6 HOURS

Jacki Every
Rotterdam, New York

Many people don't think of using a slow cooker to make dessert, but I like finishing up our dinner and having this hot, scrumptious apple treat waiting to be served up. I can start it in the morning and not think about it all day.

6 cups sliced peeled tart apples

1-1/4 teaspoons ground cinnamon

1/4 teaspoon ground allspice

1/4 teaspoon ground nutmeg

3/4 cup whole milk

2 tablespoons butter, softened

3/4 cup sugar

2 eggs

1 teaspoon vanilla extract

1/2 cup biscuit/baking mix

TOPPING:

1 cup biscuit/baking mix

1/3 cup packed brown sugar

3 tablespoons cold butter

1/2 cup sliced almonds

Ice cream *or* whipped cream, optional

1 In a large bowl, toss apples with cinnamon, allspice and nutmeg. Place in a greased 3-qt. slow cooker. In a small bowl, combine the milk, butter, sugar, eggs, vanilla and baking mix. Spoon over apples.

2 For topping, combine biscuit mix and brown sugar in a large bowl; cut in butter until crumbly. Add almonds; sprinkle over apples. Cover and cook on low for 6-7 hours or until the apples are tender. Serve with ice cream or whipped cream if desired.

Yield: 6-8 servings.

sweet sausage puffs

PREP: 25 MIN. • BAKE: 15 MIN.

Gloria Butler
Plain City, Ohio

*This delicious and easy appetizer is a favorite
with friends and family who visit me.*

- 1/2 cup butter
- 1 cup packed brown sugar
- 2 tablespoons water
- 1/2 cup finely chopped pecans
- 1 tube (12 ounces) refrigerated flaky buttermilk biscuits
- 40 miniature smoked sausages

1 In a heavy saucepan, melt the butter. Stir in the brown sugar and water. Bring to a boil. Stir in pecans. Remove from the heat; set aside.

2 Flatten each biscuit into a 3-in. circle; cut into quarters. Place a sausage on each piece of dough; wrap dough around sausage and seal. Place seam side down in a greased 15-in. x 10-in. x 1-in. baking pan. Pour butter mixture over bundles.

3 Bake at 375° for 15-20 minutes or until golden brown. Transfer to a chafing dish or 3-qt. slow cooker; cover and keep warm over low heat.

Yield: 40 appetizers.

> **Great mornings.** The Sweet Sausage Puffs are a tasty addition to parties, but they also make a unique contribution to Sunday brunches with friends, morning meetings or any early-day get-together. And because they stay warm in the slow cooker, transferring them to the event is always a snap!

chocolate peanut clusters

PREP: 10 MIN.
COOK: 2 HOURS + STANDING

Pam Posey
Waterloo, South Carolina

*I turn to my slow cooker to prepare these chocolate
treats. Making candies couldn't be any easier!*

- 1 jar (16 ounces) salted dry roasted peanuts
- 1 jar (16 ounces) unsalted dry roasted peanuts
- 1 package (11-1/2 ounces) milk chocolate chips
- 1 package (10 ounces) peanut butter chips
- 3 packages (10 to 12 ounces *each*) white baking chips
- 2 packages (11-1/2 ounces *each*) 60% cacao bittersweet chocolate baking chips

1 In a 5-qt. slow cooker, combine peanuts. Layer with the remaining ingredients in order given (do not stir). Cover and cook on low for 2 to 2-1/2 hours or until chips are melted.

2 Stir to combine. Drop by tablespoonfuls onto waxed paper. Let stand until set. Store in an airtight container at room temperature.

Yield: 4 pounds.

championship bean dip

PREP: 10 MIN. • COOK: 2 HOURS

Wendi Wavrin Law
Omaha, Nebraska

My friends and neighbors expect me to bring this irresistible dip to every gathering. When I arrive, they ask, "You brought your bean dip, didn't you?" If there are any leftovers, we use them to make bean and cheese burritos the next day. I've given out this recipe a hundred times.

1 can (16 ounces) refried beans

1 cup picante sauce

1 cup (4 ounces) shredded Monterey Jack cheese

1 cup (4 ounces) shredded cheddar cheese

3/4 cup sour cream

1 package (3 ounces) cream cheese, softened

1 tablespoon chili powder

1/4 teaspoon ground cumin

Tortilla chips and salsa

1 In a large bowl, combine the first eight ingredients; transfer to a 1-1/2-qt. slow cooker. Cover and cook on high for 2 hours or until heated through, stirring once or twice. Serve with tortilla chips and salsa.

Yield: 4-1/2 cups.

cranberry appetizer meatballs

PREP: 25 MIN. • BAKE: 15 MIN.

Jim Ulberg
Elk Rapids, Michigan

A tangy, non-traditional sauce nicely coats these meatballs for a memorable fall party snack.

2 eggs, lightly beaten

1 cup dry bread crumbs

1/3 cup minced fresh parsley

1/3 cup ketchup

2 tablespoons finely chopped onion

2 tablespoons soy sauce

2 garlic cloves, minced

1/2 teaspoon salt

1/4 teaspoon pepper

2 pounds ground beef

CRANBERRY SAUCE:

1 can (14 ounces) whole-berry cranberry sauce

1 bottle (12 ounces) chili sauce

1 tablespoon brown sugar

1 tablespoon prepared mustard

1 tablespoon lemon juice

2 garlic cloves, minced

1 In a bowl, combine eggs, bread crumbs, parsley, ketchup, onion, soy sauce, garlic, salt and pepper. Crumble beef over mixture and mix well. Shape into 1-in. balls.

2 Place meatballs on a rack in a shallow baking pan. Bake, uncovered, at 400° for 15 minutes or until no longer pink. Transfer with a slotted spoon to a 3-qt. slow cooker or chafing dish.

3 Combine sauce ingredients in a saucepan; simmer 10 minutes, stirring occasionally. Pour over meatballs. Transfer to a slow cooker, and serve warm.

Yield: about 7 dozen.

chili con queso dip

PREP/TOTAL TIME: 25 MIN.

Sarah Mohrman
Fort Wayne, Indiana

This cheesy dip never lets on that it has 2 grams of fat per serving. Chilies and garlic kick up the flavor, making it a real crowd pleaser.

1 can (14-1/2 ounces) no-salt-added diced tomatoes

1 can (10 ounces) diced tomatoes and green chilies

1 small onion, chopped

1 teaspoon olive oil

2 garlic cloves, minced

1 package (8 ounces) fat-free cream cheese, cubed

6 ounces reduced-fat process cheese (Velveeta), cubed

1 teaspoon chili powder

2 tablespoons minced fresh cilantro

Baked tortilla chip scoops

1 Pour both cans of tomatoes into a colander over a small bowl; drain, reserving 1/3 cup liquid. Discard remaining liquid.

2 In a large skillet, saute onion in oil until tender. Add garlic; cook 1 minute longer. Stir in cream cheese until melted. Add the tomatoes, process cheese, chili powder and reserved liquid. Cook and stir over low heat until cheese is melted. Stir in cilantro.

3 Transfer to a slow cooker, and keep warm. Serve with tortilla scoops.

Yield: 3 cups.

creamy artichoke dip

PREP: 20 MIN. • COOK: 1 HOUR

Mary Spencer
Waukesha, Wisconsin

This creamy dip is a family favorite. My sister got the recipe from a friend and she passed it along. It's loaded with cheese, artichokes and just the right amount of spice for crowd-pleasing fun.

- 2 cans (14 ounces *each*) water-packed artichoke hearts, rinsed, drained and coarsely chopped
- 2 cups (8 ounces) shredded part-skim mozzarella cheese
- 1 package (8 ounces) cream cheese, cubed
- 1 cup shredded Parmesan cheese
- 1/2 cup mayonnaise
- 1/2 cup shredded Swiss cheese
- 2 tablespoons lemon juice
- 2 tablespoons plain yogurt
- 1 tablespoon seasoned salt
- 1 tablespoon chopped seeded jalapeno pepper
- 1 teaspoon garlic powder
- Tortilla chips

1 In a 3-qt. slow cooker, combine the first 11 ingredients. Cover and cook on low for 1 hour or until heated through. Serve with tortilla chips.

Yield: 5 cups.

EDITOR'S NOTE: When cutting hot peppers, disposable gloves are recommended. Avoid touching your face.

mexican fondue

PREP: 15 MIN. • COOK: 1-1/2 HOURS

Nella Parker
Hersey, Michigan

A handful of items and a few moments of prep work are all you'll need for this festive fondue. Not only does it take advantage of canned goods and other convenience items, but the slow cooker does all the work.

- 1 can (14-3/4 ounces) cream-style corn
- 1 can (14-1/2 ounces) diced tomatoes, drained
- 3 tablespoons chopped green chilies
- 1 teaspoon chili powder
- 1 package (16 ounces) process cheese (Velveeta), cubed
- French bread cubes

1 Coat a 1-1/2-qt. slow cooker with cooking spray. In a small bowl, combine the corn, tomatoes, green chilies and chili powder. Stir in cheese. Pour into slow cooker.

2 Cover and cook on high for 1-1/2 hours, stirring every 30 minutes or until cheese is melted. Serve with bread cubes.

Yield: 4-1/2 cups.

black and blue cobbler

PREP: 15 MIN.
COOK: 2 HOURS + STANDING

Martha Creveling
Orlando, Florida

It never occurred to me that I could bake a cobbler in my slow cooker until I saw some recipes and decided to try my favorite fruity dessert recipe. It took a bit of experimenting, but the tasty results are "berry" well worth it.

1 cup all-purpose flour

1-1/2 cups sugar, *divided*

1 teaspoon baking powder

1/4 teaspoon salt

1/4 teaspoon ground cinnamon

1/4 teaspoon ground nutmeg

2 eggs, lightly beaten

2 tablespoons whole milk

2 tablespoons canola oil

2 cups fresh *or* frozen blackberries

2 cups fresh *or* frozen blueberries

3/4 cup water

1 teaspoon grated orange peel

Whipped cream *or* vanilla ice cream, optional

1 In a large bowl, combine the flour, 3/4 cup sugar, baking powder, salt, cinnamon and nutmeg. Combine the eggs, milk and oil; stir into dry ingredients just until moistened. Spread the batter evenly onto the bottom of a greased 5-qt. slow cooker.

2 In a large saucepan, combine the berries, water, orange peel and remaining sugar; bring to a boil. Remove from the heat; immediately pour over batter. Cover and cook on high for 2 to 2-1/2 hours or until a toothpick inserted into the batter comes out clean.

3 Turn cooker off. Uncover and let stand for 30 minutes before serving. Serve with whipped cream or ice cream if desired.

Yield: 6 servings.

mulled merlot

PREP: 10 MIN. • COOK: 1 HOUR

Taste of Home Test Kitchen

This recipe for spiced wine is sure to warm up all your winter guests!

4 cinnamon sticks (3 inches)

4 whole cloves

2 bottles (750 milliliters *each*) merlot

1/2 cup sugar

1/2 cup orange juice

1/2 cup brandy

1 medium orange, thinly sliced

1 Place cinnamon sticks and cloves on a double thickness of cheesecloth; bring up corners of cloth and tie with string to form a bag.

2 In a 3-qt. slow cooker, combine the wine, sugar, orange juice, brandy and orange slices. Add spice bag. Cover and cook on high for 1 hour or until heated through. Discard spice bag and orange slices. Serve warm in mugs.

Yield: 9 servings.

spiced tea mix

PREP/TOTAL TIME: 10 MIN.

Deb McKinney
Cedar Falls, Iowa

My family has relied on this homespun mix to make hot spiced tea and a heartwarming punch for years. My parents served steaming mugs at Thanksgiving.

1 jar (21.1 ounces) orange breakfast drink mix

1 jar (6 ounces) sugar-free instant lemon iced tea mix

2/3 cup sweetened lemonade drink mix

2 teaspoons ground cinnamon

1 teaspoon ground cloves

ADDITIONAL INGREDIENTS FOR HOT SPICE TEA:

1 cup boiling water

ADDITIONAL INGREDIENTS FOR HOT SPICED PUNCH:

2 quarts apple juice *or* cider

1-1/2 cups cranberry juice

3 cinnamon sticks (3-1/2 inches)

1 In an airtight container, combine the first five ingredients. Store in a cool dry place for up to 6 months. **Yield: about 7-1/2 cups total.**

2 To prepare tea: Dissolve 1 tablespoon of the tea mix in boiling water; stir well. **Yield: 1 serving.**

3 To prepare punch: In a 3-qt. slow cooker, combine the juices, 1/4 to 1/3 cup tea mix and cinnamon sticks. Cover and cook on low for 4 hours. **Yield: about 12 servings (6 ounces each).**

1. In a 5-qt. slow cooker, combine water, sugar and juices; stir until the sugar is dissolved. If desired, place cloves in a double thickness of cheesecloth; bring up corners of cloth and tie with string to form a bag. Add spice bag and red-hots to slow cooker. Cover and cook on low for 2-3 hours or until heated through. Before serving, discard spice bag and stir punch.

Yield: 3-1/2 quarts.

mini hot dogs 'n' meatballs

PREP: 5 MIN. • COOK: 3 HOURS

Andrea Chamberlain
Macedon, New York

Hot appetizers don't come much easier than this recipe. It always vanishes in minutes whenever I serve it. In fact, it's so popular I usually double the recipe and use a larger slow cooker.

- 1 package (12 ounces) frozen fully cooked Italian meatballs
- 1 package (16 ounces) miniature hot dogs *or* smoked sausages
- 1 package (3-1/2 ounces) sliced pepperoni
- 1 jar (26 ounces) meatless spaghetti sauce
- 1 bottle (18 ounces) barbecue sauce
- 1 bottle (12 ounces) chili sauce

1. In a 5-qt. slow cooker, combine all of the ingredients. Cover and cook on low for 3 hours or until heated through.

Yield: 8 cups.

hot cranberry punch

PREP: 10 MIN. • COOK: 2 HOURS

Laura Burgess
Ballwin, Missouri

I serve this rosy spiced beverage at parties and family gatherings during the winter. Friends like the tangy twist it gets from red-hot candies. It's a nice change from the usual hot chocolate.

- 8 cups hot water
- 1-1/2 cups sugar
- 4 cups cranberry juice
- 3/4 cup orange juice
- 1/4 cup lemon juice
- 12 whole cloves, optional
- 1/2 cup red-hot candies

kiwi tiki torches

PREP: 30 MIN. • COOK: 10 MIN.

Elaine Sweet
Dallas, Texas

Kiwi, pineapple and strawberries taste wonderful with the melted chocolate in this dish. It's an easy dessert that really dresses up a meal.

1 fresh pineapple, peeled and cut into 1-inch chunks

4 medium kiwifruit, peeled and cut into 3/4-inch chunks

2 cups fresh strawberries, halved

WHITE CHOCOLATE DIPPING SAUCE:

1 cup heavy whipping cream

6 white chocolate Toblerone candy bars (3.52 ounces *each*), broken into pieces

1/4 cup finely chopped macadamia nuts

1 to 2 teaspoons rum extract

1/3 cup flaked coconut, toasted

1 Alternately thread the pineapple, kiwi and strawberries onto 12 metal or wooden skewers; set aside.

2 In a large saucepan over medium heat, bring the cream to a boil. Remove from the heat; stir in candy bars until melted. Return to the heat. Stir in the nuts and extract; heat through.

3 Transfer to a fondue pot or 1-1/2-qt. slow cooker; keep warm. Sprinkle with coconut. Serve with fruit kabobs.

Yield: 12 servings.

p. 321

p. 306

p. 314

p. 315

layered tortellini-spinach salad

PREP/TOTAL TIME: 25 MIN.

Genise Krause
Sturgeon Bay, Wisconsin

Layers of red cabbage, green spinach, cherry tomatoes and cheese-filled tortellini make this salad a real centerpiece. You can alter the amount of dressing to your liking, if you wish.

- 1 package (19 ounces) frozen cheese tortellini
- 2 packages (6 ounces *each*) fresh baby spinach
- 6 cups shredded red cabbage
- 1 pint cherry tomatoes, quartered
- 3 tablespoons thinly sliced green onions
- 1 package (1 pound) sliced bacon, cooked and crumbled
- 1 bottle (16 ounces) ranch salad dressing

1 Cook tortellini according to package directions. Meanwhile, in a large salad bowl, layer the spinach, cabbage, tomatoes and onions.

2 Drain tortellini and rinse in cold water; place over onions. Top with bacon. Drizzle with salad dressing; do not toss. Cover and refrigerate until serving.

Yield: 18 servings.

cranberry spinach salad

PREP/TOTAL TIME: 20 MIN.

Anne Smithson
Cary, North Carolina

A few moments are all you need to toss together this pretty spinach salad and classic tangy dressing. It's a perfect way to round out holiday meals.

8 cups fresh baby spinach

1 cup dried cranberries

2 medium pears, chopped

1/4 cup cider vinegar

5 tablespoons sugar

1 teaspoon dried minced onion

1/2 teaspoon Worcestershire sauce

1/2 teaspoon ground mustard

1/4 teaspoon paprika

1/4 cup olive oil

1 tablespoon sesame seeds

1 teaspoon poppy seeds

2 tablespoons chopped pecans, toasted

1 In a large bowl, combine the spinach, cranberries and pears. In a blender, combine the vinegar, sugar, onion, Worcestershire sauce, mustard and paprika; cover and process until blended. While processing, gradually add oil in a steady stream. Add sesame seeds and poppy seeds. Pour over salad and toss to coat. Sprinkle with pecans.

Yield: 8 servings.

Mix It Up. Feel free to experiment with different toppings to shake up the flavor of this salad. You can substitute raisins, currents, dried cherries, prunes or figs for the cranberries, and walnuts or almonds for the pecans.

romaine salad with avocado dressing

PREP/TOTAL TIME: 25 MIN.

Sandra Forsyth
Edmonton, Alberta

This eye-catching salad looks great on a buffet table and tastes even better. The crunchy corn chips are a nice change from croutons.

  1 medium ripe avocado, peeled and cubed

  1/2 cup mayonnaise

  1/4 cup canola oil

  3 tablespoons lemon juice

  2 garlic cloves, peeled

  1/2 teaspoon salt

  1/4 teaspoon hot pepper sauce

  1 bunch romaine, torn

  3 medium tomatoes, cut into wedges

  1 cup (4 ounces) shredded cheddar cheese

  1 can (2-1/4 ounces) sliced ripe olives, drained

  2 green onions, chopped

  Corn chips

1 For the dressing, place the first seven ingredients in a blender; cover and process until blended.

2 In a large bowl, combine the romaine, tomatoes, cheese, olives and onions. Pour dressing over salad; toss to coat. Sprinkle with corn chips.

Yield: 12 servings.

creamy german potato salad

PREP/TOTAL TIME: 30 MIN.

Tracy Zettelmeier
Mukwonago, Wisconsin

Have you ever bought marvelous-looking German potato salad, only to discover that it tastes less than marvelous? This is my mom's recipe, and it's been a staple in our family for many years. The whipping cream makes it taste like no other.

- 4-1/2 pounds red potatoes (about 18 medium)
- 1/2 pound bacon strips, diced
- 1 medium onion, chopped
- 4 teaspoons all-purpose flour
- 3/4 cup sugar
- 3/4 cup cider vinegar
- 1 cup heavy whipping cream

1 Cut potatoes into 1/2-in. cubes; place in a stock pot and cover with water. Bring to a boil. Reduce heat; cover and simmer for 10-12 minutes or until tender.

2 In a Dutch oven, cook bacon over medium heat until crisp. Using a slotted spoon, remove to paper towels; drain, reserving 5 tablespoons drippings. Set bacon aside.

3 In the same pan, saute onion in drippings until tender. Stir in flour until blended. Gradually stir in sugar and vinegar. Bring to a boil; cook and stir for 2 minutes until thickened.

4 Remove from the heat; gradually whisk in cream. Set aside. Drain potatoes. Transfer to a large bowl; add the reserved onion mixture and bacon. Stir gently to coat. Serve warm.

Yield: 13 servings (3/4 cup each).

floret salad

PREP: 30 MIN. + CHILLING

Denise Elder
Hanover, Ontario

Colorful and crunchy, this crowd-pleasing salad can be made a day in advance. Everyone likes the little zip in the creamy dressing. Sometimes I add diced green and red pepper to the mixture or throw in a little celery.

- 6 cups fresh broccoli florets
- 6 cups fresh cauliflowerets
- 3 medium red onions, halved and sliced
- 2 cups mayonnaise
- 1 cup (8 ounces) sour cream
- 1/4 cup packed brown sugar
- 1/4 cup cider vinegar
- 1 tablespoon Worcestershire sauce
- 3 teaspoons dill weed
- 2 teaspoons salt
- Dash Louisiana-style hot sauce

1 In a bowl, combine the broccoli, cauliflower and onions. In another bowl, combine the remaining ingredients. Pour over vegetables; toss to coat. Cover and refrigerate for 4 hours before serving.

Yield: 25 servings (2/3 cup each).

1 In a large bowl, combine the romaine, nectarines, pecans and feta cheese. In a small bowl, whisk the dressing ingredients. Pour over salad and toss to coat.

Yield: 8 servings.

strawberry summer salad

PREP/TOTAL TIME: 20 MIN.

Randi Gross
Lethbridge, Alberta

My daughter wanted me to submit this family-favorite salad that combines crisp romaine, juicy strawberries and crunchy slivered almonds. We love it served with steak and baked potatoes. It's perfect for warm summer days.

7 cups torn romaine

2 cups sliced fresh strawberries

2 celery ribs, finely chopped

2 green onions, finely chopped

1/4 cup canola oil

2 tablespoons sugar

2 tablespoons cider vinegar

1/4 teaspoon salt

1/4 teaspoon pepper

1/8 teaspoon hot pepper sauce

1/2 cup slivered almonds, toasted

1 In a large bowl, combine the romaine, strawberries, celery and onions. In a small bowl, whisk the oil, sugar, vinegar, salt, pepper and pepper sauce. Pour over salad and toss to coat. Sprinkle with almonds.

Yield: 8 servings.

nectarine pecan salad

PREP/TOTAL TIME: 25 MIN.

Marina Sanders
Altamont, Manitoba

This fast, four-ingredient salad is complemented with an easy shake-to-make dressing that's inexpensive and, best of all, made out of items you probably already have in your pantry.

8 cups torn romaine

5 medium nectarines *or* peaches, chopped

2/3 cup chopped pecans, toasted

1/2 cup crumbled feta cheese

DRESSING:

2 tablespoons plus 1-1/2 teaspoons canola oil

2 tablespoons white vinegar

2 tablespoons plus 1-1/2 teaspoons sugar

1 tablespoon sesame seeds

1 tablespoon poppy seeds

3/4 teaspoon dried minced onion

1/4 teaspoon Worcestershire sauce

1/8 teaspoon paprika

green bean tossed salad

PREP: 20 MIN. + CHILLING

Shirley Kosto
Chugiak, Alaska

I decided to add green beans to spruce up a salad recipe that had oranges, onion, avocado and lettuce, and this is the tasty result.

- 1-1/2 pounds fresh green beans, trimmed
- 1 can (11 ounces) mandarin oranges, drained
- 1 medium red onion, thinly sliced
- 6 to 8 tablespoons olive oil
- 1/4 cup cider vinegar
- 3 to 4 teaspoons sugar
- 1/2 to 1 teaspoon salt
- 1/4 teaspoon pepper
- 4 cups torn mixed salad greens
- 1 ripe avocado, peeled and sliced
- 1/2 cup chopped pecans

1 Place the beans in a large saucepan and cover with water; bring to a boil. Cook, uncovered, for 8-10 minutes or until beans are crisp-tender. Drain and rinse in cold water.

2 In a large bowl, combine the beans, oranges and onion. In a small bowl, whisk the oil, vinegar, sugar, salt and pepper. Pour over bean mixture and toss to coat. Cover and refrigerate for at least 2 hours. Just before serving, add the salad greens, avocado and pecans; toss gently.

Yield: 8-9 servings.

antipasto picnic salad

PREP: 30 MIN. • COOK: 15 MIN.

Michele Larson
Baden, Pennsylvania

You'll love this blend of meats, veggies and pasta. It tastes delicious at room temperature or cold.

- 1 package (16 ounces) medium pasta shells
- 2 jars (16 ounces *each*) giardiniera
- 1 pound fresh broccoli florets
- 1/2 pound cubed part-skim mozzarella cheese
- 1/2 pound hard salami, cubed
- 1/2 pound deli ham, cubed
- 2 packages (3-1/2 ounces *each*) sliced pepperoni, halved
- 1 large green pepper, cut into chunks
- 1 can (6 ounces) pitted ripe olives, drained

DRESSING:
- 1/2 cup olive oil
- 1/4 cup red wine vinegar
- 2 tablespoons lemon juice
- 1 teaspoon Italian seasoning
- 1 teaspoon coarsely ground pepper
- 1/2 teaspoon salt

1 Cook the pasta according to package directions. Meanwhile, drain giardiniera, reserving 3/4 cup liquid. In a large bowl, combine the giardiniera, broccoli, mozzarella, salami, ham, pepperoni, green pepper and olives. Drain pasta and rinse in cold water; stir into meat mixture.

2 For dressing, in a small bowl, whisk the oil, vinegar, lemon juice, Italian seasoning, pepper, salt and reserved giardiniera liquid. Pour over salad and toss to coat. Refrigerate until serving.

Yield: 25 servings.

cucumber salad

PREP: 15 MIN. + CHILLING

Mary Lou Boyce
Wilmington, Delaware

Add a fresh-tasting touch to your menu with this favorite salad. The crunchy cucumbers are tossed with onion, green pepper and a sweet-tart dressing seasoned with celery seed.

- 7 cups thinly sliced peeled cucumbers
- 2 cups sugar
- 1 large onion, chopped
- 1 medium green pepper, chopped
- 1 cup cider vinegar
- 1 tablespoon salt
- 1 tablespoon celery seed

1 In a large serving bowl, combine all ingredients. Cover and refrigerate for at least 1 hour, stirring occasionally. Serve with a slotted spoon.

Yield: 8-10 servings.

bean and carrot salad

PREP/TOTAL TIME: 30 MIN.

Colleen Edelsward
Woodinville, Washington

Anytime I find a recipe full of vegetables that my family will eat, I'm a happy mom. My husband comes back for seconds when I serve this. The carrots and beans are great finger food for kids.

1/2 cup baby carrots, cut in half lengthwise

2 cups cut fresh green beans

1/4 cup chopped radishes

1/4 cup chopped red onion

DRESSING:

1 tablespoon lemon juice

1-1/2 teaspoons olive oil

1/2 teaspoon sugar

1/2 teaspoon Dijon mustard

1/4 teaspoon minced garlic

1/8 teaspoon salt

1/8 teaspoon ground cumin

1-1/2 teaspoons sesame seeds, toasted

1 In a small saucepan, cook carrots in a small amount of boiling water for 4 minutes. Add the beans; cook 4-5 minutes longer or until vegetables are crisp-tender. Drain; chill in ice water. Drain and pat dry; place in a large bowl. Add radishes and onion.

2 In a small bowl, whisk the lemon juice, oil, sugar, mustard, garlic, salt and cumin. Pour over bean mixture; toss to coat. Cover and refrigerate until serving. Sprinkle with sesame seeds.

Yield: 4 servings.

peppery vegetable salad

PREP: 20 MIN. + CHILLING

Andrea Sheatz
Knox, Pennsylvania

I'm always looking for great recipes since our large garden provides a beautiful harvest each year. This colorful combination is loaded with crunch and well-seasoned flavor.

15 poblano *and/or* banana peppers, seeded and coarsely chopped (about 7 cups)

1-1/2 cups fresh cauliflowerets, cut into bite-size pieces

3 small carrots, coarsely chopped

1 large sweet red pepper, coarsely chopped

1 cup pitted ripe olives

3 garlic cloves, minced

1 cup water

1 cup white vinegar

3/4 cup olive oil

4 teaspoons dried oregano

1 teaspoon salt

1 In a large bowl, combine the peppers, cauliflower, carrots, red pepper, olives and garlic. In a large bowl, whisk remaining ingredients. Pour over vegetable mixture and toss to coat. Cover and refrigerate overnight. Serve with a slotted spoon.

Yield: 12 servings.

EDITOR'S NOTE: When cutting hot peppers, disposable gloves are recommended. Avoid touching your face.

rainbow pasta salad

PREP: 1 HOUR + CHILLING

Benjamin & Sue Ellen Clark
Warsaw, New York

This colorful salad is hearty enough to be a light meal in itself. It's a great make-ahead dish, since the full flavors of the herbs and veggies need a little time to blend.

2 packages (12 ounces *each*) tricolor spiral pasta

2 packages (16 ounces *each*) frozen California-blend vegetables, thawed

2 pints grape tomatoes

1 large zucchini, halved and thinly sliced

1 large yellow summer squash, quartered and thinly sliced

1 large red onion, finely chopped

1 block (8 ounces) cheddar cheese, cubed

1 block (8 ounces) Monterey Jack cheese, cubed

2 packages (4 ounces *each*) crumbled tomato and basil feta cheese

1 bottle (16 ounces) Italian salad dressing

3 tablespoons minced fresh parsley

1 tablespoon minced fresh basil

1 teaspoon Italian seasoning

1 teaspoon seasoned salt

1/2 teaspoon pepper

1 can (3.8 ounces) sliced ripe olives, drained

Grated Romano cheese, optional

1 Cook pasta according to package directions. Rinse with cold water; drain well. In two large bowls, combine the California vegetables, tomatoes, zucchini, yellow squash, onion, cheeses and pasta.

2 In a small bowl, combine the salad dressing, parsley, basil, Italian seasoning, seasoned salt and pepper. Pour over pasta mixture; toss to coat. Stir in olives. Cover and refrigerate for 8 hours or overnight.

3 Toss before serving. Serve with Romano cheese if desired.

Yield: 36 servings.

buttermilk salad dressing

PREP/TOTAL TIME: 10 MIN.

Patricia Mele
Lower Burrell, Pennsylvania

When serving salad to a crowd, this easy recipe comes in handy. It makes a full quart of creamy, delicious dressing to accompany your favorite greens and vegetables.

- 2 cups buttermilk
- 2 cups mayonnaise
- 1 tablespoon onion powder
- 1 tablespoon dried parsley flakes
- 1-1/2 teaspoons garlic powder
- 1/2 teaspoon salt
- 1/2 teaspoon celery salt
- 1/4 teaspoon pepper

1 In a large bowl, whisk all ingredients until smooth. Cover dressing and refrigerate until serving.

Yield: 4 cups.

rhubarb pear gelatin

PREP: 25 MIN. + CHILLING

Linda Strubhar
Cataldo, Idaho

When rhubarb is in season, this is one of my family's favorite ways to eat it. I tried this mixture of ingredients on my own, and my family of 12 couldn't get enough of it.

- 2 packages (6 ounces *each*) strawberry gelatin
- 2 cups miniature marshmallows, *divided*
- 4 cups sliced fresh *or* frozen rhubarb
- 2 cups water
- 2/3 cup sugar
- 2 cups cold water
- 1 can (15-1/4 ounces) sliced pears, drained and chopped

1 Place gelatin and 1 cup marshmallows in a large bowl; set aside.

2 In a large saucepan, combine the rhubarb, water and sugar. Bring to a boil. Reduce heat; cover and simmer for 3-4 minutes or until the rhubarb is tender. Remove from the heat; pour over marshmallow mixture, stirring to dissolve gelatin. Stir in the cold water, pears and remaining marshmallows.

3 Transfer to a 13-in. x 9-in. dish. Refrigerate for at least 6 hours or until firm.

Yield: 12 servings.

broccoli & sweet potato salad

PREP: 15 MIN
BAKE: 30 MIN. + COOLING

Mary Ann Dell
Phoenixville, Pennsylvania

A symphony of flavor is yours the minute you bite into this refreshing, colorful salad. The veggies are lightly coated with a simple dressing and accented with thyme and feta cheese.

4 cups cubed peeled sweet potatoes (about 2 large)

2 medium sweet red peppers, sliced

6 fresh thyme sprigs

7 teaspoons olive oil, *divided*

4 cups fresh broccoli florets

1/2 cup crumbled feta cheese

2 tablespoons sunflower kernels

2 tablespoons cider vinegar

1/2 teaspoon salt

1/4 teaspoon pepper

1 Place the sweet potatoes, red peppers and thyme in a greased 15-in. x 10-in. x 1-in. baking pan. Drizzle with 3 teaspoons oil. Bake, uncovered, at 400° for 30-45 minutes or until the potatoes are tender, stirring once. Cool; discard thyme sprigs.

2 Fill a large saucepan half full of water; bring to a boil. Add broccoli; cover and boil for 2 minutes. Drain and immediately place in ice water. Drain and pat dry.

3 In a large bowl, combine the roasted vegetables, broccoli, cheese and sunflower kernels. In a small bowl, whisk the vinegar, salt, pepper and remaining oil. Pour over vegetable mixture and toss to coat.

Yield: 8 servings.

super italian chopped salad

PREP/TOTAL TIME: 25 MIN.

Kim Molina
Duarte, California

Antipasto ingredients are sliced and diced to make this substantial salad. I like to buy sliced meat from the deli and chop it all up so you can get a bit of everything in each bite.

3 cups torn romaine

1 can (15 ounces) garbanzo beans *or* chickpeas, rinsed and drained

1 jar (6-1/2 ounces) marinated artichoke hearts, drained and chopped

1 medium green pepper, chopped

2 medium tomatoes, chopped

1 can (2-1/4 ounces) sliced ripe olives, drained

5 slices deli ham, chopped

5 thin slices hard salami, chopped

5 slices pepperoni, chopped

3 slices provolone cheese, chopped

2 green onions, chopped

1/4 cup olive oil

2 tablespoons red wine vinegar

1/4 teaspoon salt

1/8 teaspoon pepper

2 tablespoons grated Parmesan cheese

Pepperoncinis, optional

1 In a large bowl, combine the first 11 ingredients. For dressing, in a small bowl, whisk the oil, vinegar, salt and pepper. Pour over salad; toss to coat. Sprinkle with cheese. Top with pepperoncinis if desired.

Yield: 10 servings.

EDITOR'S NOTE: Look for pepperoncinis (pickled peppers) in the pickle and olive section of your grocery store.

southwestern spinach salad

PREP/TOTAL TIME: 25 MIN.

Dixie Terry
Goreville, Illinois

This recipe came from a newspaper a few years ago and quickly became a keeper. It's a delightful salad that will surprise your taste buds.

1/2 cup picante sauce

1/4 cup prepared Italian salad dressing

1/4 teaspoon ground cumin

4 cups fresh baby spinach

1 can (15 ounces) black beans, rinsed and drained

1 cup sliced fresh mushrooms

1 medium sweet red pepper, julienned

1/2 cup sliced red onion

8 bacon strips, cooked and crumbled

4 hard-cooked eggs, sliced

Additional picante sauce, optional

1 In a small bowl, combine the picante sauce, salad dressing and cumin.

2 In a salad bowl, combine the spinach, beans, mushrooms, pepper, onion and bacon. Drizzle with dressing; toss to coat. Garnish with eggs. Serve with additional picante sauce if desired.

Yield: 6 servings.

company's coming salad

PREP/TOTAL TIME: 30 MIN.

Dolores Lucken
Ferdinand, Indiana

Sugared almonds give my delicious salad an over-the-top kick that guests will adore.

- 2 tablespoons sugar
- 1/2 cup sliced almonds
- 1 package (5 ounces) spring mix salad greens
- 6 cups torn romaine
- 1 can (11 ounces) mandarin oranges, drained
- 2 celery ribs, thinly sliced
- 1 small red onion, chopped
- 2 green onions, thinly sliced

DRESSING:

- 3 tablespoons canola oil
- 2 tablespoons cider vinegar
- 5 teaspoons sugar
- 1 tablespoon minced fresh parsley
- 1/4 teaspoon salt

1 In a small heavy skillet, cook and stir the sugar over medium-low heat until melted. Stir in almonds; cook for 1 minute or until lightly browned. Spread onto foil coated with cooking spray; set aside.

2 In a large salad bowl, combine the mixed greens, romaine, oranges, celery and onions. In a small bowl, whisk the dressing ingredients. Drizzle over salad; add almonds and toss to coat.

Yield: 8 servings.

peachy rice salad

PREP/TOTAL TIME: 20 MIN.

Linda Goshorn
Bedford, Virginia

We especially love this refreshing rice salad in summer, when fresh peaches are available. Yogurt and honey make a light dressing while celery and walnuts add crunch.

1/3 cup plain yogurt

2 tablespoons honey

4 teaspoons lemon juice

1/2 teaspoon salt

2 cups cold cooked rice

2 medium peaches, peeled and diced *or* 1-1/2 cups frozen unsweetened peach slices, thawed and diced

1/2 cup sliced celery

1/4 cup coarsely chopped walnuts, toasted

1 In a large bowl, combine the yogurt, honey, lemon juice and salt. Stir in the rice, peaches and celery. Cover and refrigerate. Just before serving, stir in walnuts.

Yield: 4 servings.

rice noodle salad

PREP/TOTAL TIME: 25 MIN.

Krista Frank
Rhododendron, Oregon

This salad is easy, sweet, spicy, nutty and light. To make it a main dish, I add marinated and grilled teriyaki chicken.

1 package (8.8 ounces) thin rice noodles

2 cups fresh spinach, cut into strips

1 large carrot, shredded

1/2 cup pineapple tidbits

1/4 cup minced fresh cilantro

1 green onion, chopped

SESAME PEANUT DRESSING:

1/4 cup unsalted peanuts

1/4 cup water

1/4 cup lime juice

2 tablespoons soy sauce

1 tablespoon brown sugar

1 tablespoon canola oil

1 teaspoon sesame oil

1/2 teaspoon ground ginger

1/4 teaspoon crushed red pepper flakes

1 Cook noodles according to package directions. Meanwhile, in a large salad bowl, combine the spinach, carrot, pineapple, cilantro and onion.

2 In a blender, combine the dressing ingredients; cover and process until blended. Drain noodles and rinse in cold water; drain well. Add to spinach mixture. Drizzle with dressing and toss to coat.

Yield: 8-10 servings.

maple salad dressing

PREP/TOTAL TIME: 10 MIN.

Janet Lawton
St. Albans, Vermont

Sweet and tangy like French dressing, this quick-to-fix mixture will jazz up most any green salad. I know you'll love it!

7 tablespoons maple syrup

1/4 cup cider vinegar

1/4 cup ketchup

3 tablespoons plus 1 teaspoon canola oil

2 tablespoons water

1/2 teaspoon prepared horseradish

1/4 teaspoon salt

1/8 teaspoon celery salt

1 In a small bowl, whisk all the ingredients. Cover and refrigerate until serving.

Yield: 1-1/4 cups.

veggie barley salad

PREP: 30 MIN. + CHILLING

Kathy Rairigh
Milford, Indiana

When I took this salad to a family potluck, it was such a hit! I often fix it with basil-flavored vinegar that I make each summer. The longer this chills, the tastier it gets.

1-1/4 cups reduced-sodium chicken broth *or* vegetable broth

3/4 cup water

1 cup quick-cooking barley

1 medium tomato, seeded and chopped

1 small zucchini, halved and thinly sliced

1 small sweet yellow pepper, chopped

2 tablespoons minced fresh parsley

DRESSING:

3 tablespoons olive oil

2 tablespoons white wine vinegar

1 tablespoon water

1 tablespoon lemon juice

1 tablespoon minced fresh basil

1/2 teaspoon salt

1/4 teaspoon pepper

1/4 cup slivered almonds, toasted

1 In a small saucepan, bring the broth, water and barley to a boil. Reduce heat; cover and simmer for 10-12 minutes or until barley is tender. Remove from the heat; let stand for 5 minutes.

2 In a large serving bowl, combine the tomato, zucchini, yellow pepper and parsley. Stir in barley. In a small bowl, whisk the oil, vinegar, water, lemon juice, basil, salt and pepper. Pour over barley mixture; toss to coat. Cover and refrigerate for at least 3 hours. Just before serving, stir in almonds.

Yield: 6 servings.

easy caesar salad

PREP/TOTAL TIME: 15 MIN.

Dianne Nash
Kaslo, British Columbia

Make your own Caesar salad in just minutes. This recipe is easy to prepare and tasty, too!

> 1/4 cup grated Parmesan cheese
>
> 1/4 cup mayonnaise
>
> 2 tablespoons whole milk
>
> 1 tablespoon lemon juice

1 tablespoon Dijon-mayonnaise blend

1 garlic clove, minced

Dash cayenne pepper

1 bunch romaine, torn

Salad croutons and additional grated Parmesan cheese, optional

1 In a small bowl, whisk the first seven ingredients. Place romaine in a large bowl. Drizzle with dressing and toss to coat. Serve with salad croutons and additional cheese if desired.

Yield: 8 servings.

tangy carrot salad

PREP: 20 MIN. + CHILLING

Peggy Gleichman
McAlester, Oklahoma

This is one of my favorite carrot recipes. Our family and friends always ask for it!

1 pound carrots, cut into 1/4-inch slices

2 celery ribs, chopped

1 small onion, chopped

1/3 cup reduced-fat mayonnaise

1/4 cup white vinegar

4 teaspoons sugar

1/2 teaspoon garlic salt

1/4 teaspoon pepper

1 Place carrots in a steamer basket; place in a small saucepan over 1 in. of water. Bring to a boil; cover and steam for 7-10 minutes or until crisp-tender. Rinse in cold water.

2 In a small bowl, combine the carrots, celery and onion. In another bowl, combine the mayonnaise, vinegar, sugar, garlic salt and pepper. Add to carrot mixture and stir gently to coat completely. Cover and refrigerate for at least 2 hours. Serve with a slotted spoon.

Yield: 4 servings.

corn and black bean salad

PREP: 15 MIN. + CHILLING

Krista Frank
Rhododendron, Oregon

This colorful, crunchy salad is chock-full of easy-to-swallow nutrition that all ages will love. Try it with a variety of summer entrees.

1 can (15-1/4 ounces) whole kernel corn, drained

1 can (15 ounces) black beans, rinsed and drained

2 large tomatoes, finely chopped

1 large red onion, finely chopped

1/4 cup minced fresh cilantro

2 garlic cloves, minced

DRESSING:

2 tablespoons sugar

2 tablespoons white vinegar

2 tablespoons canola oil

1-1/2 teaspoons lime juice

1/4 teaspoon salt

1/4 teaspoon ground cumin

1/4 teaspoon pepper

1 In a large bowl, combine the first six ingredients. In a small bowl, whisk the dressing ingredients; pour over corn mixture and toss to coat. Cover and refrigerate for at least 1 hour. Stir before serving. Serve with a slotted spoon.

Yield: 8 servings.

scrumptious scrambled salad

PREP: 45 MIN. + CHILLING

Becky Muldrow
Highlands, Texas

This recipe makes a large bowl of absolutely delicious salad, so it's perfect for picnics, potlucks or backyard barbecues. It always disappears as fast as I make it.

2 large bunches romaine, torn

12 green onions, thinly sliced

1-1/2 cups sliced water chestnuts, coarsely chopped

1 package (16 ounces) frozen peas, thawed

2-1/4 cups mayonnaise

1/2 cup plus 1 tablespoon evaporated milk

1/4 cup plus 1-1/2 teaspoons cider vinegar

3/4 teaspoon garlic powder

2 cups (8 ounces) shredded cheddar cheese

3 medium tomatoes, chopped

1 pound sliced bacon, cooked, crumbled and drained

3 hard-cooked eggs, sliced

1 In a very large salad bowl, layer the romaine, onions, water chestnuts and peas. Combine the mayonnaise, milk, vinegar and garlic powder; spread over peas. Sprinkle with cheese. Cover and refrigerate for 8 hours or overnight.

2 Just before serving, add the tomatoes, bacon and eggs; toss gently.

Yield: 24 servings.

marinated vegetable salad

PREP: 20 MIN. + CHILLING

Sarah Newman
Mahtomedi, Minnesota

Toss some good-for-you veggies together with a coating of fat-free dressing, and you've got this ideal side dish in no time. The salad is so easy, and marinating the vegetables overnight gives them a great flavor and texture.

2 cups fresh broccoli florets

2 cups fresh cauliflowerets

1 medium cucumber, halved and thinly sliced

1 cup sliced fresh mushrooms

1 cup cherry tomatoes, halved

1/3 cup finely chopped red onion

1/2 cup fat-free Italian salad dressing

1 In a large bowl, gently combine the broccoli, cauliflower, cucumber, mushrooms, tomatoes and onion. Add dressing and toss to coat. Cover and refrigerate for 8 hours or overnight.

Yield: 6 servings.

roasted pepper mushroom salad

PREP: 30 MIN. + CHILLING

Bonnie Hawkins
Elkhorn, Wisconsin

This is a very pretty dish to serve at any type of get-together. I always make a double batch so everyone can have seconds.

- 1 large sweet red pepper
- 1 large green pepper
- 2 cups whole fresh mushrooms
- 1 small red onion, sliced
- 1/2 cup pitted ripe olives
- 1/3 cup Italian salad dressing
- 1 garlic clove, minced
- 1 teaspoon dried basil
- 1/2 teaspoon salt
- 1/2 teaspoon dried oregano
- 1/2 teaspoon pepper
- Lettuce leaves

1 Broil the peppers 4 in. from the heat until skins blister, about 10 minutes. With tongs, rotate the peppers a quarter turn. Broil and rotate until all sides are blistered and blackened. Immediately place the peppers in a bowl; cover and let stand for 15-20 minutes.

2 Peel off and discard charred skin. Remove stems and seeds. Cut peppers into thin slices. In a large bowl, combine the peppers, mushrooms, onion and olives.

3 In a small bowl, combine the salad dressing, garlic, basil, salt, oregano and pepper. Pour over the vegetables; toss to coat. Cover and refrigerate for 8 hours or overnight. Serve on lettuce leaves.

Yield: 6 servings.

colorful gazpacho salad

PREP: 20 MIN. + CHILLING

Brenda Hoffman
Stanton, Michigan

The combination of flavors from the tomatoes, jicama and cilantro make this salad great for picnics, potlucks, cookouts and salad buffets. It is simply delicious.

> 5 medium tomatoes, seeded and chopped
>
> 1 cup chopped peeled cucumber
>
> 3/4 cup chopped red onion
>
> 1 small sweet red pepper, chopped
>
> 1/2 cup fresh *or* frozen corn
>
> 1 tablespoon lime juice
>
> 1 tablespoon red wine vinegar
>
> 2 teaspoons water

> 2 garlic cloves, minced
>
> 1 teaspoon olive oil
>
> 1/4 teaspoon salt
>
> 1/4 teaspoon pepper
>
> 1/8 teaspoon crushed red pepper flakes
>
> 8 cups torn romaine
>
> 1 cup diced peeled jicama
>
> 1/2 cup minced fresh cilantro

1 In a large bowl, combine the tomatoes, cucumber, onion, red pepper and corn. In a small bowl, whisk the lime juice, vinegar, water, garlic, oil, salt, pepper and pepper flakes. Drizzle over tomato mixture; toss to coat. Refrigerate until chilled.

2 Just before serving, combine the romaine, jicama and cilantro. Place 1 cup on each of eight salad plates; top each with 1/3 cup tomato mixture.

Yield: 8 servings.

dilly potato salad

PREP: 40 MIN. + CHILLING

Angela Leinenbach
Mechanicsville, Virginia

Everyone has a favorite potato salad, and this is mine. I hope you will be adventurous and give it a try. I've received lots of compliments on it and requests for the recipe whenever I prepare it for summertime gatherings.

4 pounds red potatoes, halved

5 hard-cooked eggs

1 cup chopped dill pickles

1 small onion, chopped

1-1/2 cups mayonnaise

1 teaspoon celery seed

1/2 teaspoon salt

1/4 teaspoon pepper

Paprika

1 Place potatoes in a large saucepan; cover with water. Bring to a boil. Reduce heat; cover and cook for 15 to 20 minutes or until tender. Drain and cool.

2 Cut potatoes into 3/4-in. cubes. Chop four eggs; slice remaining egg for garnish. In a large bowl, combine the potatoes, chopped eggs, pickles and onion.

3 In a small bowl, combine the mayonnaise, celery seed, salt and pepper. Pour over potato mixture and stir gently to coat. Sprinkle with paprika; garnish with sliced egg. Cover and refrigerate for at least 2 hours before serving.

Yield: 12-14 servings.

fiesta salad

PREP/TOTAL TIME: 10 MIN.

Heather Byers
Pittsburgh, Pennsylvania

I was making a Mexican themed dinner and figured I'd make a salad with fresh produce. I threw in anything that reminded me of Mexican food. Thankfully, it turned out, and the combination of salsa and ranch dressing is one we now use on sandwiches, burgers and more.

- 2 cups torn romaine
- 3/4 cup frozen corn, thawed
- 1/3 cup canned black beans, rinsed and drained
- 1 medium tomato, chopped
- 1 celery rib, chopped
- 1 medium carrot, thinly sliced
- 1/4 cup torn curly endive
- 1/3 cup salsa
- 2 tablespoons reduced-fat sour cream
- 2 tablespoons reduced-fat ranch salad dressing

1 In a salad bowl, combine the first seven ingredients. In a small bowl, combine the salsa, sour cream and ranch dressing. Drizzle over salad and toss to coat.

Yield: 4 servings.

tangy cabbage slaw

PREP/TOTAL TIME: 10 MIN.

Rose Purrington
Windom, Minnesota

People enjoy the crunchy texture and the sweet-and-sour zip of this slaw. Plus, it can be easily made ahead of time.

  1 package (3 ounces) chicken ramen noodles

  3-3/4 cups coleslaw mix

  1/3 cup slivered almonds

  3 tablespoons sliced green onions

  1/2 cup canola oil

  1/3 cup white wine vinegar

  3 tablespoons sugar

1 In a large bowl, break noodles into small pieces; set seasoning packet aside. Add the coleslaw mix, almonds and onions.

2 In a small bowl, whisk the oil, vinegar, sugar and contents of seasoning packet. Pour over coleslaw mixture and toss to coat. Serve with a slotted spoon. Refrigerate leftovers.

Yield: 4-6 servings.

greek macaroni salad

PREP: 15 MIN. + CHILLING

Cheryl Maczko
Eglon, West Virginia

I've found that I can't go wrong taking this colorful bean and pasta salad to a potluck, patio party or picnic. It is easy to put together.

  1 cup uncooked elbow macaroni

  4 medium plum tomatoes, chopped

  1 can (15 ounces) garbanzo beans *or* chickpeas, rinsed and drained

  1 medium onion, chopped

  1 can (6 ounces) pitted ripe olives

  1 package (4 ounces) crumbled feta cheese

  1 teaspoon salt

  1/2 teaspoon pepper

  1 garlic clove, minced

  1/2 cup olive oil

  1/4 cup lemon juice

1 Cook macaroni according to package directions; drain and rinse in cold water. In a large bowl, combine the macaroni, tomatoes, beans, onion, olives, feta cheese, salt, pepper and garlic.

2 In a small bowl, whisk the oil and the lemon juice. Pour over salad; toss to coat. Cover and refrigerate until chilled. Stir before serving.

Yield: 8 servings.

p. 337

p. 359

p. 348

p. 357

savory dill and caraway scones

PREP: 20 MIN. • BAKE: 15 MIN.

Sally Sibthorpe
Shelby Township, Michigan

These tender, tasty scones will melt in your mouth. The unique flavors of dill and caraway ensure that you won't soon forget this treat.

2 cups all-purpose flour

4-1/2 teaspoons sugar

1 tablespoon onion powder

1 tablespoon snipped fresh dill *or* 1 teaspoon dill weed

2 teaspoons caraway seeds

1 teaspoon baking powder

3/4 teaspoon salt

1/2 teaspoon baking soda

1/2 teaspoon coarsely ground pepper

6 tablespoons cold butter

1 egg yolk

3/4 cup sour cream

1/2 cup ricotta cheese

4 teaspoons heavy whipping cream

Additional caraway seeds, optional

1 In a large bowl, combine the first nine ingredients. Cut in butter until mixture resembles coarse crumbs. Combine the egg yolk, sour cream and ricotta cheese; stir into crumb mixture just until moistened. Turn onto a floured surface; knead 10 times.

2 Pat into two 6-in. circles. Cut each into six wedges. Separate wedges and place on a greased baking sheet. Brush tops with cream; sprinkle with additional caraway seeds if desired. Bake at 400° for 15-18 minutes or until golden brown. Serve warm.

Yield: 1 dozen.

applesauce bread

PREP: 20 MIN.
BAKE: 50 MIN. + COOLING

Sherry Craw
Mattoon, Illinois

This recipe contains quite a bit of applesauce, which provides natural sweetness so you use less sugar. As a bonus, it requires only a minimal amount of oil.

1 cup all-purpose flour
1 cup whole wheat flour
1/2 cup sugar
1-1/2 teaspoons ground cinnamon, *divided*
1 teaspoon baking soda
1/2 teaspoon salt
1/2 teaspoon baking powder
1/4 teaspoon ground nutmeg
2 egg whites

1 egg
1-1/4 cups unsweetened applesauce
1/4 cup canola oil
3 tablespoons fat-free milk
1/4 cup packed brown sugar

1 In a large bowl, combine the flours, sugar, 1 teaspoon cinnamon, baking soda, salt, baking powder and nutmeg. In a small bowl, whisk the egg whites, egg, applesauce, oil and milk. Stir into the dry ingredients just until moistened.

2 Transfer to a 9-in. x 5-in. loaf pan coated with cooking spray. Combine the brown sugar and remaining cinnamon; sprinkle over the top.

3 Bake at 350° for 50-60 minutes or until a toothpick inserted near the center comes out clean. Cool for 10 minutes before removing from pan to a wire rack.

Yield: 1 loaf (16 slices).

bacon spinach muffins

PREP: 20 MIN. • BAKE: 20 MIN.

Rebecca Lindamood
Belfast, New York

A new addition to my repertoire, these rustic muffins with just a touch of feta cheese are very popular. They make a fabulous accompaniment to soups and salads, are super-quick to whip up from scratch and so satisfying!

6 bacon strips, diced

1/2 cup butter, softened

2 tablespoons sugar

1 egg

1/2 cup sour cream

1/2 cup whole milk

2 cups all-purpose flour

1/2 teaspoon baking powder

1/2 teaspoon baking soda

1/2 teaspoon salt

1/2 cup crumbled feta cheese

1/4 cup finely chopped onion

1 package (10 ounces) frozen chopped spinach, thawed and squeezed dry

1 In a small skillet, cook bacon over medium heat until crisp. Remove to paper towels to drain. Meanwhile, in a small bowl, cream butter and sugar until light and fluffy; beat in egg.

2 Combine sour cream and milk. Combine the flour, baking powder, baking soda and salt; add to creamed mixture alternately with the sour cream mixture just until moistened. Fold in the bacon, feta cheese, onion and 1/4 cup spinach (save remaining spinach for another use).

3 Fill greased or paper-lined muffin cups three-fourths full. Bake at 375° for 18-22 minutes or until a toothpick inserted near the center comes out clean. Cool for 5 minutes before removing from pan to a wire rack. Serve warm.

Yield: 1 dozen.

herb quick bread

PREP: 15 MIN.
BAKE: 40 MIN. + COOLING

Donna Roberts
Manhattan, Kansas

This simple loaf is especially good with soups and stews, but slices are also tasty alongside fresh, green salads. The herbs make it a flavorful treat any time of the year.

3 cups all-purpose flour

3 tablespoons sugar

1 tablespoon baking powder

1 tablespoon caraway seeds

1/2 teaspoon salt

1/2 teaspoon dried thyme

1/2 teaspoon ground nutmeg

1 egg

1 cup fat-free milk

1/3 cup canola oil

1 In a large bowl, combine the first seven ingredients. In a small bowl, whisk the egg, milk and oil; stir into dry ingredients just until moistened.

2 Transfer to a 9-in. x 5-in. loaf pan coated with cooking spray. Bake at 350° for 40-50 minutes or until a toothpick inserted near the center comes out clean. Cool for 10 minutes before removing from pan to a wire rack to cool completely.

Yield: 1 loaf (14 slices).

irish soda bread muffins

PREP/TOTAL TIME: 30 MIN.

Lorraine Ballsieper
Deep River, Connecticut

Irish soda bread is traditionally prepared in a loaf shape, but these currant-dotted muffins have the same terrific flavor.

2-1/4 cups all-purpose flour

1/2 cup plus 1 tablespoon sugar, *divided*

2 teaspoons baking powder

1/2 teaspoon salt

1/4 teaspoon baking soda

1 teaspoon caraway seeds

1 egg

1 cup buttermilk

1/4 cup butter, melted

1/4 cup canola oil

3/4 cup dried currants *or* raisins

1 In a large bowl, combine the flour, 1/2 cup sugar, baking powder, salt, baking soda and caraway seeds. In another bowl, beat the egg, buttermilk, butter and oil. Stir into the dry ingredients just until moistened. Fold in the currants.

2 Fill greased muffin cups three-fourths full. Sprinkle with remaining sugar. Bake at 400° for 15 minutes or until a toothpick inserted near the center comes out clean. Cool for 5 minutes before removing from pan to wire rack. Serve warm.

Yield: 1 dozen.

3/4 cup shredded part-skim mozzarella cheese

1/3 cup grated Parmesan cheese, *divided*

1 In a large skillet, cook onions in butter over medium heat for 10-12 minutes or until very tender. Remove and keep warm. In the same skillet, cook steak for 2-3 minutes or until no longer pink.

2 Return onions to the pan. Stir in the flour, brown sugar and salt until blended; gradually add the broth. Bring to a boil; cook and stir for 4-6 minutes or until the mixture is thickened.

3 Separate biscuits; split each horizontally into three portions. Press onto the bottom and up the sides of eight ungreased muffin cups, overlapping the sides and tops of the dough pieces. Fill each with about 2 tablespoons beef mixture.

4 Combine the mozzarella cheese and 1/4 cup Parmesan cheese; sprinkle over filling. Fold the dough over completely to enclose filling. Sprinkle with the remaining Parmesan cheese.

5 Bake at 375° for 12-15 minutes or until golden brown. Let stand for 2 minutes before removing from pan. Serve warm.

Yield: 4 servings.

onion-beef muffin cups

PREP: 25 MIN. • BAKE: 15 MIN.

Barbara Carlucci
Orange Park, Florida

Refrigerated biscuits make these delicious bites so quick and easy! They're one of my tried-and-true lunch recipes and always bring raves. I usually double the recipe just to be sure I have leftovers.

3 medium onions, thinly sliced

1/4 cup butter, cubed

1 beef top sirloin steak (1-inch thick and 6 ounces), cut into 1/8-inch slices

1 teaspoon all-purpose flour

1 teaspoon brown sugar

1/4 teaspoon salt

1/2 cup beef broth

1 tube (16.3 ounces) large refrigerated flaky biscuits

Jumbo vs. Mini. Generally, the oven temperature won't need to be adjusted if you are using mini or jumbo muffin pans, but the baking time will most likely need to be altered. Mini muffins can take anywhere from 10 to 15 minutes while jumbo muffins can take from 20 to 40 minutes. The baking time will vary according to the recipe due to the oven temperature and the amount of batter in each muffin cup.

parmesan knots

PREP/TOTAL TIME: 15 MIN.

Jane Paschke
Duluth, Minnesota

These novel knots are handy because they can be made ahead of time and reheated when needed.

1 tube (12 ounces) refrigerated buttermilk biscuits

1/4 cup canola oil

3 tablespoons grated Parmesan cheese

1 teaspoon garlic powder

1 teaspoon dried oregano

1 teaspoon dried parsley flakes

1 Cut each biscuit into thirds. Roll each piece into a 3-in. rope and tie into a knot; tuck ends under. Place 2 in. apart on a greased baking sheet. Bake at 400° for 8-10 minutes or until golden brown.

2 In a large bowl, combine the remaining ingredients; add the warm knots and gently toss to coat.

Yield: 2-1/2 dozen.

spinach spirals

PREP: 15 MIN. • BAKE: 25 MIN.

Isabel Mancini
Youngstown, Ohio

When I bring this quick and tasty bread to a potluck, someone always asks for the recipe.

1 package (10 ounces) frozen chopped spinach, thawed and squeezed dry

1 cup (4 ounces) shredded Monterey Jack cheese

1 egg, lightly beaten

2 tablespoons dried minced onion

1 tube (13.8 ounces) refrigerated pizza crust

1 tablespoon butter, melted

2 tablespoons grated Parmesan cheese

1 In a small bowl, combine the spinach, Monterey Jack cheese, egg and onion. On a baking sheet coated with cooking spray, roll pizza dough into a 14-in. x 10-in. rectangle; seal any holes. Spread spinach mixture to within 1/2 in. of edges.

2 Roll up jelly-roll style, starting with a long side; seal ends and place seam side down. Brush with butter; sprinkle with Parmesan cheese. Bake at 400° for 25-27 minutes or until golden brown. Slice and serve warm.

Yield: 14 slices.

mini cheddar loaves

PREP: 10 MIN.
BAKE: 35 MIN. + COOLING

Melody Rowland
Chattanooga, Tennessee

It's hard to believe you need only four ingredients to bake up a batch of these beautiful miniature loaves. Sliced warm from the oven, this golden bread is simple and delicious.

3-1/2 cups biscuit/baking mix

2-1/2 cups (10 ounces) shredded sharp cheddar cheese

2 eggs

1-1/4 cups whole milk

1 In a large bowl, combine biscuit mix and cheese. Beat eggs and milk; stir into cheese mixture just until moistened. Pour into four greased and floured 5-3/4-in. x 3-in. x 2-in. loaf pans.

2 Bake at 350° for 35-40 minutes or until a toothpick inserted near the center comes out clean. Cool for 10 minutes. Remove from pans; slice and serve warm.

Yield: 4 mini loaves.

sweet potato bread

PREP: 15 MIN.
BAKE: 1 HOUR + COOLING

Rebecca Cook Jones
Henderson, Nevada

This moist and spicy bread gives a true feeling of fall. My family isn't fond of traditional sweet potatoes, so I make this yummy bread instead.

  1-3/4 cups all-purpose flour

  1-1/2 cups sugar

  1 teaspoon baking soda

  1 teaspoon ground cinnamon

  1 teaspoon ground nutmeg

  3/4 teaspoon salt

  1/4 teaspoon ground allspice

  1/4 teaspoon ground cloves

  2 eggs

  1-1/2 cups mashed sweet potatoes
  (about 2 medium)

  1/2 cup canola oil

  6 tablespoons orange juice

  1/2 cup chopped pecans

1 In a large bowl, combine the first eight ingredients. In a small bowl, whisk the eggs, sweet potatoes, oil and orange juice. Stir into dry ingredients just until moistened. Fold in pecans.

2 Transfer to a greased 9-in. x 5-in. loaf pan. Bake at 350° for 60-65 minutes or until a toothpick inserted near the center comes out clean. Cool for 10 minutes before removing from pan to a wire rack.

Yield: 1 loaf.

parmesan-ranch pan rolls

PREP: 30 MIN. + RISING
BAKE: 20 MIN.

Trisha Kruse
Eagle, Idaho

My mom taught me this easy recipe, which is great for feeding a crowd. There is never a crumb left over. Mom used her own bread dough, but using frozen dough is my shortcut.

  2 loaves (1 pound *each*) frozen bread dough,
  thawed

  1 cup grated Parmesan cheese

  1/2 cup butter, melted

  1 envelope buttermilk ranch salad dressing mix

  1 small onion, finely chopped

1 On a lightly floured surface, divide dough into 18 portions; shape each into a ball. In a small bowl, combine the cheese, butter and ranch dressing mix.

2 Roll balls in cheese mixture; arrange in two greased 9-in. square baking pans. Sprinkle with onion. Cover and let rise in a warm place until doubled, about 45 minutes.

3 Bake at 350° for 20-25 minutes or until tops are golden brown. Remove from pans to wire racks.

Yield: 1-1/2 dozen.

> **Grated Parmesan.** If you grate your own Parmesan cheese, be sure to use the finest section on your grating tool. You can also use a blender or food processor. Simply cut the cheese into 1-inch cubes and process 1 cup of the cubes at a time on high until finely grated.

basil cheddar scones

PREP: 20 MIN. • BAKE: 20 MIN.

Taste of Home Test Kitchen

For a hostess gift, tuck these oven-fresh savory scones into a napkin-lined gift basket, along with a package of pasta and jar of spaghetti sauce.

2-1/4 cups all-purpose flour

2 teaspoons baking powder

1/2 cup cold butter, cubed

1 egg

1 cup whole milk

1 cup (4 ounces) shredded cheddar cheese

1/4 cup prepared pesto sauce

1 In a large bowl, combine flour and baking powder. Cut in the butter until mixture resembles coarse crumbs. In another bowl, combine the egg, milk, cheese and pesto. Stir into flour mixture just until moistened.

2 Turn onto a lightly floured surface; knead 8-10 times. Transfer to a greased baking sheet. Pat into a 10-in. circle; cut into eight wedges but do not separate.

3 Bake at 400° for 20-25 minutes or until golden brown. Serve warm.

Yield: 8 scones.

parmesan zucchini bread

PREP: 10 MIN.
BAKE: 1 HOUR + COOLING

Christine Wilson
Sellersville, Pennsylvania

This loaf has a rugged, textured look that adds to its old-fashioned appeal. The mild Parmesan flavor nicely complements the zucchini, which adds bits of green color to every tender slice.

    3 cups all-purpose flour
    3 tablespoons grated Parmesan cheese
    1 teaspoon salt
    1/2 teaspoon baking powder
    1/2 teaspoon baking soda
    2 eggs
    1 cup buttermilk
    1/3 cup sugar
    1/3 cup butter, melted
    1 cup shredded peeled zucchini
    1 tablespoon grated onion

1 In a large bowl, combine the flour, cheese, salt, baking powder and baking soda. In another bowl, whisk the eggs, buttermilk, sugar and butter. Stir into dry ingredients just until moistened. Fold in the zucchini and onion.

2 Pour into a greased and floured 9-in. x 5-in. loaf pan. Bake at 350° for 1 hour or until a toothpick inserted near the center comes out clean. Cool for 10 minutes before removing from pan to a wire rack.

Yield: 1 loaf (16 slices).

peppy cheese bread

PREP: 10 MIN. • BAKE: 4 HOURS

Dusti Christensen
Goodridge, Minnesota

*As a stay-at-home mother of two little girls, I pack
a lot of activity into my days. The bread machine
makes it a snap for me to turn out this attractive
loaf that gets zip from cayenne pepper, pepperoni
and Mexican cheese.*

1 cup water (70° to 80°)

1 tablespoon butter

2 tablespoons sugar

2 teaspoons ground mustard

1/2 teaspoon salt

1/2 teaspoon cayenne pepper

1/4 teaspoon garlic powder

3 cups bread flour

2-1/4 teaspoons active dry yeast

1-1/2 cups (6 ounces) shredded Mexican
cheese blend

1 cup chopped pepperoni

1 In bread machine pan, place the first
nine ingredients in order suggested by
the manufacturer. Select the basic bread
setting. Choose the crust color and loaf
size if available. Bake according to bread
machine directions (check the dough after
5 minutes of mixing; add 1 to 2 tablespoons
of water or flour if needed).

2 Just before the final kneading (your bread
machine may audibly signal this), add the
cheese and pepperoni.

**Yield: 1 loaf (about 1-1/2 pounds, 16
slices).**

EDITOR'S NOTE: We recommend you do not use a
bread machine's time-delay feature for this recipe.

mini blue cheese rolls

PREP/TOTAL TIME: 25 MIN.

Myrtle Albrecht
Shingle Springs, California

These savory bites are a fun and easy way to dress up refrigerated breadsticks.

- 1/4 cup butter, cubed
- 1/2 cup crumbled blue cheese
- 1 tube (11 ounces) refrigerated breadsticks

1 In a saucepan, melt butter and blue cheese over low heat. Unroll dough. Separate into six sections. Cut each double breadstick into six pieces; place in a foil-lined 11-in. x 7-in. baking pan. Pour cheese mixture over dough.

2 Bake at 400° for 20 minutes or until butter is absorbed and rolls are lightly browned. Carefully lift foil out of pan; transfer rolls to a serving plate. Serve warm.

Yield: 4-6 servings.

caramelized onion breadsticks

PREP: 45 MIN. + RISING
BAKE: 15 MIN.

Jennifer Bermingham
Shillington, Pennsylvania

I'm a sixth grade special education teacher with very little time on my hands. These easy-to-make breadsticks go especially well with my hearty vegetable beef soup.

- 1 large sweet onion, halved and thinly sliced
- 6 tablespoons butter, *divided*
- 1 teaspoon sugar
- 1 loaf (1 pound) frozen bread dough, thawed

1 In a large skillet over medium-low heat, cook onion in 4 tablespoons butter for 5 minutes or until tender. Add sugar; cook over low heat for 30-40 minutes longer or until onion is golden brown, stirring frequently.

2 On a lightly floured surface, roll bread dough into an 18-in. x 12-in. rectangle. Spoon onion mixture lengthwise over half of the dough; fold plain half of dough over onion mixture. Cut into eighteen 1-in. strips. Twist each strip twice; pinch ends to seal.

3 Place 2 in. apart on greased baking sheets. Melt the remaining butter; brush over breadsticks. Cover and let rise in a warm place until doubled, about 40 minutes.

4 Bake at 350° for 12-15 minutes or until lightly browned. Serve warm.

Yield: 1-1/2 dozen.

sun-dried tomato cheese biscuits

PREP/TOTAL TIME: 20 MIN.

Lisa Huff
Clive, Iowa

On busy nights, I whip up these yummy biscuits.

- 1-1/2 cups biscuit/baking mix
- 1/3 cup shredded part-skim mozzarella cheese
- 1/4 cup grated Parmesan cheese
- 1 teaspoon Italian seasoning
- 1/4 teaspoon onion powder
- 1/4 teaspoon garlic powder
- 1/2 cup buttermilk
- 3 tablespoons oil-packed sun-dried tomatoes, drained and finely chopped
- 1-1/2 teaspoons butter, melted

1 In a large bowl, combine the biscuit mix, cheeses, Italian seasoning, onion powder and garlic powder. Stir in buttermilk and tomatoes just until moistened.

2 Drop by 1/4 cupfuls 2 in. apart onto a greased baking sheet. Bake at 425° for 8-12 minutes or until golden brown. Brush with butter. Serve warm.

Yield: 6 biscuits.

Baking Biscuits. For biscuits to bake properly, arrange the oven rack so that the baking sheet is in the center. Use a hot oven (425°-450°) and a baking time of 8-12 minutes for standard-size biscuits. Insulated baking sheets will not allow the bottom of biscuits to brown like regular baking sheets do.

mushroom cheese bread

PREP: 25 MIN. • BAKE: 20 MIN.

Lori Stefanishion
Drumheller, Alberta

I serve this satisfying bread as a side with meat, fish and main-dish soups and salads. The savory slices are lifesavers when you need a last-minute appetizer or brunch item.

6 cups sliced fresh mushrooms

1 tablespoon butter

4 green onions, chopped

1 loaf (1 pound) French bread

1 carton (8 ounces) spreadable garlic and herb cream cheese

2 cups (8 ounces) shredded Italian cheese blend

1 cup mayonnaise

1 cup grated Parmesan cheese

1 In a large skillet, saute mushrooms in butter until tender. Add onions; cook and stir until liquid has evaporated. Set aside.

2 Cut French bread in half lengthwise and then widthwise; spread cut sides with cream cheese. Combine the Italian cheese, mayonnaise and Parmesan cheese; spread over bread. Top with mushroom mixture.

3 Place on a baking sheet. Bake at 350° for 20 minutes or until cheese is melted. If desired, broil 4-6 in. from the heat for 2-4 minutes or until golden brown. Slice and serve warm.

Yield: 16 servings.

popovers

PREP: 20 MIN. • BAKE: 45 MIN.

Lourdes Dewick
Fort Lauderdale, Florida

Popovers have a crisp exterior and an almost hollow interior. As they bake, the liquid in the batter turns to steam, making the batter pop up.

1 tablespoon shortening

2 eggs

1 cup whole milk

1 tablespoon butter, melted

1 cup all-purpose flour

1/2 teaspoon salt

1 Using 1/2 teaspoon shortening for each cup, grease the bottom and sides of six 6-oz. custard cups or the cups of a popover pan. If using custard cups, place on a 15-in. x 10-in. x 1-in. baking pan.

2 In a small bowl, beat eggs; blend in milk and butter. Beat in flour and salt until smooth (do not overbeat).

3 Fill cups half full. Bake at 450° for 15 minutes. Reduce heat to 350°; bake 30 minutes longer or until very firm. Remove from oven and prick each popover to allow steam to escape. Serve immediately.

Yield: 6 servings.

pecan lemon loaf

PREP: 20 MIN.
BAKE: 50 MIN. + COOLING

Laura Comitz
Enola, Pennsylvania

A pretty glaze gives this tender, nutty bread an extra boost of lemony flavor. I make it at least once a week. For variety, I substitute grated orange peel and orange juice for the lemons.

1/2 cup butter, softened

1-1/2 cups sugar, *divided*

2 eggs

2 cups all-purpose flour

1 teaspoon baking powder

1/2 teaspoon salt

3/4 cup sour cream

1 cup chopped pecans, toasted

1 tablespoon grated lemon peel

1/4 cup lemon juice

1 In a large bowl, cream butter and 1 cup sugar until light and fluffy. Beat in eggs. Combine the flour, baking powder and salt; add to creamed mixture alternately with sour cream, beating well after each addition. Fold in pecans and lemon peel.

2 Transfer to a greased 9-in. x 5-in. loaf pan. Bake at 350° for 50-60 minutes or until a toothpick inserted near the center comes out clean.

3 In a small saucepan, combine lemon juice and remaining sugar. Cook and stir over medium heat until sugar is dissolved. Pour over warm bread. Cool completely on a wire rack before removing from pan.

Yield: 1 loaf (16 slices).

grandma's honey muffins

PREP/TOTAL TIME: 30 MIN.

Darlis Wilfer
West Bend, Wisconsin

I can remember my Grandma Wheeler making these sweet and delicious muffins.

- 2 cups all-purpose flour
- 1/2 cup sugar
- 3 teaspoons baking powder
- 1/2 teaspoon salt
- 1 egg
- 1 cup 2% milk
- 1/4 cup butter, melted
- 1/4 cup honey

1 In a large bowl, combine the flour, sugar, baking powder and salt. In a small bowl, combine the egg, milk, butter and honey. Stir into dry ingredients just until moistened.

2 Fill greased or paper-lined muffin cups three-fourths full. Bake at 400° for 15-18 minutes or until a toothpick inserted near the center comes out clean. Remove from pan to a wire rack. Serve warm.

Yield: 1 dozen.

sweet & savory breadsticks

PREP/TOTAL TIME: 25 MIN.

Taste of Home Test Kitchen

These easy breadsticks are a complete winner. And with just five ingredients, they come together quickly. We're sure you'll love them!

1 tube (11-1/2 ounces) refrigerated corn bread twists

1/4 cup butter, melted

1/3 cup packed brown sugar

1/2 teaspoon garlic salt

1/4 teaspoon onion powder

1 Unroll and separate bread twists into 16 pieces. Place the butter in a shallow bowl. Combine the brown sugar, garlic salt and onion powder in another shallow bowl. Roll bread pieces in butter, then in the brown sugar mixture.

2 Twist two pieces together. Pinch ends to seal. Place on an ungreased baking sheet. Repeat. Bake at 375° for 12-14 minutes or until golden brown. Serve warm.

Yield: 4 servings.

cheesy round bread

PREP: 15 MIN. + RISING
BAKE: 40 MIN.

Ruthe Krohne
Fort Wayne, Indiana

This bread, which looks similar to focaccia, has a light olive and garlic flavor. We enjoy generous slices with soup.

1 package (16 ounces) hot roll mix

3/4 cup warm water (120° to 130°)

1 egg

1 tablespoon butter, softened

1-1/2 teaspoons garlic salt

1/2 teaspoon dried oregano

1/2 teaspoon paprika

3/4 cup shredded cheddar cheese

1/2 cup chopped ripe olives, well drained

1 egg white, lightly beaten

1 In a large bowl, combine the contents of the roll mix and yeast packets. Add warm water and mix well. Stir in the egg, butter and seasonings until blended.

2 Turn onto a floured surface. Knead in cheese and olives. Place in a greased bowl, turning once to grease top. Cover and let rise in a warm place until doubled, about 1 hour.

3 Punch dough down. Press into a 12-in. pizza pan. Cover and let rise in a warm place until doubled, about 30 minutes.

4 With a sharp knife, make three or four slashes across top of loaf. Brush with egg white. Bake at 325° for 40-45 minutes or until golden brown. Cool for 5 minutes before removing from pan to a wire rack.

Yield: 16 servings.

sour cream & chive biscuits

PREP/TOTAL TIME: 20 MIN.

Priscilla Gilbert
Indian Harbour Beach, Florida

Chives add a nice, mild onion flavor to just about any dish, whether it be soup, dip, baked potatoes or buttery spread. They are a really nice touch in these tender biscuits.

3 cups biscuit/baking mix

3 tablespoons minced chives

2/3 cup water

2/3 cup sour cream

1 In a large bowl, combine biscuit mix and chives. Stir in water and sour cream just until moistened.

2 Drop by heaping tablespoonfuls onto a baking sheet coated with cooking spray. Bake at 450° for 8-10 minutes or until lightly browned. Serve warm.

Yield: 16 biscuits.

cinnamon zucchini bread

PREP: 25 MIN.
BAKE: 50 MIN. + COOLING

Kathie Meyer
Round Rock, Texas

The only way Mom could get me to eat veggies was to bake this zucchini bread. When I grew up, I lightened her original recipe, so I can still eat it without feeling guilty.

- 3/4 cup sugar
- 1/4 cup unsweetened applesauce
- 1/4 cup canola oil
- 2 egg whites
- 1 teaspoon vanilla extract
- 1-1/2 cups all-purpose flour
- 1-1/2 teaspoons ground cinnamon
- 1 teaspoon baking powder
- 1/2 teaspoon salt
- 1/2 teaspoon ground nutmeg
- 1/4 teaspoon baking soda
- 1-1/4 cups shredded peeled zucchini
- 1/2 cup raisins

1 In a small bowl, beat the sugar, applesauce, oil, egg whites and vanilla until well blended. Combine the flour, cinnamon, baking powder, salt, nutmeg and baking soda; gradually beat into sugar mixture. Fold in zucchini and raisins.

2 Transfer to an 8-in. x 4-in. loaf pan coated with cooking spray. Bake at 350° for 50-60 minutes or until toothpick inserted near the center comes out clean. Cool for 10 minutes before removing from pan to a wire rack to cool completely.

Yield: 1 loaf (12 slices).

cheddar skillet corn bread

PREP/TOTAL TIME: 30 MIN.

Terri Adrian
Lake City, Florida

Here's a tasty spin on traditional corn bread. It may become your new favorite!

- 2 tablespoons butter
- 2 packages (8-1/2 ounces *each*) corn bread/muffin mix
- 2 eggs, lightly beaten
- 1/2 cup whole milk
- 1/2 cup plain yogurt
- 1 can (14-3/4 ounces) cream-style corn
- 1/2 cup shredded cheddar cheese

HONEY BUTTER:

- 1/2 cup butter, softened
- 2 tablespoons honey

1 Place the butter into a deep 10-in. ovenproof skillet. Place in 400° oven for 4-6 minutes or until butter is melted.

2 Meanwhile, in a large bowl, combine the corn bread mix, eggs, milk and yogurt until blended. Stir in corn and cheese. Pour into hot skillet. Bake at 400° for 20-25 minutes or until a toothpick inserted near the center comes out clean. Cut into wedges.

3 In a small bowl, cream butter and honey. Serve with warm corn bread.

Yield: 1 loaf (12 wedges).

garlic poppy seed spirals

PREP/TOTAL TIME: 25 MIN.

Stacey Scherer
Macomb, Michigan

This is a fast, easy way to dress up plain crescent rolls. Adjust the seasoning to suit your family's taste...or use a little powdered ranch dressing mix as a tasty alternative.

3 tablespoons butter, melted

1 teaspoon garlic powder

1 teaspoon dried minced onion

1/2 teaspoon poppy seeds

1 tube (8 ounces) refrigerated crescent rolls

1 In a small bowl, combine the butter, garlic powder, onion and poppy seeds; set aside. Remove crescent dough from tube; do not unroll. Cut dough into 10 slices; dip one side in butter mixture.

2 Place rolls buttered side up in an ungreased 9-in. round baking pan. Brush with the remaining butter mixture. Bake rolls at 350° for 14-16 minutes or until golden brown. Serve warm.

Yield: 10 servings.

Poppy Seeds. Poppy seeds add a unique nutty flavor and a crunchy texture to breads, rolls, biscuits, breadsticks, muffins, quick breads, cakes and other baked goods. Try adding a few pinches of this versatile ingredient to other dishes you commonly prepare, such as salad dressing, marinades, fruit salads, coleslaw or chicken salad, just to name a few.

dilled wheat bread

PREP: 10 MIN. • BAKE: 3 HOURS

Jenny Witcraft
Cleveland, Ohio

I like to serve this everyday bread with just about any meal, but it is especially good alongside hearty soups and stews.

- 1-1/4 cups water (70° to 80°)
- 1 tablespoon butter, softened
- 2 tablespoons sugar
- 2 teaspoons dill weed
- 1-1/2 teaspoons salt
- 2 cups whole wheat flour
- 1-1/4 cups all-purpose flour
- 1-1/2 teaspoons active dry yeast

1 In bread machine pan, place all ingredients in order suggested by manufacturer. Select basic bread setting. Choose crust color and loaf size if available. Bake according to bread machine directions (check dough after 5 minutes of mixing; add 1 to 2 tablespoons of water or flour if needed).

Yield: 1 loaf (1-3/4 pounds, 12 slices).

squash corn bread

PREP: 15 MIN. • BAKE: 20 MIN.

Marlene Huffstetler
Chapin, South Carolina

Enjoy the fresh flavor of summer squash in squares of this moist and hearty corn bread. It is good enough to eat by itself!

- 5 medium yellow summer squash (about 2 pounds), chopped
- 2 packages (8-1/2 ounces *each*) corn bread/muffin mix
- 4 eggs, lightly beaten
- 2/3 cup 4% cottage cheese
- 1/2 cup shredded cheddar cheese
- 1/2 cup chopped onion
- 1/4 teaspoon salt
- 1/4 teaspoon pepper

1 Place squash in a steamer basket; place in a large saucepan over 1 in. of water. Bring to a boil; cover and steam for 3-5 minutes or until tender. Drain and squeeze dry.

2 In a large bowl, combine corn bread mixes and eggs. Fold in the squash, cheeses, onion, salt and pepper.

3 Pour into two 8-in. square baking pans coated with cooking spray. Bake at 400° for 20-25 minutes or until a toothpick inserted near the center comes out clean.

4 Serve warm or cool for 10 minutes before removing from pan to a wire rack to cool completely. Wrap in foil and freeze for up to 3 months. To use frozen bread: Thaw at room temperature. Serve warm.

Yield: 2 dozen.

golden sesame braid

PREP: 35 MIN. + RISING
BAKE: 20 MIN. + COOLING

Marty Rummel
Trout Lake, Washington

I've made this pretty braid for every celebration in our family for over 30 years. It makes a festive addition to a holiday meal. Everyone looks forward to its soft, fragrant, golden presence.

> 2 packages (1/4 ounce *each*) active dry yeast
>
> 1-1/4 cups warm water (110° to 115°)
>
> 1/4 cup canola oil
>
> 1/4 cup sugar
>
> 1 teaspoon salt
>
> 2 eggs
>
> 2 to 3 drops yellow food coloring
>
> 4-1/2 to 5 cups all-purpose flour
>
> 1 egg yolk
>
> 1 tablespoon cold water
>
> 1 tablespoon sesame seeds

1 In a large bowl, dissolve yeast in warm water. Add the oil, sugar, salt, eggs, food coloring and 3 cups flour. Beat on medium speed for 3 minutes. Stir in enough remaining flour to form a soft dough (dough will be sticky).

2 Turn onto a floured surface; knead until smooth and elastic, about 6-8 minutes. Place in a bowl coated with cooking spray, turning once to coat top. Cover and let rise in a warm place until doubled, about 1 hour.

3 Punch dough down. Turn onto a lightly floured surface; divide into fourths. Shape each portion into an 18-in. rope. Place ropes parallel to one another on a baking sheet coated with cooking spray.

4 Beginning from the right side, braid dough by placing the first rope over the second rope, under the third and over the fourth. Repeat three or four times, beginning each time from the right side. Pinch ends to seal and tuck under. Cover and let rise until doubled, about 45 minutes.

5 Beat egg yolk and cold water; brush over braid. Sprinkle with sesame seeds. Bake at 350° for 20-25 minutes or until golden brown. Remove from pan to a wire rack to cool.

Yield: 1 loaf (32 slices).

spinach flatbreads

PREP/TOTAL TIME: 20 MIN.

Kristen Westbrook
Pittsburgh, Pennsylvania

Instead of the same old side of garlic bread, serve up wedges of toasty, mouthwatering flatbreads. I always seemed to have spinach that would spoil before I could use it all. So I started making these delicious and quick flatbreads. They're low-fat and can double as a light lunch.

> 2/3 cup sliced onion
>
> 4 teaspoons olive oil, *divided*
>
> 4 whole pita flatbreads
>
> 2 cups fresh baby spinach
>
> 1-1/2 cups (6 ounces) shredded part-skim mozzarella cheese
>
> 1/4 teaspoon pepper

1 In a small skillet, saute the onion in 2 teaspoons oil for 2-3 minutes or until tender; set aside. Place pitas on a baking sheet coated with cooking spray. Brush with the remaining oil.

2 Layer with the spinach, sauteed onion and cheese. Sprinkle with pepper. Bake at 425° for 6-8 minutes or until the cheese is melted.

Yield: 4 servings.

nutmeg blueberry muffins

PREP: 20 MIN. • BAKE: 25 MIN.

Colleen Belbey
Warwick, Rhode Island

These tender muffins feature a crunchy topping.

1/2 cup butter, softened

1 cup plus 1 tablespoon sugar, *divided*

2 eggs

1/2 cup whole milk

1 teaspoon vanilla extract

2 cups all-purpose flour

2 teaspoons baking powder

1/4 teaspoon salt

2 cups fresh *or* frozen unsweetened blueberries

1/4 teaspoon ground nutmeg

1 In a large bowl, cream the butter and 1 cup sugar until light and fluffy. Add eggs, one at a time, beating well after each addition. Stir in the milk and vanilla. Combine the flour, baking powder and salt; add to the creamed mixture just until moistened. Fold in the blueberries.

2 Fill paper-lined muffin cups three-fourths full. Combine nutmeg and remaining sugar; sprinkle over the top.

3 Bake at 375° for 25-30 minutes or until a toothpick inserted near center comes out clean. Cool for 5 minutes before removing from pan to a wire rack. Serve warm.

Yield: 1 dozen.

EDITOR'S NOTE: If using frozen blueberries, use without thawing to avoid discoloring the batter.

green onion drop biscuits

PREP/TOTAL TIME: 30 MIN.

Taste of Home Test Kitchen

These golden gems take just minutes to stir up. They're perfect with slow cooker dishes.

- 2 cups all-purpose flour
- 1/2 cup thinly sliced green onions
- 2 teaspoons sugar
- 2 teaspoons baking powder
- 1/2 teaspoon salt
- 1/4 teaspoon baking soda
- 6 tablespoons cold butter, cubed
- 1 egg
- 3/4 cup buttermilk

1 In a bowl, combine flour, onions, sugar, baking powder, salt and baking soda. Cut in butter until mixture resembles coarse crumbs. Combine egg and buttermilk; stir into crumb mixture just until moistened.

2 Drop by 1/4 cupfuls 2 in. apart onto a greased baking sheet. Bake at 400° for 12-15 minutes or until golden brown. Serve warm.

Yield: 10 biscuits.

mini toffee rolls

PREP: 20 MIN. • BAKE: 15 MIN.

Carol Gillespie
Chambersburg, Pennsylvania

*I found this delicious recipe in a magazine years
ago and adapted the original to make it my own.
The rich, bite-sized treats are full of cinnamon
flavor and great with coffee!*

6 tablespoons butter, softened

1/2 cup packed brown sugar

1 teaspoon ground cinnamon

1/3 cup English toffee bits *or* almond
brickle chips

2 tubes (8 ounces *each*) refrigerated
crescent rolls

1 cup confectioners' sugar

4-1/2 teaspoons whole milk

1/4 teaspoon vanilla extract

1 In a small bowl, cream the butter, brown
sugar and cinnamon until light and fluffy.
Stir in toffee bits.

2 Separate each tube of crescent dough into
four rectangles; seal perforations. Spread
evenly with butter mixture. Roll up each
rectangle jelly-roll style, starting with a
long side.

3 Cut each into six 1-in. slices; place cut side
down into two greased 8-in. square baking
dishes. Bake at 375° for 14-16 minutes or
until golden brown.

4 In a small bowl, combine the confectioners'
sugar, milk and vanilla until smooth. Drizzle
over warm rolls.

Yield: 4 dozen.

general recipe index

This handy index lists the recipes by food category and major ingredient so you can easily locate recipes that suit your needs.

APPETIZERS

Barbecue Chicken Wings, 287

Bavarian Meatballs, 20

Beer Cheese Fondue, 290

Caramel Apple Fondue, 286

Championship Bean Dip, 294

Cheesy Pizza Fondue, 273

Chili con Queso Dip, 295

Chipotle Ham 'n' Cheese Dip, 272

Cider Cheese Fondue, 284

Cranberry Appetizer Meatballs, 294

Creamy Artichoke Dip, 297

Hot Chili Cheese Dip, 270

Hot Crab Dip, 280

Hot Crab Spread, 274

Italian Appetizer Meatballs, 281

Mexican Fondue, 297

Mini Hot Dogs 'n' Meatballs, 300

Nacho Salsa Dip, 276

Party Meatballs, 269

Raspberry Fondue Dip, 283

Reuben Spread, 268

Saucy Cocktail Meatballs, 289

Slow Cooker Mexican Dip, 288

Sunshine Chicken Wings, 282

Sweet Sausage Puffs, 293

Sweet-and-Sour Chicken Wings, 277

Warm Broccoli Cheese Dip, 274

Zesty Smoked Links, 278

APPLES

Applesauce Bread, 333

Brats with Sauerkraut, 29

Caramel Apple Fondue, 286

Cider Mushroom Brisket, 114

Cider Pork Roast, 149

Cranberry-Stuffed Apples, 284

Hot Fruit Salad, 261

Nutty Apple Streusel Dessert, 292

Peachy Spiced Cider, 282

Pork Chop Supper, 169

Slow-Cooked Pork Loin, 165

Slow Cooker Cider, 290

Slow Cooker Pork and Apple Curry, 164

Spiced Tea Mix, 299

Warm Spiced Cider Punch, 289

Wassail Bowl Punch, 271

APRICOTS

Apricot-Orange Salsa Chicken, 230

Apricot Pork Roast, 152

Cranberry-Apricot Pork Roast with Potatoes, 170

ARTICHOKES

Creamy Artichoke Dip, 297

AVOCADOS

Green Bean Tossed Salad, 309

Romaine Salad with Avocado Dressing, 306

BACON

Bacon Spinach Muffins, 334

Baked Potato Soup, 31

Creamy German Potato Salad, 307

Hash Brown Egg Brunch, 159

Makeover Hash Brown Soup, 38

Scrumptious Scrambled Salad, 324

Slow-Cooked Pork & Beans, 260

Texican Chili, 33

BARLEY

Beef Barley Soup, 21

Beef Barley Stew, 124

Vegetable Barley Soup, 61

Veggie Barley Salad, 320

BEANS (GREEN & LIMA)

Bean and Carrot Salad, 312

Green Beans and New Potatoes, 255

alphabetical index

This handy index lists every recipe in alphabetical order, so you can easily find your favorite dish.

cook time index

On a schedule? Let this index help! Stop here to find which recipes fit into your time frame.

Appetizers and Desserts Served from a Slow Cooker

1 Hour Cooking Time

Appetizers

Beverages

1-1/2 Hours Cooking Time

Appetizers

Side Dish

Soup

2 Hours Cooking Time

Appetizers

Beverages

Desserts

Main Dish

Salad

Side Dish

2-1/2 Hours Cooking Time

Appetizer

Main Dish

Side Dish

2-3/4 Hours Cooking Time

Side Dish

3 Hours Cooking Time

Appetizers

Beverage

Main Dishes

Beef

4 Hours Cooking Time

Main Dishes

Poultry (continued)

Chicken with Veggies 'n' Gravy, 189

Citrus Chicken, 226

Creamy Chicken and Carrots, 205

Fruited Chicken, 228

Herbed Chicken with Wild Rice, 196

Herbed Slow Cooker Chicken, 199

Italian Chicken and Peppers, 201

Lemon Chicken Breasts, 229

Moist & Tender Turkey Breast, 190

Mushroom Chicken Cacciatore, 207

Prosciutto Chicken Cacciatore, 237

Satisfying Chicken and Veggies, 198

Saucy Chicken Thighs, 212

Slow-Cooked Italian Chicken, 202

Southern Barbecue Spaghetti
  Sauce, 200

Soy-Garlic Chicken, 201

Stuffed Chicken Rolls, 208

Stuffed Sweet Peppers, 214

Sweet 'n' Sour Curry Chicken, 191

Sweet Pepper Chicken, 222

Teriyaki Chicken, 204

Turkey Sloppy Joes, 10

Venison

Venison Meatballs, 246

Sandwiches

Ham Barbecue, 58

Italian Sausage Sandwiches, 54

Slow Cooker Sloppy Joes, 38

Soups & Chili

Beef Vegetable Soup, 63

Hearty Sausage-Chicken Chili, 29

Smoked Sausage Gumbo, 25

4-1/4 Hours Cooking Time

Dessert

Strawberry Rhubarb Sauce, 278

Main Dishes

Chicken

Fiesta Chicken Burritos, 232

Forgotten Jambalaya, 225

Lemon Chicken, 187

Pork

Sweet 'n' Sour Pork Chops, 177

Soups

Small-Batch Veggie Meatball Soup, 13

Vegetable Lentil Soup, 21

4-1/2 Hours Cooking Time

Main Dishes

Beef

Steak 'n' Gravy, 88

Chicken & Poultry

Saucy Chicken with Veggies and
  Rice, 226

Pork

Asian Pork Roast, 161

Honey-Glazed Ham, 155

Sweet 'n' Sour Sausage, 169

Soup

Chunky Chicken Soup, 44

4-3/4 Hours Cooking Time

Main Dish

Spicy Seafood Stew, 241

5 Hours Cooking Time

Main Dishes

Beef

Hearty Beef Vegetable Stew, 101

Herbed Beef with Noodles, 71

Burgundy Pot Roast, 84

Slow-Cooked Meat Loaf, 89

Slow Cooker Enchiladas, 128

Steak Strips with Dumplings, 126

Sweet-Sour Meatballs, 79

Meatless

Sweet Potato Lentil Stew, 243

Pork

Cider Pork Roast, 149

Country Pork Chop Supper, 146

Country-Style Pork Loin, 179

Cranberry-Apricot Pork Roast with
  Potatoes, 170

Creamy Ham & Potatoes, 175

Maple Pork Ribs, 174

Peachy Pork Chops, 183

Sesame Pork Ribs, 142

Slow-Cooked Pork Loin, 165

Spicy Sausage Hash Browns, 145

Poultry

Busy Mom's Chicken Fajitas, 194

Chicken, Bean and Rice Nachos, 188

Coconut Curry Chicken, 197

Greek Chicken Dinner, 213

Moist Drumsticks, 188

Nostalgic Chicken and
  Dumplings, 222

Pepper Jack Chicken, 218

Soft Chicken Tacos, 209

Substitutions & Equivalents

Equivalent Measures

3 teaspoons	=	1 tablespoon	16 tablespoons	=	1 cup
4 tablespoons	=	1/4 cup	2 cups	=	1 pint
5-1/3 tablespoons	=	1/3 cup	4 cups	=	1 quart
8 tablespoons	=	1/2 cup	4 quarts	=	1 gallon

Food Equivalents

Grains

Macaroni	1 cup (3-1/2 ounces) uncooked	=	2-1/2 cups cooked
Noodles, Medium	3 cups (4 ounces) uncooked	=	4 cups cooked
Popcorn	1/3 to 1/2 cup unpopped	=	8 cups popped
Rice, Long Grain	1 cup uncooked	=	3 cups cooked
Rice, Quick-Cooking	1 cup uncooked	=	2 cups cooked
Spaghetti	8 ounces uncooked	=	4 cups cooked

Crumbs

Bread	1 slice	=	3/4 cup soft crumbs, 1/4 cup fine dry crumbs
Graham Crackers	7 squares	=	1/2 cup finely crushed
Buttery Round Crackers	12 crackers	=	1/2 cup finely crushed
Saltine Crackers	14 crackers	=	1/2 cup finely crushed

Fruits

Bananas	1 medium	=	1/3 cup mashed
Lemons	1 medium	=	3 tablespoons juice, 2 teaspoons grated peel
Limes	1 medium	=	2 tablespoons juice, 1-1/2 teaspoons grated peel
Oranges	1 medium	=	1/4 to 1/3 cup juice, 4 teaspoons grated peel

Vegetables

Cabbage	1 head	=	5 cups shredded	Green Pepper	1 large	=	1 cup chopped
Carrots	1 pound	=	3 cups shredded	Mushrooms	1/2 pound	=	3 cups sliced
Celery	1 rib	=	1/2 cup chopped	Onions	1 medium	=	1/2 cup chopped
Corn	1 ear fresh	=	2/3 cup kernels	Potatoes	3 medium	=	2 cups cubed

Nuts

Almonds	1 pound	=	3 cups chopped	Pecan Halves	1 pound	=	4-1/2 cups chopped
Ground Nuts	3-3/4 ounces	=	1 cup	Walnuts	1 pound	=	3-3/4 cups chopped

Easy Substitutions

When you need...	Use...	
Baking Powder	1 teaspoon	1/2 teaspoon cream of tartar + 1/4 teaspoon baking soda
Buttermilk	1 cup	1 tablespoon lemon juice or vinegar + enough milk to measure 1 cup (let stand 5 minutes before using)
Cornstarch	1 tablespoon	2 tablespoons all-purpose flour
Honey	1 cup	1-1/4 cups sugar + 1/4 cup water
Half-and-Half Cream	1 cup	1 tablespoon melted butter + enough whole milk to measure 1 cup
Onion	1 small, chopped (1/3 cup)	1 teaspoon onion powder or 1 tablespoon dried minced onion
Tomato Juice	1 cup	1/2 cup tomato sauce + 1/2 cup water
Tomato Sauce	2 cups	3/4 cup tomato paste + 1 cup water
Unsweetened Chocolate	1 square (1 ounce)	3 tablespoons baking cocoa + 1 tablespoon shortening or oil
Whole Milk	1 cup	1/2 cup evaporated milk + 1/2 cup water